To Melissa

IN THE HEART OF THE SEA

THE EPIC TRUE STORY THAT INSPIRED *MOBY DICK*

Nathaniel Philbrick

CHIVERS PRESS
BATH

First published 2000
by
HarperCollins
This Large Print edition published by
Chivers Press
by arrangement with
HarperCollinsPublishers Ltd
2001

ISBN 0 7540 1622 6

British Library Cataloguing in Publication Data available

Printed and bound in Great Britain by
BOOKCRAFT, Midsomer Norton, Somerset

And in the greatness of thine excellency
thou has overthrown them that rose up
against thee: Thou sentest forth thy wrath,
which consumed them as stubble. And with
the blast of thy nostrils the waters were
gathered together, the floods stood upright
as a heap, and the depths were congealed in
the heart of the sea.

—EXODUS 15:7–8

This is the end of the whaleroad and the
  whale
Who spewed Nantucket bones in the
  thrashed swell . . .
This is the end of running on the waves;
We are poured out like water. Who will
  dance
The mast-lashed master of Leviathans
Up from this field of Quakers in their
  unstoned graves?

—ROBERT LOWELL,
'The Quaker Graveyard in Nantucket'

CONTENTS

PREFACE

Like a giant bird of prey, the whaleship moved lazily up the western coast of South America, zigging and zagging across a living sea of oil. For that was the Pacific Ocean in 1821, a vast field of warm-blooded oil deposits known as sperm whales.

Harvesting sperm whales—the largest toothed whales in existence—was no easy matter. Six men would set out from the ship in a small boat, row up to their prey, harpoon it, then attempt to stab it to death with a lance. The sixty-ton creature could destroy the whaleboat with a flick of its tail, throwing the men into the cold ocean water, often miles from the ship.

Then came the prodigious task of transforming a dead whale into oil: ripping off its blubber, chopping it up, and boiling it into the high-grade oil that lit the streets and lubricated the machines of the Industrial Age. That all of this was conducted on the limitless Pacific Ocean meant that the whalemen of the early nineteenth century were not merely seagoing hunters and factory workers but also explorers, pushing out farther and farther into a scarcely charted wilderness larger than all the earth's landmasses combined.

For more than a century, the headquarters of this global oil business had been a little island called Nantucket, twenty-four miles off the coast of southern New England. One of the defining paradoxes of Nantucket's whalemen was that many

xi

of them were Quakers, a religious sect stoically dedicated to pacifism, at least when it came to the human race. Combining rigid self-control with an almost holy sense of mission, these were what Herman Melville would call 'Quakers with a vengeance.'

It was a Nantucket whaleship, the *Dauphin,* just a few months into what would be a three-year voyage, that was making her way up the Chilean coast. And on that February morning in 1821, the lookout saw something unusual—a boat, impossibly small for the open sea, bobbing on the swells. The ship's captain, the thirty-seven-year-old Zimri Coffin, trained his spyglass on the mysterious craft with keen curiosity.

He soon realized that it was a whaleboat—double-ended and about twenty-five feet long—but a whaleboat unlike any he had ever seen. The boat's sides had been built up by about half a foot. Two makeshift masts had been rigged, transforming the rowing vessel into a rudimentary schooner. The sails—stiff with salt and bleached by the sun—had clearly pulled the boat along for many, many miles. Coffin could see no one at the steering oar. He turned to the man at the *Dauphin*'s wheel and ordered, 'Hard up the helm.'

Under Coffin's watchful eye, the helmsman brought the ship as close as possible to the derelict craft. Even though their momentum quickly swept them past it, the brief seconds during which the ship loomed over the open boat presented a sight that would stay with the crew the rest of their lives.

First they saw bones—human bones—littering the thwarts and floorboards, as if the whaleboat were the seagoing lair of a ferocious, man-eating beast. Then they saw the two men. They were curled up in opposite ends of the boat, their skin covered with sores, their eyes bulging from the hollows of their skulls, their beards caked with salt and blood. They were sucking the marrow from the bones of their dead shipmates.

Instead of greeting their rescuers with smiles of relief, the survivors—too delirious with thirst and hunger to speak—were disturbed, even frightened. They jealously clutched the splintered and gnawed-over bones with a desperate, almost feral intensity, refusing to give them up, like two starving dogs found trapped in a pit.

Later, once the survivors had been given some food and water (and had finally surrendered the bones), one of them found the strength to tell his story. It was a tale made of a whaleman's worst nightmares: of being in a boat far from land with nothing left to eat or drink and—perhaps worst of all—of a whale with the vindictiveness and guile of a man.

*   *   *

Even though it is little remembered today, the sinking of the whaleship *Essex* by an enraged sperm whale was one of the most well-known marine disasters of the nineteenth century. Nearly every child in America read about it in school. It was the event that inspired the climactic scene of Herman Melville's *Moby-Dick*.

But the point at which Melville's novel ends— the sinking of the ship—was merely the starting point for the story of the real-life *Essex* disaster. The sinking seemed to mark the beginning of a kind of terrible laboratory experiment devised to see just how far the human animal could go in its battle against the savage sea. Of the twenty men who escaped the whale-crushed ship, only eight survived. The two men rescued by the *Dauphin* had sailed almost 4,500 nautical miles across the Pacific—farther by at least 500 miles than Captain William Bligh's epic voyage in an open boat after being abandoned by the *Bounty* mutineers and more than five times farther than Sir Ernest Shackleton's equally famous passage to South Georgia Island.

For nearly 180 years, most of what was known about the calamity came from the 128-page *Narrative of the Wreck of the Whaleship* Essex, written by Owen Chase, the ship's first mate. Fragmentary accounts from other survivors existed, but these lacked the authority and scope of Chase's narrative, which was published with the help of a ghostwriter only nine months after the first mate's rescue. Then, around 1960, an old notebook was found in the attic of a home in Penn Yan, New York. Not until twenty years later, in 1980, when the notebook reached the hands of the Nantucket whaling expert Edouard Stackpole, was it realized that its original owner, Thomas Nickerson, had been the *Essex*'s cabin boy. Late in life, Nickerson, then the proprietor of a boardinghouse on Nantucket, had been urged to write an account of the disaster by a professional writer named Leon Lewis, who may have been one of Nickerson's guests. Nickerson sent Lewis the notebook containing his only draft of the narrative in 1876. For whatever reason, Lewis never prepared the manuscript for publication and eventually gave the notebook to a neighbor, who died with it still in his possession. Nickerson's account was finally published as a limited-edition monograph by the Nantucket Historical Association in 1984.

In terms of literary quality, Nickerson's narrative cannot compare to Chase's polished account. Ragged and meandering, the manuscript is the work of an amateur, but an amateur who was *there*, at the helm of the *Essex* when she was struck by the whale. At fourteen, Nickerson had been the youngest member of the ship's crew, and his account remains that of a wide-eyed child on the verge of manhood, of an orphan (he lost both his parents before he was two) looking for a home. He was seventy-one when he finally put pen to paper, but Thomas Nickerson could look back to that distant time as if it were yesterday, his memories bolstered by information he'd learned in conversations with other survivors. In the account that follows, Chase will get his due, but for the first time his version of events is challenged by that of his cabin boy, whose testimony can now be heard 180 years after the sinking of the *Essex*.

*   *   *

When I was a child, my father, Thomas Philbrick, a professor of English at the University of Pittsburgh and author of several books about American sea fiction, often put my brother and me to bed with the story of the whale that attacked a ship. My uncle, the late Charles Philbrick, winner of the Wallace Stevens Poetry Prize in 1958, wrote a five-hundred-line poem about the *Essex*, 'A Travail Past,' published posthumously in 1976. It powerfully evoked what he called 'a past we forget that we need to know.' Ten years later, as it happened, in 1986, I moved with my wife and two children to the *Essex*'s home port, Nantucket Island.

I soon discovered that Owen Chase, Herman Melville, Thomas Nickerson, and Uncle Charlie were not the only ones to have written about the *Essex*. There was Nantucket's distinguished historian Edouard Stackpole, who died in 1993, just as my own research was beginning. There was Thomas Heffernan, author of *Stove by a Whale: Owen Chase and the* Essex (1981), an indispensable work of scholarship that was completed just before the discovery of the Nickerson manuscript. Finally, there was Henry Carlisle's compelling novel *The Jonah Man* (1984), which tells the story of the *Essex* from the viewpoint of the ship's captain, George Pollard.

Even after I'd read these accounts of the disaster, I wanted to know more. I wondered why the whale had acted as it did, how starvation and dehydration had affected the men's judgment; what had happened out there? I immersed myself in the documented experiences of other whalemen from the era; I read about cannibalism, survival at sea, the psychology and physiology of starvation, navigation, oceanography, the behavior of sperm whales, the construction of ships—anything that might help me better understand what these men experienced on the wide and unforgiving Pacific Ocean.

I came to realize that the *Essex* disaster had provided Melville with much more than an ending to one of the greatest American novels ever written. It had spoken to the same issues of class, race, leadership, and man's relationship to nature that would occupy him throughout *Moby-Dick*. It had also given Melville an archetypal but real place from which to launch the imaginary voyage of the *Pequod*: a tiny island that had once commanded the attention of the world. Relentlessly acquisitive, technologically advanced, with a religious sense of its own destiny, Nantucket was, in 1821, what America would become. No one dreamed that in a little more than a generation the island would founder—done in, like the *Essex*, by a too-close association with the whale.

CREW OF THE *ESSEX*

CAPTAIN
George Pollard, Jr.

FIRST MATE
Owen Chase

SECOND MATE
Matthew Joy

BOATSTEERERS
Benjamin Lawrence—Obed Hendricks
Thomas Chappel

STEWARD
William Bond

SAILORS
Owen Coffin—Isaac Cole—Henry Dewitt
Richard Peterson—Charles Ramsdell—Barzillai Ray
Samuel Reed—Isaiah Sheppard—Charles Shorter
Lawson Thomas—Seth Weeks—Joseph West
William Wright

CABIN BOY
Thomas Nickerson

CHAPTER ONE

NANTUCKET

It was, he later remembered, 'the most pleasing moment of my life'—the moment he stepped aboard the whaleship *Essex* for the first time. He was fourteen years old, with a broad nose and an open, eager face, and like every other Nantucket boy, he'd been taught to 'idolize the form of a ship.' The *Essex* might not look like much, stripped of her rigging and chained to the wharf, but for Thomas Nickerson she was a vessel of opportunity. Finally, after what had seemed an endless wait, Nickerson was going to sea.

The hot July sun beat down on her old, oil-soaked timbers until the temperature below was infernal, but Nickerson explored every cranny, from the brick altar of the tryworks being assembled on deck to the lightless depths of the empty hold. In between was a creaking, compartmentalized world, a living thing of oak and pine that reeked of oil, blood, tobacco juice, food, salt, mildew, tar, and smoke. '[B]lack and ugly as she was,' Nickerson wrote, 'I would not have exchanged her for a palace.'

In July of 1819 the *Essex* was one of a fleet of more than seventy Nantucket whaleships in the Pacific and Atlantic Oceans. With whale-oil prices steadily climbing and the rest of the world's economy sunk in depression, the village of Nantucket was on its way to becoming one of the richest towns in America.

The community of about seven thousand people lived on a gently sloping hill crowded with houses and topped by windmills and church towers. It resembled, some said, the elegant and established port of Salem—a remarkable compliment for an island more than twenty miles out into the Atlantic, below Cape Cod. But if the town, high on its hill, radiated an almost ethereal quality of calm, the waterfront below bustled with activity. Sprouting from among the long, low warehouses and ropewalks, four solid-fill wharves reached out more than a hundred yards into the harbor. Tethered to the wharves or anchored in the harbor were, typically, fifteen to twenty whaleships, along with dozens of smaller vessels, mainly sloops and schooners, that brought trade goods to and from the island. Each wharf, a labyrinth of anchors, try-pots, spars, and oil casks, was thronged with sailors, stevedores, and artisans. Two-wheeled, horse-drawn carts known as calashes continually came and went.

It was a scene already familiar to Thomas Nickerson. The children of Nantucket had long used the waterfront as their playground. They rowed decrepit whaleboats up and down the harbor and clambered up into the rigging of the ships. To off-islanders it was clear that these children were a 'distinctive class of juveniles, accustomed to consider themselves as predestined mariners . . . They climbed ratlines like monkeys—little fellows of ten or twelve years—and laid out on the yardarms with the most perfect nonchalance.' The *Essex* might be Nickerson's first ship, but he had been preparing for the voyage almost his entire life.

He wasn't going alone. His friends Barzillai Ray,

Owen Coffin, and Charles Ramsdell, all between the ages of fifteen and eighteen, were also sailing on the *Essex*. Owen Coffin was the cousin of the *Essex*'s new captain and probably steered his three friends to his kinsman's ship. Nickerson was the youngest of the group.

The *Essex* was old and, at 87 feet long and 238 tons displacement, quite small, but she had a reputation on Nantucket as a lucky ship. Over the last decade and a half, she had done well by her Quaker owners, regularly returning at two-year intervals with enough oil to make them wealthy men. Daniel Russell, her previous captain, had been successful enough over the course of four voyages to be given command of a new and larger ship, the Aurora. Russell's promotion allowed the former first mate, George Pollard, Jr., to take over command of the *Essex*, and one of the boatsteerers (or harpooners), Owen Chase, to move up to first mate. Three other crew members were elevated to the rank of boatsteerer. Not only a lucky but apparently a happy vessel, the *Essex* was, according to Nickerson, 'on the whole rather a desirable ship than otherwise.'

Since Nantucket was, like any seafaring town of the period, a community obsessed with omens and signs, such a reputation counted for much. Still, there was talk among the men on the wharves when earlier that July, as the *Essex* was being repaired and outfitted, a comet appeared in the night sky.

⁑   *   *

Nantucket was a town of roof dwellers. Nearly every house, its shingles painted red or left to

3

weather into gray, had a roof-mounted platform known as a walk. While its intended use was to facilitate putting out chimney fires with buckets of sand, the walk was also an excellent place to look out to sea with a spyglass, to search for the sails of returning ships. At night, the spyglasses of Nantucket were often directed toward the heavens, and in July of 1819, islanders were looking toward the northwest sky. The Quaker merchant Obed Macy, who kept meticulous records of what he determined were the 'most extraordinary events' in the life of his island, watched the night sky from his house on Pleasant Street. 'The comet (which appears every clear night) is thought to be very large from its uncommonly long tail,' he wrote, 'which extends upward in opposition to the sun in an almost perpendicular direction and heaves off to the eastward and nearly points for the North Star.'

From earliest times, the appearance of a comet was interpreted as a sign that something unusual was about to happen. The *New Bedford Mercury*, the newspaper Nantucketers read for lack of one of their own, commented, 'True it is, that the appearance of these eccentric visitors have always preceded some remarkable event.' But Macy resisted such speculation: '[T]he philosophical reasoning we leave to the scientific part of the community, still it is beyond a doubt that the most learned is possessed of very little undoubted knowledge of the subject of cometicks.'

At the wharves and shipping offices there was much speculation, and not just about the comet. All spring and summer there had been sightings up and down the New England coast of what the *Mercury* described as 'an extraordinary sea

4

animal'—a serpent with black, horselike eyes and a fifty-foot body resembling a string of barrels floating on the water. Any sailor, especially if he was young and impressionable like Thomas Nickerson, must have wondered, if only fleetingly, if this was, in fact, the best time to be heading out on a voyage around Cape Horn.

Nantucketers had good reason to be superstitious. Their lives were governed by a force of terrifying unpredictability—the sea. Due to a constantly shifting network of shoals, including the Nantucket Bar just off the harbor mouth, the simple act of coming to and from the island was an often harrowing and sometimes catastrophic lesson in seamanship. Particularly in winter, when storms were the most violent, wrecks occurred almost weekly. Buried throughout the island were the corpses of anonymous seamen who had washed up on its wave-thrashed shores. Nantucket, which means 'faraway land' in the language of the island's native inhabitants, the Wampanoag, was a mound of sand eroding into an inexorable ocean, and all its residents, even if they had never left the island, were all too aware of the inhumanity of the sea.

Nantucket's English settlers, who began arriving in 1659, had been mindful of the sea's dangers. They had hoped to support themselves not as fishermen but as farmers and sheepherders on this grassy, pond-speckled crescent without wolves. But as the increasing size of the livestock herds, combined with the growing number of farms, threatened to transform the island into a wind-blown wasteland, Nantucketers inevitably looked seaward.

Every fall, hundreds of 'right whales' appeared

5

to the south of the island and remained until the early spring. So named because they were 'the right whale to kill,' right whales grazed the waters off Nantucket much like seagoing cattle, straining the nutrient-rich surface of the ocean through the bushy plates of baleen in their perpetually grinning mouths. While English settlers at Cape Cod and eastern Long Island had already been hunting right whales for decades, no one on Nantucket had had the courage to pursue the whales in boats. Instead they left the harvesting of whales that washed up onto the shore (known as drift whales) to the Wampanoag.

Around 1690, a group of Nantucketers was standing on a hill overlooking the ocean where some whales were spouting and playing with one another. One of the onlookers nodded toward the whales and the ocean beyond. 'There,' he asserted, 'is a green pasture where our children's grandchildren will go for bread.' In fulfillment of his prophecy, a Cape Codder by the name of Ichabod Paddock was soon thereafter lured across Nantucket Sound to instruct the islanders in the art of killing whales.

Their first boats were only twenty feet long, and they launched them from the beaches along the island's south shore. Typically a whaleboat's crew was comprised of five Wampanoag oarsmen, with a single white Nantucketer at the steering oar. Once they'd killed the whale, they towed it back to the beach, where they removed the blubber and boiled it into oil. By the beginning of the eighteenth century, English Nantucketers had instituted a system of debt servitude that provided them with a steady supply of Wampanoag labor. Without the island's native inhabitants, who outnumbered Nantucket's white population well into the 1720s, the island would never have become a successful whaling port.

In the year 1712, a Captain Hussey, cruising in his little boat for right whales along Nantucket's south shore, was blown out to sea in a fierce northerly gale. Many miles out, he glimpsed several whales of a type he had never seen before. Unlike a right whale's vertical spout, this whale's spout arched forward. In spite of the high winds and rough seas, Hussey managed to harpoon and kill one of the whales, its blood and oil stilling the waves in an almost biblical fashion. This creature, Hussey quickly realized, was a sperm whale, one of which had washed up on the island's southwest shore only a few years before. Not only was the oil derived from the sperm whale's blubber far superior to that of the right whale, providing a brighter and cleaner-burning light, but its block shaped head contained a vast reservoir of even better oil, called spermaceti, that could be simply ladled into an awaiting cask. (It was spermaceti's resemblance to seminal fluid that gave rise to the sperm whale's name.) The sperm whale might be faster and more aggressive than the right whale, but it was far more enriching. With no other means of support, Nantucketers dedicated themselves to the single-minded pursuit of the sperm whale, and they soon outstripped their whaling rivals on the mainland and Long Island.

By 1760, the Nantucketers had practically wiped out the local whale population. But no matter—by that point they had enlarged their whaling sloops and equipped them with brick tryworks capable of processing the oil on the open ocean. Now, since it would not need to return to port as often to deliver bulky blubber, their fleet had a far greater range. By the outbreak of the American Revolution, Nantucketers had made it to the verge of the Arctic Circle, to the west coast of Africa, the east coast of South America, and as far south as the Falkland Islands.

In a speech before Parliament in 1775, the British statesman Edmund Burke looked to the island's inhabitants as the leaders of a new American breed—a 'recent people' whose success in whaling had exceeded the collective might of all of Europe. Living on an island that was almost the same distance from the mainland as England was from France, Nantucketers developed a British sense of themselves as a distinct and superior people, privileged citizens of what Ralph Waldo Emerson called the 'Nation of Nantucket.'

The Revolution and the War of 1812, when the British navy marauded offshore shipping, proved disastrous to the whale fishery. Fortunately, Nantucketers possessed enough capital and inherent whaling expertise to survive these trials. By 1819, Nantucket was well on its way to reclaiming and, as the whalers ventured into the Pacific, even surpassing its former glory. But the rise of the Pacific sperm-whale fishery had an unfortunate side effect. Instead of voyages that had once averaged about nine months, two- and three-year voyages had become the norm. Never before had the division between Nantucket's whalemen and their people been so great. Long gone were the days when Nantucketers could watch from shore as the men and boys of the island pursued the whale.

Nantucket was now the whaling capital of the world, but there were more than a few islanders who had never even seen a whale.

In the summer of 1819 people were still talking about the time when, nine years earlier, a pod of right whales was spotted to the north of the island. Whaleboats were quickly dispatched. A crowd gathered on shore to watch in fascination as two whales were killed and towed back into the harbor. For the people of Nantucket, it was an epiphany. Here at last were two of the creatures they had heard so much about, creatures upon which their livelihood depended. One of the whales was pulled up onto the wharf, and before the day was out, thousands of people-including, perhaps, the five-year-old Thomas Nickerson—had come to see it. One can only imagine the intensity of the Nantucketers' curiosity as they peered at the giant creature, and poked and prodded it, and said to themselves, 'So *this* is it.'

Nantucket had created an economic system that no longer depended on the island's natural resources. The island's soil had long since been exhausted by overfarming. Nantucket's large Wampanoag population had been reduced to a handful by epidemics, forcing shipowners to look to the mainland for crew. Whales had almost completely disappeared from local waters. And still the Nantucketers prospered. As one visitor observed, the island had become a 'barren sandbank, fertilized with whale-oil only.'

* * *

Throughout the seventeenth century, English
9

Nantucketers resisted all attempts to establish a church on the island, partly because a woman by the name of Mary Coffin Starbuck forbade it. It was said that nothing of consequence was done on Nantucket without Mary's approval. Mary Coffin and Nathaniel Starbuck had been the first English couple to be married on the island, in 1662, and had established a lucrative outpost for trading with the Wampanoag. Whenever an itinerant minister came to Nantucket looking to establish a congregation, he was firmly rebuffed by Mary Starbuck. Then, in 1702, Mary succumbed to a charismatic Quaker minister named John Richardson. Speaking before a group assembled in the Starbucks' living room, Richardson succeeded in moving Mary to tears. It was Mary Starbuck's conversion to Quakerism that established the unique fusion of spirituality and covetousness that would make possible Nantucket's rise as a whaling port.

Quakers or, more properly, members of the Society of Friends, depended on their own experience of God's presence, the 'Inner Light,' for guidance rather than relying on a Puritan minister's interpretation of scripture. But Nantucket's ever growing number of Quakers were hardly free-thinking individuals. Friends were expected to conform to rules of behavior determined during yearly meetings, encouraging a sense of community that was as carefully controlled as that of any New England society. If there was a difference, it was the Quaker belief in pacifism and a conscious spurning of worldly ostentation—two principles that were not intended to interfere, in any way, with a person's ability to make money. Instead of building fancy houses or buying fashionable clothes, Nantucket's Quakers reinvested their profits in the whale fishery. As a result, they were able to weather the downturns that laid to waste so many mainland whaling merchants, and Mary Starbuck's children, along with their Macy and Coffin cousins, quickly established a Quaker whaling dynasty.

Nantucketers saw no contradiction between their livelihood and their religion. God Himself had granted them dominion over the fishes of the sea. Peleg Folger, a Nantucket whaleman turned Quaker elder, expressed it in verse:

Thou didst, O Lord, create the mighty whale,
That wondrous monster of a mighty length;
Vast is his head and body, vast his tail,
Beyond conception his unmeasured strength.

But, everlasting God, thou dost ordain
That we, poor feeble mortals should engage
(Ourselves, our wives and children to maintain),
This dreadful monster with a martial rage.

Even if Nantucket's Quakers dominated the island economically and culturally, room was made for others, and by the early nineteenth century there were two Congregational church towers bracketing the town north and south. Yet all shared in a common, spiritually infused mission—to maintain a peaceful life on land while raising bloody havoc at sea. Pacifist killers, plain-dressed millionaires, the whalemen of Nantucket were simply fulfilling the Lord's will.

The town that Thomas Nickerson knew had a
ramshackle feel about it. All it took was one walk
through its narrow sandy streets to discover that
despite the stately church towers and the
occasional mansion, Nantucket was a far cry from
Salem. 'The good citizens of [Nantucket] do not
seem to pride themselves upon the regularity of
their streets [or] the neatness of their sidewalks,'
observed a visiting Quaker. The houses were
shingled and unpretentious and, as often as not,
included items scavenged from ships. '[H]atchways
make very convenient bridges for gutters . . . ; a
plank from the stern of a ship—having the name on
it—answers the double purpose of making a
fence—and informing the stranger if he can be at a
loss—in what town he is.'

Instead of using the official street names that
had been assigned for tax purposes in 1798,
Nantucketers spoke of 'Elisha Bunker's street' or
'Captain Mitchell's.' 'The inhabitants live together
like one great family,' wrote the Nantucketer
Walter Folger, who happened to be a part-owner of
the *Essex*, 'not in one house, but in friendship.
They not only know their nearest neighbors, but
each one knows all the rest. If you should wish to
see any man, you need but ask the first inhabitant
you meet, and he will be able to conduct you to his
residence, to tell what occupation he is of, and any
other particulars you may wish to know.'

But even within this close-knit familial
community, there were distinctions, and Thomas
Nickerson was on the outside looking in. The
unhappy truth was that while Nickerson's mother,

Rebecca Gibson, was a Nantucketer, his father, Thomas Nickerson, had been from Cape Cod, and Thomas Junior had been born in Harwich in 1805. Six months later, his parents moved him and his sisters across the sound to Nantucket. It was six months too late. Nantucketers took a dim view of off-islanders. They called them 'strangers' or, even worse, 'coofs,' a term of disparagement originally reserved for Cape Codders but broadened to include all of those unlucky enough to have been born on the mainland.

It might have earned Thomas Nickerson some regard on the island if his mother had at least come from old Nantucket stock, with a last name like Coffin, Starbuck, Macy, Folger, or Gardner. Such was not the case. On an island where many families could claim direct descent from one of the twenty or so 'first settlers,' the Gibsons and Nickersons were without the network of cousins that sustained most Nantucketers. 'Perhaps there is not another place in the world, of equal magnitude,' said Obed Macy, 'where the inhabitants [are] so connected by consanguinity as in this, which add[s] much to the harmony of the people and to their attachment to the place.' Nickerson's friends and shipmates Owen Coffin, Charles Ramsdell, and Barzillai Ray could count themselves as part of this group. Thomas might play with them, go to sea with them, but deep down he understood that no matter how hard he might try, he was, at best, only a coof.

Where a person lived in Nantucket depended on his station in the whaling trade. If he was a shipowner or merchant, he more than likely lived on Pleasant Street, set back on the hill, farthest from the clamor and stench of the wharves. (In

13

subsequent decades, as their ambitions required greater space and visibility, these worthies would gravitate toward Main Street). Captains, in contrast, tended to choose the thoroughfare with the best view of the harbor: Orange Street. With a house on the east side of Orange, a captain could watch his ship being outfitted at the wharf and keep track of activity in the harbor. Mates, as a rule, lived at the foot of this hill ('under the bank,' it was called) on Union Street, in the actual shadow of the homes they aspired one day to own.

On the corner of Main and Pleasant Streets was the Friends' immense South Meeting House, built in 1792 from pieces of the even bigger Great Meeting House that once loomed over the stoneless field of the Quaker Burial Ground at the end of Main Street. Just because Nickerson had been brought up a Congregationalist didn't mean he had never been inside this or the other Quaker meeting house on Broad Street. One visitor claimed that almost half the people who attended a typical Quaker meeting were not members of the Society of Friends. Earlier that summer, on June 29, Obed Macy recorded that two thousand people (more than a quarter of the island's population) had attended a public Quaker meeting at the South Meeting House.

While many of the attendees were there for the good of their souls, those in their teens and early twenties tended to have other motives. No other place on Nantucket offered a better opportunity for young people to meet members of the opposite sex. Nantucketer Charles Murphey described in a poem how young men such as himself used the long gaps of silence typical of a Quaker meeting

14

To sit with eager eyes directed
On all the beauty there collected
And gaze with wonder while in sessions
On all the various forms and fashions.

Yet another gathering spot for amorous young people was the ridge of hills behind the town where the four windmills stood. Here couples could enjoy a spectacular view of the town and Nantucket Harbor, with the brand-new lighthouse at the end of Great Point visible in the distance.

What is surprising is how rarely Nantucketers, even young and adventurous Nantucketers like Nickerson and company, strayed beyond the gates of the little town. 'As small as [the island] is,' one whale-oil merchant admitted in a letter, 'I was never at the extreme east or west, and for some years I dare say have not been one mile from town.' In a world of whales, sea serpents, and ominous signs in the night sky, all Nantucketers, whalemen and landsmen alike, looked to the town as a sanctuary, a fenced-in place of familiar ways and timeless ancestral alliances, a place to call home.

*   *   *

Passions stirred beneath Nantucket's Quaker facade. Life might seem restrained and orderly as hundreds, sometimes thousands, of people made their way to meeting each Thursday and Sunday, the men in their long dark coats and wide-brimmed hats, the women in long dresses and meticulously crafted bonnets. But factors besides Quakerism and a common heritage also drove the Nantucket

15

psyche—in particular, an obsession with the whale. No matter how much the inhabitants might try to hide it, there was a savagery about this island, a bloodlust and pride that bound every mother, father, and child in a clannish commitment to the hunt.

The imprinting of a young Nantucketer began at the earliest age. The first words a baby was taught included the language of the chase—'townor,' for instance, a Wampanoag word meaning that the whale has been sighted for a second time. Bedtime stories told of killing whales and eluding cannibals in the Pacific. One mother approvingly recounted how her nine-year-old son attached a fork to the end of a ball of darning cotton and then proceeded to harpoon the family cat. The mother happened into the room just as the terrified pet attempted to escape, and unsure of what she had found herself in the middle of, she picked up the cotton ball. Like a veteran boatsteerer, the boy shouted, 'Pay out, mother! Pay out! There she sounds through the window!'

There was rumored to be a secret society of young women on the island whose members pledged to marry only men who had already killed a whale. To help these young women identify them as hunters, boatsteerers wore chockpins (small oak pins used to keep the harpoon line in the bow groove of a whaleboat) on their lapels. Boatsteerers, superb athletes with prospects of lucrative captaincies, were considered the most eligible of Nantucket bachelors.

Instead of toasting a person's health, a Nantucketer offered invocations of a darker sort:

16

Death to the living,
Long life to the killers,
Success to sailors' wives
And greasy luck to whalers.

Despite the bravado of this little ditty, death was a fact of life with which all Nantucketers were thoroughly familiar. In 1810 there were forty-seven fatherless children on Nantucket, while almost a quarter of the women over the age of twenty-three (the average age of marriage) had been widowed by the sea.

In old age, Nickerson still visited the graves of his parents in the Old North Burial Ground. In 1819, during the last few weeks before his departure aboard the *Essex*, he undoubtedly made his way to this fenced-in patch of sun-scorched grass and walked among its canted stones. Nickerson's father had been the first of the parents to die, on November 9, 1806, at the age of thirty-three. His gravestone read:

Crush'd as the moth beneath thy hand
We moulder to the dust
Our feeble powers can ne'er withstand
And all our beauty's lost.

Nickerson's mother, who had borne five children, died less than a month later at the age of twenty-eight. Her oldest living daughter was eight years old; her only son was not yet two. Her inscription read:

This mortal life decays apace
How soon the bubble's broke

17

Adam and all his numerous race
Are Vanity and Smoke.

Nickerson, who was raised by his grandparents, wasn't the only orphan aboard the *Essex*. His friend Barzillai Ray had also lost both his parents. Owen Coffin and Charles Ramsdell had each lost a father. This may have been their closest bond: each of them, like so many Nantucketers, was a fatherless child for whom a ship's officer would be much more than a demanding taskmaster; he would be, quite possibly, the first male authority figure the boys had ever known.

*　　*　　*

Perhaps no community before or since has been so divided by its commitment to work. For a whaleman and his family, it was a punishing regimen: two to three years away, three to four months at home. With their men gone for so long, Nantucket's women were obliged not only to raise the children but also to run many of the island's businesses. It was largely the women who maintained the complex web of personal and commercial relationships that kept the community functioning. J. Hector St. John de Crèvecoeur, whose classic *Letters from an American Farmer* describes his lengthy stay on the island a few years prior to the outbreak of the Revolution, suggested that the Nantucket women's 'prudence and good management . . . justly entitles them to a rank superior to that of other wives.'

Quakerism contributed to the women's strength. In its emphasis on the spiritual and intellectual equality of the sexes, the religion fostered an attitude that was in keeping with what all Nantucketers saw plainly demonstrated to them every day: that women, who on Nantucket tended to be better educated than the island's men, were just as intelligent, just as capable as their male counterparts.

By necessity and choice, the island's women maintained active social lives, visiting one another with a frequency Crèvecoeur described as incessant. These visits involved more than the exchange of mere gossip. They were the setting in which much of the business of the town was transacted. The nineteenth-century feminist Lucretia Coffin Mott, who was born and raised on Nantucket, remembered how a husband back from a voyage commonly followed in the wake of his wife, accompanying her to get-togethers with other wives. Mott, who eventually moved to Philadelphia, commented on how odd such a practice would have struck anyone from the mainland, where the sexes operated in entirely different social spheres.

Some of the Nantucket wives adapted quite well to the three-years-away, three-months-at-home rhythm of the whale fishery. The islander Eliza Brock recorded in her journal what she called the 'Nantucket Girl's Song':

> Then I'll haste to wed a sailor, and send him off
>   to sea,
> For a life of independence, is the pleasant life
>   for me.
> But every now and then I shall like to see his
>   face,
> For it always seems to me to beam with manly

grace,
With his brow so nobly open, and his dark and
kindly eye,
Oh my heartbeats fondly towards him whenever
he is nigh.
But when he says 'Goodbye my love, I'm off
across the sea,'
First I cry for his departure, then laugh because
I'm free.

The mantle of power and responsibility settled upon the Nantucket woman's shoulders on her wedding day. '[N]o sooner have they undergone this ceremony,' said Crèvecoeur, 'than they cease to appear so cheerful and gay; the new rank they hold in the society impresses them with more serious ideas than were entertained before . . . [T]he new wife . . . gradually advises and directs [the household]; the new husband soon goes to sea; he leaves her to learn and exercise the new government in which she is entered.'

To the undying outrage of subsequent generations of Nantucket loyalists, Crèvecoeur claimed that many of the island's women had developed an addiction to opium: 'They have adopted these many years the Asiatic custom of taking a dose of opium every morning, and so deeply rooted is it that they would be at a loss how to live without this indulgence.' Why they took the drug is perhaps impossible to determine from this distance in time. Still, the portrait that emerges—of a community of achievers attempting to cope with a potentially devastating loneliness—makes the women's dependence on opium perhaps easier to understand. The ready availability of the drug on

20

the island (opium was included in every whaleship's medical chest) combined with the inhabitants' wealth may also help to explain why the drug was so widely used in Nantucket.

There is little doubt that intimacy—physical as well as emotional—between a wife and a husband must have been difficult to establish under the tremendously compressed circumstances of the few months available between voyages. An island tradition claims that Nantucket women dealt with their husbands' long absences by relying on sexual aids known as 'he's-at-homes.' Although this claim, like that of drug use, seems to fly in the face of the island's staid Quaker reputation, in 1979 a six-inch plaster penis (along with a batch of letters from the nineteenth century and a laudanum bottle) was discovered hidden in the chimney of a house in the island's historic district. Just because they were 'superior wives' didn't mean that the island's women were without normal physical desires. Like their husbands, Nantucket's women were ordinary human beings attempting to adapt to a most extraordinary way of life.

*   *   *

Thomas Nickerson may have enjoyed his first moments aboard the *Essex*, exploring her dark, hot interior, but the thrill was soon over. For the next three weeks, during the warmest summer anyone could remember, Nickerson and the gradually accumulating crew of the *Essex* labored to prepare the ship. Even in winter, Nantucket's wharves, topped by a layer of oil-soaked sand, stank to the point that people said you didn't see Nantucket

21

when you first rounded the lighthouse at Brant Point, you smelled it. That July and August the stench rising from the wharf must have been pungent enough to gag even a veteran whaleman.

At that time on Nantucket it was standard practice to have the newly signed members of a whaleship's crew help prepare the vessel for the upcoming voyage. Nowhere else in New England was a sailor expected to help rig and provision his ship. That was what riggers, stevedores, and provisioners were for. But on Nantucket, whose Quaker merchants were famous for their ability to cut costs and increase profits, a different standard prevailed.

Whalemen did not work for wages; they were paid a share, or lay—a predetermined portion of the total take—at the end of the voyage. This meant that whatever work a shipowner could extract from a sailor prior to a voyage was, in essence, free or, to Nickerson's mind, 'a donation of . . . labor' on the part of the sailor. A shipowner might advance a seaman some money to help him purchase the clothing and equipment necessary for the voyage, but it was deducted (with interest) from his lay at the conclusion of the voyage.

As cabin boy, Thomas Nickerson had what was known as a very 'long' (or meager) lay. Although the ship papers from the *Essex*'s 1819 voyage have vanished, we know that Nickerson's predecessor, the cabin boy Joseph Underwood of Salem, received a 1/198 lay for the previous voyage. Given that the *Essex*'s cargo of 1,200 barrels of sperm oil sold for about $26,500, Underwood was paid, once the expenses of the voyage were deducted from the gross and his personal expenses were deducted from his own portion, a grand total of about $150 for two years' work. Although this was a pitiful wage, the cabin boy had been provided with room and board for two years and now had the experience to begin a career as a whaleman.

By the end of July, the *Essex*'s upperworks—just about everything at deck level and above—had been completely rebuilt, including a new layer of pine decking and a cookhouse. At some point— probably before Nickerson joined the crew—the *Essex* was laid over on her side for coppering. Immense block-and-tackle systems were strung from the ship's masts to the wharf to haul the ship onto her side. The exposed bottom was then sheathed in copper to protect the ship from marine growth, which could turn her four-inch-thick oak hull planking into a soft, porous veneer.

At twenty years of age, the *Essex* was reaching the point when many vessels began to exhibit serious structural deterioration. Whale oil seems to have acted as a preservative, providing most whaleships with lives much longer than that of atypical merchant vessel. Still, there were limits. Rot, teredo worms, and a condition called iron sickness, in which the ship's rusted iron fastenings weakened the oak, were all potential problems.

The ever lengthening voyages around Cape Horn were another concern. 'The ship[s] being so long at sea without much repairs,' Obed Macy would write in his journal, 'must shorten the durations of the ships [by] many years.' Indeed, the *Essex* had undergone several days of repairs in South America during her previous voyage. She was an old ship caught up in a new era of whaling, and no one knew how much longer she would last.

23

Owners were always reluctant to invest any more money in the repair of a ship than was absolutely necessary. While they had no choice but to rebuild the *Essex*'s upperworks, there could well have been suspicious areas below the waterline that they chose to address at a later time, if not ignore. That summer, the *Essex*'s principal owners, Gideon Folger and Sons, were awaiting delivery of a new, much larger whaleship, the *Aurora*. This was not the year to spend an inordinate amount of money on a tired old vessel like the *Essex*.

*   *   *

Nantucket's shipowners could be as fierce in their own bloodless way as any whaleman. They might 'act the Quaker,' but that didn't keep them from pursuing profits with a lethal enthusiasm.

In *Moby-Dick*, one of the *Pequod*'s owners is Bildad, a pious Quaker whose religious scruples do not prevent him from extorting cruelly long lays from the crew (he offers Ishmael a 1/777 lay!)— With his Bible in one hand and ledgerbook in the other, Bildad resembles a lean, Quakerly John D. Rockefeller, his mind and soul devoted to the cold calculus of making a whaling voyage pay.

There were some observers who claimed that, rather than leading the islanders to prosperity and grace, Quakerism was at the root of whatever evil flourished in the sharp business practices of Nantucket's shipowners. According to William Comstock, who penned an account of a whaling cruise from Nantucket in the 1820s, 'Unfortunately, the anger which [the Quakers] are forbidden to express by outward actions, finding no

24

vent, stagnates the heart, and, while they make professions of love and goodwill . . . , the rancor and intense malevolence of their feelings poisons every generous spring of human kindness.'

Gideon Folger and Paul Macy, two major shareholders in the *Essex*, were prominent members of the island's Quaker upper class. Yet, according to Nickerson, Macy, in charge of outfitting the *Essex* that summer of 1819, attempted to cut costs by severely underprovisioning the ship. In this practice he was not alone. '[T]he owners of whaleships too frequently neglect to victual their ships properly,' Comstock wrote, 'depending on the Captain to stint his crew in proportion to his means, by which a few dollars are saved to the rich owners, while the poor hard laboring sailor famishes with hunger.' While it would be unfair to point to Paul Macy as responsible, even in part, for the grief that eventually awaited the men of the *Essex*, the first step toward that future began with Macy's decision to save a little money in beef and hardtack.

On Nantucket in the early nineteenth century, people didn't invest in bonds or the stock market, but rather in whaleships. By purchasing shares in several ships rather than putting their money in a single vessel, islanders spread both the risk and the reward throughout the community. Agents such as Macy and Folger could expect a total return on their whaling investments of somewhere between 28 and 44 percent per year.

Making this level of profitability all the more remarkable was the state of the world's economy in 1819. As Nantucket continued to add ship after ship to her fleet, mainland businesses were

25

collapsing by the hundreds. Claiming that the 'days of our fictitious affluence is past,' a Baltimore newspaper reported that spring on 'dishonored credits, deserted dwellings, inactive streets, declining commerce, and exhausted coffers.' Nantucket remained an astonishing exception. Just as its isolated situation many miles out to sea enabled it to enjoy the warming influence of the Gulf Stream (providing for the longest growing season in the region), Nantucket existed, at least for the time being, in its own benign climate of prosperity.

Between July 4 and July 23, ten whaleships left the island, most heading out in pairs. The wharves were busy with laborers long into the night, all caught up in the disciplined frenzy of preparing whaleships for sea. But Gideon Folger, Paul Macy, and the *Essex*'s captain, George Pollard, knew that all the preparations would be for naught if they couldn't find a crew of twenty-one men.

Since there were only so many Nantucketers to go around, shipowners relied on off-islanders with no previous sailing experience, known as 'green hands,' to man their vessels. Many came from nearby Cape Cod. Shipping agents in cities up and down the East Coast also provided the owners with green hands, often sending them to Nantucket in groups aboard packet ships.

A green hand's first impression of the island was seldom positive. The young boys loitering on the waterfront inevitably harassed the new arrivals with the cry 'See the greenies, come to go ileing.' ('Oil' was pronounced 'ile' on Nantucket.) Then followed a walk from Straight Wharf to the base of Main Street, where a clothing and dry goods store served

26

as the 'grand resort and rendezvous of seafaring men.' Here men looking for a berth or just killing time (known as 'watching the pass' on Nantucket) spent the day in a haze of tobacco smoke, lounging on an assortment of benches and wooden boxes.

On this island of perpetual motion, job-seeking seamen were expected to whittle. It was the way a man whittled that let people know what kind of berth he expected. A whaleman with at least one voyage under his belt knew enough to draw his knife always away from him. This signaled that he was looking for a boatsteerer's berth. Boatsteerers, on the other hand, whittled in the opposite direction, toward themselves; this indicated that they believed they were ready to become a mate. Not knowing the secret codes that Nantucketers had developed, a green hand simply whittled as best he knew how.

Many of the green hands felt as if they had found themselves in a foreign country where the people spoke a different language. All Nantucketers, even the women and little children, used nautical terms as if they were able-bodied seamen. According to one visitor, 'Every child can tell *which way the wind blows*, and any old woman in the street will talk of *cruising about, hailing an old messmate,* or *making one bring to,* as familiarly as the captain of a whaleship, just arrived from the northwest coast, will describe dimension to a *landlubber* by the span of his *jibboom*, or the length of his *mainstay.*' For the green hands, whose first taste of the sea may have been on the packet ship to Nantucket, it was all a bewildering blur, particularly since many of the islanders also employed the distinctive 'thee and thou' phrasing

27

of the Quakers.

Compounding the confusion was the Nantucketers' accent. It wasn't just 'ile' for 'oil'; there was a host of peculiar pronunciations, many of which varied markedly from what was found even as nearby as Cape Cod and the island of Martha's Vineyard. A Nantucket whaleman kept his clothing in a 'chist.' His harpoons were kept 'shurp,' especially when 'atteking' a 'lirge' whale. A 'keppin' had his own 'kebbin' and was more often than not a 'merrid' man, while a 'met' kept the ship's log for the entire 'viege.'

Then there were all these strange phrases that a Nantucketer used. If he bungled a job, it was a 'foopaw,' an apparent corruption of the French *faux pas* that dated back to the days after the Revolution when Nantucketers established a whaling operation in Dunkirk, France. A Nantucketer didn't just go for a walk on a Sunday afternoon, he went on a 'rantum scoot,' which meant an excursion with no definite destination. Fancy victuals were known as 'manavelins.' If someone was cross-eyed, he was 'born in the middle of the week and looking both ways for Sunday.'

Green hands were typically subjected to what one man remembered as 'a sort of examination' by both the shipowner and the captain. Recalled another, 'We were catechized, in brief, concerning our nativity and previous occupation, and the build and physical points of each were looked to, not forgetting the eyes, for a sharp-sighted man was a jewel in the estimation of the genuine whaling captain.' Some green hands were so naive and poorly educated that they insisted on the longest lay possible, erroneously thinking that the higher number meant higher pay. The owners were all too willing to grant their wishes.

Whaling captains competed with one another for men. But, as with everything on Nantucket, there were specific rules to which everyone had to adhere. Since first-time captains were expected to dcfcr to all others, the only men available to Captain Pollard of the *Essex* would have been those in whom no one else had an interest. By the end of July, Pollard and the owners were still short by more than half a dozen men.

*   *   *

On August 4, Obed Macy stopped by the Marine Insurance Company at the corner of Main and Federal Streets to look at the thermometer mounted on its shingled exterior. In his journal he recorded, '93 degrees and very little wind, which has rendered it almost insupportable to be exposed to the rays of the sun.'

The next day, August 5, the fully rigged *Essex* was floated over the Nantucket Bar into deep water. Now the loading could begin in earnest, and a series of smaller craft called lighters began ferrying goods from the wharf to the ship. First to be stowed were the ground-tier casks—large, iron-hooped containers each capable of holding 268 gallons of whale oil. They were filled with seawater to keep them swollen and tight. On top of thcsc were stowed casks of various sizes filled with freshwater. Firewood took up a great dcal of space, as did the thousands of shooks, or packed bundles of staves, which would be used by the ship's cooper

29

to create more oil casks. On top of that was enough food, all stored in casks, to last two and a half years. If the men were fed the same amount as merchant seamen (which is perhaps assuming too much when it came to a Nantucket whaler), the *Essex* would have contained at least fourteen tons of meat (salt beef and pork), more than eight tons of bread, and thousands of gallons of freshwater. Then there were massive amounts of whaling equipment (harpoons, lances, etc.), as well as clothing, charts, sails (including at least one spare set), navigational instruments, medicine, rum, gin, lumber, and so on. In addition to the three newly painted whaleboats that were suspended from the ship's davits, there were at least two spare boats: one stored upside down on a rack over the quarterdeck, another mounted on spare spars that projected over the stern.

By the time the men were done loading the *Essex* six days later—their labors briefly interrupted by a tremendous shower of rain duly noted by Obed Macy on August 9—the ship was almost as heavily laden as it would be with whale oil on her return to Nantucket. Explained one Nantucketer, '[T]he gradual consumption of provisions and stores keeps pace with the gradual accumulation of oil . . . , and a whaleship is always full, or nearly so, all the voyage.'

Something, however, was still missing: the men needed to fill the seven empty berths in the *Essex*'s forecastle. At some point, Gideon Folger put out the call to an agent in Boston for as many black sailors as the agent could find.

*   *   *

30

Although he wasn't black, Addison Pratt came to Nantucket under circumstances similar to the ones that brought seven African Americans to the island and to service on the *Essex*. In 1820, Pratt found himself in Boston, looking for a ship:

> I soon commenced hunting for a voyage, but it was dull times with commerce as seamen's wages were but ten dollars per month, and there were more sailors than ships in port, and I found it dull times for green hands. But after looking around for a few days I heard there were hands wanted to go on a whaling voyage to the Pacific Ocean. I made no delay, but hastened to the office and put down my name and received twelve dollars of advance money, which I laid out in sea clothes . . . Six more hands were shipped for the same vessel, and we were all sent on board of a packet bound to Nantucket.

As Pratt's account suggests, a whaling voyage was the lowest rung on the maritime ladder for a seaman. Nantucketers like Thomas Nickerson and his friends might look to their first voyage as a necessary step in the beginning of a long and profitable career. But for the men who were typically rounded up by shipping agents in cities such as Boston, it was a different story. Instead of the beginning of something, shipping out on a whaling voyage was often a last and desperate resort. The seven black sailors who agreed to sign on for a voyage aboard the *Essex*—Samuel Reed, Richard Peterson, Lawson Thomas, Charles

31

Shorter, Isaiah Sheppard, William Bond, and Henry Dewitt—had even fewer choices than Addison Pratt would in 1820. None of their names appear in Boston or New York directories from this period, indicating that they were not landowners. Whether or not they called Boston home, most of them had probably spent more than a few nights in the boardinghouses in the waterfront area of the North End of the city—a place notorious as a gathering place for itinerant seamen, black and white, looking for a berth.

As they boarded the packet for Nantucket, the seven African Americans knew at least one thing: they might not be paid well for their time aboard a Nantucket whaler, but they were assured of being paid no less than a white person with the same qualifications. Since the time when Native Americans had made up the majority of Nantucket's labor force, the island's shipowners had always paid men according to their rank, not their color. Some of this had to do with the Quakers' anti-slavery leanings, but much of it also had to do with the harsh realities of shipboard life. In a tight spot, a captain didn't care if a seaman was white or black; he just wanted to know he could count on the man to complete his appointed task.

Still, black sailors who were delivered to the island as green hands were never regarded as equals by Nantucketers. In 1807, a visitor to the island reported:

[T]he Indians having disappeared, Negroes are now substituted in their place. Seamen of color are more submissive than the whites; but

32

as they are more addicted to frolicking, it is difficult to get them aboard the ship, when it is about to sail, and to keep them aboard, after it has arrived. The Negroes, though they are to be prized for their habits of obedience, are not as intelligent as the Indians; and none of them attain the rank of [boatsteerer or mate].

It wasn't lofty social ideals that brought black sailors to this Quaker island, but rather the whale fishery's insatiable and often exploitative hunger for labor. '[A]n African is treated like a brute by the officers of their ship,' reported William Comstock, who had much to say about the evils of Nantucket's Quaker shipowners. 'Should these pages fall into the hands of any of my colored brethren, let me advise them to fly Nantucket as they would the Norway Maelstrom.' Even Nickerson admitted that Nantucket whaling captains had a reputation as 'Negro drivers.' Significantly, Nantucketers referred to the packet that delivered green hands from New York City as the 'Slaver.'

*   *   *

By the evening of Wednesday, August 11, all save for Captain Pollard were safely aboard the *Essex*. Anchored beside her, just off the Nantucket Bar, was another whaleship, the *Chili*. Commanded by Absalom Coffin, the *Chili* was also to leave the following day. It was an opportunity for what whalemen referred to as a 'gam'—a visit between two ships' crews. Without the captains to inhibit the revelry (and with the Bar between them and town), they may have seized this chance for a final, uproarious fling before the grinding discipline of shipboard life took control of their lives.

At some point that evening, Thomas Nickerson made his way down to his bunk and its mattress full of mildewed corn husks. As he faded off to sleep on the gently rocking ship, he surely felt what one young whaleman described as a great, almost overwhelming 'pride in my floating home.'

That night he was probably unaware of the latest bit of gossip circulating through town—of the strange goings-on out on the Commons. Swarms of grasshoppers had begun to appear in the turnip fields. '[T]he whole face of the earth has been spotted with them . . . ,' Obed Macy would write. '[N]o person living ever knew them so numerous.' A comet in July and now a plague of locusts?

As it turned out, things would end up badly for the two ships anchored off the Nantucket Bar on the evening of August 11, 1819. The *Chili* would not return for another three and a half years, and then with only five hundred barrels of sperm oil, about a quarter of what was needed to fill a ship her size. For Captain Coffin and his men, it would be a disastrous voyage.

But nothing could compare to what fate had in store for the twenty-one men of the *Essex*.

CHAPTER TWO

KNOCKDOWN

On the morning of Thursday, August 12, 1819, a harbor vessel delivered Captain George Pollard, Jr., to the *Essex*. At twenty-eight, Pollard was a young, but not spectacularly young, first-time captain. Over the last four years he had spent all but seven months aboard the *Essex*, as second mate and then first mate. Except for her former captain, Daniel Russell, no one knew this ship better than George Pollard.

Pollard carried a letter from the *Essex*'s principal owners telling the new captain, in spare, direct prose, exactly what was expected of him. His predecessor, Daniel Russell, had received a similar letter prior to an earlier voyage. It had read:

Respected Friend,
    As thou art master of the Ship *Essex* now lying without the bar at anchor, our orders are, that thou shouldst proceed to sea the first fair wind and proceed for the Pacifick Ocean, and endeavour to obtain a load of Sperm Oil and when accomplished to make the best dispatch for this place. Thou art forbidden to hold any illicit trade. Thou art forbidden to carry on thyself or to suffer any person belonging to the ship *Essex* to carry on any trade except it should be necessary for the preservation of the ship *Essex* or her crew: wishing thee a short and prosperous voyage,

with a full portion of happiness we remain thy friends.

In behalf of the owners of the ship *Essex*,
Gideon Folger, Paul Macy

Pollard felt the full weight of the owners' expectations. But he was thinking not only about the voyage ahead but also about what he was leaving behind. Just two months before, he and nineteen-year-old Mary Riddell had been married in the Second Congregational Church, of which Mary's father, a well-to-do cordwainer, or ropemaker, was a deacon.

As he scrambled up the *Essex*'s side, then made his way aft to the quarterdeck, Captain Pollard knew that the entire town was watching him and his men. All summer, ships had been leaving the island, sometimes as many as four or five a week, but with the departure of the *Essex* and the *Chili*, there would be a lull of about a month or so before another whaleship would depart. For the entertainment-starved inhabitants of Nantucket, this would be it for a while.

Leaving the island was difficult aboard any whaleship, since most of the crew had no idea of what they were doing. It could be an agony of embarrassment for a captain, as the green hands bumbled their way around the deck or clung white-knuckled to the spars. The whole affair was carried out in the knowledge that the town's old salts and, of course, the owners were watching and criticizing from the shade of the windmills up on Mill Hill.

With, perhaps, a nervous glance townward, Captain George Pollard gave the order to prepare the ship for weighing the anchors.

A whaleship, even a small and old whaleship, was a complex and sophisticated piece of equipment. The *Essex* had three masts and a bowsprit. To the mast were fastened a multitude of horizontal spars known as yards, from which the rectangular sails were set. There was so much cordage, dedicated to either supporting the spars or controlling the sails (more than twenty in number), that, from the perspective of a green hand staring up from the deck, the *Essex* looked like the web of a giant rope-spinning spider.

That each one of these pieces of rope had a name was plainly laughable to a green hand. How could anyone, even after a three-year voyage, pretend to have any idea of what went where? For young Nantucketers such as Nickerson and his friends, it was particularly devastating since they had begun this adventure assuming they knew much more than they apparently did. '[All] was bustle, confusion and awkwardness, that is, on the part of the crew,' Nickerson remembered. 'The officers were smart active men and were no doubt . . . piqued at having such a display of awkwardness in full view of their native town.'

Since he was required by custom to remain stationed at the quarterdeck, Pollard was all but powerless before this clumsy display. Doing his best to apply some method to the madness was the first mate, Owen Chase, stationed in the forward part of the deck. It was his duty to implement Pollard's orders, and he shouted and cajoled the men as if every hesitation or mistake on their part were a personal insult.

Pollard and Chase had been together aboard the *Essex* since 1815, when Chase, at eighteen, had signed on as a common sailor. Chase had moved quickly through the ranks. By the next voyage he was a boat-steerer, and now, at only twenty-two, he was the first mate. (Matthew Joy, the *Essex*'s second mate, was four years older than Chase.) If all went well during this voyage, Chase would have a good chance of becoming a captain before he was twenty-five.

At five feet ten, Chase was tall for the early nineteenth century; he towered over Captain Pollard, a small man with a tendency toward stoutness. While Pollard's father was also a captain, Chase's father was a farmer. Perhaps because his father was a farmer on an island where seagoing men got all the glory, Chase was fired with more than the usual amount of ambition and, as he started his third voyage, he made no secret of his impatience to become a captain. 'Two voyages are generally considered sufficient to qualify an active and intelligent young man for command,' he would write, 'in which time, he learns from experience, and the examples which are set him, all that is necessary to be known.' He was six years younger than Captain Pollard, but Chase felt he had already mastered everything he needed to know to perform Pollard's job. The first mate's cocksure attitude would make it difficult for Pollard, a first-time captain just emerging from the long shadow of a respected predecessor, to assert his own style of command.

As the crew assembled spare hawsers and rope in preparation for weighing the anchor, Chase made sure everything was secured about the deck. Then he ordered the men to the windlass, a long, horizontally mounted wooden cylinder with a double row of holes at each end. Positioned just forward of the forecastle hatch, the windlass provided the mechanical advantage required to do the heavy lifting aboard the ship. Eight men were stationed at the two ends, four aft, four forward, each holding a wooden handspike.

Working the windlass in a coordinated fashion was as challenging as it was backbreaking. 'To perform this the sailors must . . . give a sudden jerk at the same instant,' went one account, 'in which movement they are regulated by a sort of song or howl pronounced by one of their number.'

Once the men had pulled the slack out of the anchor cable, or hove short, it was time for crew members who had been positioned aloft to loosen the sails from their ties. Pollard then ordered Chase (whom, in accordance with custom, he always addressed as 'Mr. Chase') to heave up the anchor and to let him know when it was aweigh. Now the real work began—a process, given the rawness of the *Essex*'s crew, that probably took an excruciatingly long time to perform: inching the huge, mud-dripping anchor up to the bow. Eventually, however, the anchor was lashed to the bulwarks, with the ring at the end of its shank secured to a projecting timber known as a cathead.

Now Pollard's and Chase's public agony began in earnest. There were additional sails to be set in the gradually building southwesterly breeze. A crack crew would have had all the canvas flying in an instant. In the *Essex*'s case, it wasn't until they had sailed completely around Great Point—more than

nine miles from where they'd weighed anchor—
that the upper, or topgallant, sails were, according
to Nickerson, 'set and all sails trimmed in the
breeze.' All the while, Pollard and his officers knew
that the town's spyglasses had been following them
for each and every awful moment.

As cabin boy, Nickerson had to sweep the decks
and coil any stray lines. When he paused for a few
seconds to watch his beloved island fade from view
behind them, he was accosted by the first mate,
who in addition to cuffing him about the ears,
snarled, 'You boy, Tom, bring back your broom
here and sweep clean. The next time I have to
speak to you, your hide shall pay for it, my lad!'

Nickerson and his Nantucket friends may have
thought they knew Chase prior to their departure,
but they now realized that, as another young
Nantucketer had discovered, 'at sea, things appear
different.' The mate of a Nantucket whaleship
routinely underwent an almost Jekyll-and-Hyde
transformation when he left his island home,
stepping out of his mild Quaker skin to become a
vociferous martinet. 'You will often hear a
Nantucket mother boast that her son "who is *met*
of a ship is a real *spit-fire*,"' William Comstock
wrote, 'meaning that he is a cruel tyrant, which on
that island is considered the very *acme* of human
perfection.'

And so Nickerson saw Owen Chase change from
a perfectly reasonable young man with a new wife
named Peggy to a bully who had no qualms about
using force to obtain obedience and who swore in a
manner that shocked these boys who had been
brought up, for the most part, by their mothers and
grandmothers. ' [A]lthough but a few hours before

40

I had been so eager to go [on] this voyage,' Nickerson remembered, 'there [now] seemed a sudden gloom to spread over me. A not very pleasing prospect [was] truly before me, that of a long voyage and a hard overseer. This to a boy of my years who had never been used to hear such language or threats before.'

It was more than a realization that the whaling life might be harsher than he had been led to believe. Now that the island had slipped over the horizon, Nickerson began to understand, as only an adolescent on the verge of adulthood can understand, that the carefree days of childhood were gone forever: 'Then it was that I, for the first time, realized that I was alone upon a wide and an unfeeling world . . . without one relative or friend to bestow one kind word upon me.' Not till then did Nickerson begin to appreciate 'the full sacrifice that I had made.'

*   *   *

That evening the men were divided into two shifts, or watches. With the exception of the 'idlers'—those such as the cook, steward, and cooper (or barrel maker), who worked in the day and slept at night—all the men served alternating four-hour stints on deck. Like children picking teams on a playground, the mate and second mate took turns choosing the men who would serve in their watches. '[T]he first step taken by the officers,' said William Comstock, 'is, to discover who are natives of the island, and who are strangers. The honor of being a Roman citizen was not, in days of yore, so enviable a distinction, as it is on board one of these ships, to be a native of that sand bank, yclept Nantucket.' Once the Nantucketers had all been picked (with Nickerson taken by Chase), the mates chose among the Cape Codders and the blacks.

Next came the choice of oarsmen for the whaleboats, a contest that involved both mates and also Captain Pollard, who headed up his own boat. Since these were the men with whom a mate or a captain was going into battle, he took the selection of the whaleboat crew very seriously. '[T]here was much competition among the officers,' a whaleman remembered, 'and evidently some anxiety, with a little ill-concealed jealousy of feeling.'

Once again, each officer attempted to man his boat with as many fellow Nantucketers as he could. Nickerson found himself on Chase's boat, with the Nantucketer Benjamin Lawrence as a boatsteerer. Nickerson's friend (and the captain's cousin) Owen Coffin was assigned to Pollard's boat along with several other Nantucketers. Matthew Joy, who as second mate was the lowest-ranking officer, was left without a single islander on his boat. The three remaining men not chosen as oarsmen became the *Essex*'s shipkeepers. It was their duty to handle the *Essex* when whales were being hunted.

The first day of a whaling voyage included yet another ritual—the captain's speech to the crew. The tradition was said to date back to when Noah first closed the doors of the ark, and was the way the captain officially introduced himself. It was a performance that all aboard the ship—officers and green hands alike—attended with great interest.

As soon as Pollard began to speak, Nickerson was impressed by the difference between the captain and the first mate. Instead of shouting and

42

cursing at the men, Pollard spoke 'without overbearing display or ungentleman-like language.' He simply stated that the success of the voyage would depend on the crew and that the officers should be strictly obeyed. Any sailor who willfully disregarded an order, Pollard told them, would have to answer not just to the officers but to him. He then dismissed the men with the words 'Set the watch, Mr. Chase.'

* * *

The men of the *Essex* ate and slept in three different areas: the captain's and mates' cabins, in the aft portion of the ship; steerage, where the boatsteerers and young Nantucketers lived, just forward of the officers; and the forecastle—the cramped, poorly lit quarters in the extreme forward part of the vessel, separated from steerage by the blubber room. The divide between the forecastle and the other living quarters was not just physical but also racial. According to Addison Pratt, a green hand on a Nantucket ship in 1820, the forecastle was 'filled with darkies' while the white sailors who weren't officers lived in steerage. Reflecting the prejudices typical of a Nantucket whaleman, Thomas Nickerson considered himself 'fortunate indeed to escape being so closely penned up with so large a number of blacks' in the *Essex*'s forecastle.

But the forecastle had its merits. Its isolation (the only way to enter it was from a hatchway in the deck) meant that its occupants could create their own world. When he sailed on a merchant voyage in the 1830s, Richard Henry Dana, the author of

43

Two Years Before the Mast, preferred the camaraderie of the forecastle to steerage, where '[y]ou are immediately under the eye of the officers, cannot dance, sing, play, smoke, make a noise, or *growl* [i.e., complain], or take an other sailor's pleasure.' In the forecastle the African American sailors indulged in the ancient seafaring tradition of 'yarning'—swapping stories about passages, shipmates, and wrecks, along with other tales of the sea. They danced and sang songs, often accompanied by a fiddle; they prayed to their God; and, in keeping with yet another oceangoing tradition, they second-guessed the captain and his officers.

*　　　*　　　*

By the following morning, many of the green hands found themselves in the throes of seasickness, 'rolling and tumbling about the decks almost ready . . . to die or be cast in to the sea,' Nickerson remembered. Nantucketers had what they considered a sure-fire cure for seasickness, a treatment that more delicate mortals might have considered even worse than the malady. The sufferer was made to swallow a piece of pork fat tied to a string, which was then pulled back up again. If the symptoms returned, the process was repeated.

Chase was not about to coddle his queasy crew. That morning at eight bells sharp, he ordered all hands to clear the decks and prepare the ship for whaling. Even though the whale population in the waters to the southeast of the island along the edges of the Gulf Stream had been greatly

44

diminished over the years, it was still quite possible to come across what Nantucketers called a shoal of sperm whales. Woe to the crew that was not ready when a whale was sighted.

But for a whale to be sighted, a lookout had to be positioned aloft—not a pleasing prospect for a crew of seasick green hands. Every man was expected to climb to the head of the mainmast and spend two hours in search of whales. Some of the men were so weak from vomiting that they doubted they had the strength to hold on to a pitching spar for two hours. One of them, Nickerson said, even went so far as to protest that it was 'altogether absurd and unreasonable' to expect them to look for whales, and that he, for one, 'should not go, and he hoped the captain would not expect it of him.'

The fact that this unnamed sailor specifically mentioned the captain instead of the first mate suggests that he was Pollard's cousin, seventeen-year-old Owen Coffin. Miserable and genuinely fearful for his life, Coffin may have made a desperate, ill-advised appeal to his kinsman for a reprieve from the first mate's discipline. But it was futile. According to Nickerson, whose narrative is not without irony, there followed a few 'soft words' from the officers, along with 'some little challenging of their spirits,' and it wasn't long before all the green hands had taken a turn at the masthead.

*   *   *

Like a skier traversing the face of a mountain, a Nantucket whaleship took an indirect route toward Cape Horn, a course determined by the prevailing

45

winds of the Atlantic Ocean. First, pushed by the westerlies, the ship sailed south and east toward Europe and Africa. There she picked up winds called the northeast trades, which took her back across the ocean again, in the direction of South America. After crossing the equator in an often airless region known as the doldrums, she worked her way south and west through the southeast trades into an area of variable winds. Then she encountered the band of westerlies that could make rounding the Horn so difficult.

On the first leg of this southern slide down the Atlantic, there were provisioning stops at the Azores and Cape Verde Islands, where vegetables and livestock could be purchased for much less than they cost on Nantucket. These stops also gave the whalemen the opportunity to ship back any oil they might have obtained during their cruise across the Atlantic.

On August 15, three days out of Nantucket, the *Essex* was making good time toward the Azores, with the wind out of the southwest, coming directly over her starboard side, or beam. Having left Nantucket late in the season, the officers hoped to make up lost time. As usual, three topgallant sails were pulling from the upper yards, but on this day the *Essex* also carried at least one studding sail, a rectangle of canvas mounted on a special spar temporarily fitted to the end of the fore topsail yard.

Whaleships rarely set their studding sails, especially when they were in a region where whales might be sighted. Whereas ships in the China trade lived and died by how quickly they delivered their cargo, whalers were, for the most part, in no particular hurry. Use of the studding sails meant that a captain wanted to wring the last possible quarter knot of speed from his ship. The sails were difficult to set and even harder to take down, especially with an inexperienced crew. Since the sails' booms projected out beyond the yards, there was a danger of dipping them into the water if the ship should begin to roll from side to side. For a whaleship full of green hands to approach the often tempestuous waters of the Gulf Stream with her studding sails flying indicated an aggressive, if not foolhardy, attitude on the part of her commander.

With the extra sail area catching the wind, the *Essex* was moving well, probably at six to eight knots. The lookout spotted a ship ahead. Pollard ordered the helmsman to steer for her, and soon the *Essex* had caught up to what proved to be the whaleship *Midas*, five days out of New Bedford. Captain Pollard and the captain of the *Midas* exchanged shouted pleasantries, along with estimates of their longitude, and the *Essex* was soon pulling ahead, her entire crew undoubtedly enjoying the fact that their ship had proved to be what Nickerson called 'the fastest sailor of the two.'

Later that day, the weather began to deteriorate. Clouds moved into the sky, and it grew suspiciously dark to the southwest. 'The sea became very rough,' Nickerson remembered, 'which caused the ship to roll and tumble heavily.' A storm seemed imminent, but the *Essex* 'continued to carry a press of sail throughout the night and [the officers] had no cause to disturb the hands except for their respective watches.'

By the next morning they were in the Gulf Stream, and it was raining steadily. Nantucketers knew this eerily warm ocean current better than perhaps any other group of mariners. In the eighteenth century they had hunted sperm whales along its margins from Carolina to Bermuda. In 1786, Benjamin Franklin, whose mother, Abiah Folger, had been born on Nantucket, had used knowledge gleaned from his Nantucket 'cousin,' whaling captain Timothy Folger, to create the first chart of the Gulf Stream.

Many considerations, both nautical and psychological, went into a decision to shorten sail. No captain wanted to be needlessly timid, yet taking unnecessary risks, especially at the beginning of a voyage that might last as long as three years, was unwise. At some point the conditions became so rough that Pollard elected to take in the fore and mizzen topgallant sails yet to leave flying the main topgallant and also the studding sails, usually the first sails taken down in worsening weather. Pollard may have wanted to see how the *Essex* performed when pushed to the limit. They sailed on, refusing to back down.

*   *   *

According to Chase, they could see it coming: a large black cloud rushing toward them from the southwest. Now was surely the time to shorten sail. But once again they waited, deciding the cloud was an inconsequential gust. They would ride it out. As Chase would later admit, they 'miscalculated altogether as to the strength and violence of it.'

In delaying, even for a second, shortening sail in the face of an approaching squall, Pollard was now flaunting his disregard of traditional seafaring

48

wisdom. The officers of the British Navy had a maxim: 'never to be overtaken unprepared by [a squall], as never to be surprised by an enemy.' It was said that the sharper and more defined the storm cloud, the worse the wind; thunder and lightning were also bad signs. When jagged streaks of lightning began to crackle out of the forbidding black sky and thunder boomed, Pollard finally began to issue orders. But it was too late.

In the face of an approaching squall, there were two options: either to point the ship into the oncoming wind, to relieve the pressure on the sails by letting them luff, or to turn almost 180 degrees in the opposite direction, away from the wind, and let the storm blow the ship with it. This relieved the pressure on the forward sails as they became partially becalmed in the shelter of the after ones. In the merchant service, in which ships were typically undermanned, some captains favored heading into the wind—what they called luffing through a squall—in part because heading up is the natural tendency of a sailing ship in a gust. Most captains, however, favored turning away from the wind—a strategy that required them to anticipate the arrival of the squall as the crew shortened the upper and aft sails. To attempt to bear away from the wind in the last few seconds before being struck by a squall was held to show 'a poor appreciation of the squall, or a lack of watchfulness.'

This was precisely what happened to the *Essex*. As the squall approached, the helmsman was ordered to turn away from the direction of the wind and 'run before it.' Unfortunately it took time for a ship the size of the *Essex* to respond to her rudder. When the gust slammed into the ship, she

49

had just begun to turn and was sideways to the wind—the worst possible position.

For the green hands, the sound alone was terrifying: the shrieking of the wind across the rigging and then a frenzied flapping of sails and creaking of the stays and masts. The *Essex* began to lurch to leeward—slowly at first, the ponderous weight of the ship's keel and ballast, not to mention the tons of stores stowed in her hold, refusing at first to yield, but then, as the wind increased, the ship inevitably succumbed to the merciless pressure of the wind.

When a ship is heeled over by forty-five degrees or more, her hull might be compared to a fat man on the short end of a lopsided seesaw. No matter how much he weighs, if the end of the seesaw on the other side of the pivot point is long enough, it becomes a lever that will eventually lift him up into the air as the distant tip of the seesaw settles softly to the ground. In the case of the *Essex*, the masts and their wind-pressed sails became levers prying the hull toward the point of no return, forcing it over until the tips of the yards were buried in the water. The *Essex* had been rolled almost ninety degrees onto her side—knocked over on her 'beam-ends,' in the language of the sea.

Those on deck clung to the nearest fixture, fearful that they might fall down into the lee scuppers, now under knee-deep water. Those below deck did their best to shield themselves from objects falling down around them. If he hadn't abandoned it already, the ship's cook was doing his best to scramble out of the cookhouse, the heavy stove and cookware threatening to burst through its frail wooden sides. The two whaleboats on the

50

Essex's port side had disappeared beneath the waves, pressed underwater by the massive weight of the capsized ship. According to Chase, 'The whole ship's crew were, for a short time thrown into the utmost consternation and confusion.'

Yet amid all the chaos there was, at least on deck, a sudden sense of calm. When a ship suffers a knockdown, her hull acts as a barrier against the wind and rain. Even though the ship had been slammed against the water, the men were temporarily sheltered from the howling forces of the wind. Pollard took the opportunity to pull the crew back together. '[T]he cool and undismayed countenance of the captain,' Nickerson remembered, 'soon brought all to their sober senses.' The order was given to let go all the halyards and let the sheets run, but 'the ship lay so far upon her side that nothing would run down as desired.'

If the squall continued to pin her on her beamends, the ship would begin to settle into the water as the sea rushed into the hull through her open hatchways. The longer she was over on her side, the greater the chances of the ballast and stores in her hold shifting to leeward, a disastrous turn of events from which she might never recover. Already the waves had wiped the cookhouse almost completely off the deck. As a last resort, it might be necessary to cut away the masts.

The rain poured down and the lightning flashed, and time slowed to a crawl as the men clung to the weather rail. But before the axes came into play, the ship twitched back to life. The men could feel it in their hands and feet and in the pits of their stomachs—an easing of the awful strain. They

51

waited for another gust to slam the ship back down again. But no—the ballast continued to exert its gravitational pull, lifting the three masts until the yards came clear of the water. As the masts swung into the sky, seawater rushed across the deck and out the scuppers. The *Essex* shuddered to the vertical and was a ship again.

Now that the hull was no longer acting as a shield, the officers quickly realized that the squall had passed. But even if the wind had diminished, it was still blowing hard. The ship's bow was now pointed into the wind, the sails blown back against the masts. The rigging creaked in an eerie, unfamiliar way as the hull wallowed in the rain-whipped waves. The deck shifted, and the green hands temporarily lost their balance. This time the ship wasn't going over, she was going backward, water boiling up over the quarterdeck as her broad transom was pushed back against the waves, pummeling the spare whaleboat stored off the stern.

Going backward in a square-rigged ship was dangerous. The sails were plastered against the masts, making it almost impossible to furl them. The pressure placed an immense amount of strain on the stays and spars. Since the rigging had not been designed for loads coming from this direction, all three masts might come tumbling down, domino fashion, across the deck. Already the windows in the stern were threatening to burst open and flood the captain's cabin. There was also the danger of breaking the ship's tall, narrow rudder, which became useless as water pressed against it.

Eventually, the *Essex*'s bow fell off to leeward, her sails filled, and she was once again making

52

forward progress. Now the crew could do what they should have done before the storm—shorten sail.

As the men aloft wrestled with the canvas, the wind shifted into the northwest and the skies began to brighten. But the mood aboard the *Essex* sank into one of gloom. The ship had been severely damaged. Several sails, including both the main topgallant and the studding sail, had been torn into useless tatters. The cookhouse had been destroyed. The two whaleboats that had been hung off the port side of the ship had been torn from their davits and washed away, along with all their gear. The spare boat on the stern had been crushed by the waves. That left only two workable boats, and a whaleship required a minimum of three, plus two spares. Although the *Essex*'s stern boat could be repaired, they would be without a single spare boat. Captain Pollard stared at the splintered mess and declared that they would be returning to Nantucket for repairs.

His first mate, however, disagreed. Chase urged that they continue on, despite the damage. The chances were good, he insisted, that they would be able to obtain spare whaleboats in the Azores, where they would soon be stopping to procure fresh provisions. Joy sided with his fellow mate. The captain's will was normally the law of the ship. But instead of ignoring his two younger mates, Pollard paused to consider their arguments. Four days into his first command, Captain Pollard reversed himself. 'After some little reflection and a consultation with his officers,' Nickerson remembered, 'it was deemed prudent to continue on our course and trust to fortune and a kind providence to make up our loss.'

53

The excuse given to the crew was that with the wind now out of the northwest, it would have taken too long to return to Nantucket. Nickerson suspected that Chase and Joy had other motives. Both knew that the men had not taken kindly to their treatment by the mates. Seeing the knockdown as a bad omen, many of the sailors had become sullen and sour. If they returned to Nantucket, some of the crew would jump ship. Despite the seriousness of the loss of the whaleboats, it was not the time to return to port.

Not surprisingly, given that he was the object of much of the crew's discontent, Chase, in his own account of the accident, never mentions that Pollard originally proposed turning back. As Chase would have it, the knockdown was only a minor inconvenience: 'We repaired our damage with little difficulty, and continued on our course.' But Nickerson knew differently. Many of the *Essex*'s men were profoundly shaken by the knockdown and wanted to get off the ship. Whenever they passed a homeward-bound vessel, the green hands would lament, in the words of one, 'O, how I wish I was onboard with them going home again, for I am heartily sick of these whaling voyages'—even though they had not yet even seen a whale.

CHAPTER THREE

FIRST BLOOD

After a provisioning stop in the Azores, which provided plenty of fresh vegetables but no spare whaleboats, the *Essex* headed south toward the Cape Verde Islands. Two weeks later they sighted Boavista Island. In contrast to the Azores' green, abundant hills, the slopes of the Cape Verdes were brown and sere, with no trees to offer relief from the burning subtropical sun. Pollard intended to obtain some hogs at the island of Maio a few miles to the southwest.

The next morning, as they approached the island, Nickerson noticed that Pollard and his mates were strangely animated, speaking to each other with a conspiratorial excitement as they passed a spyglass back and forth, taking turns studying something on the beach. What Nickerson termed 'the cause of their glee' remained a mystery to the rest of the crew until they came close enough to the island to see that a whaleship had been run up onto the beach. Here, perhaps, was a source of some additional whaleboats—something the men of the *Essex* needed much more desperately than pork.

Before Pollard could dispatch one of his own boats to the wreck, a whaleboat was launched from the beach and made its way directly toward the *Essex.* Aboard the boat was the acting American consul, Ferdinand Gardner. He explained that the wrecked whaler was the *Archimedes* of New York. While approaching the harbor she had struck a submerged rock, forcing the captain to run her up onto the beach before she was a total loss. Gardner had purchased the wreck, but he had only a single whaleboat left to sell.

While one was better than nothing, the *Essex* would still be dangerously low on boats. With this latest addition (and an old and leaky addition at

55

that), the *Essex* would now have a total of four whaleboats. That would leave her with only one spare. In a business as dangerous as whaling, boats were so frequently damaged in their encounters with whales that many whaleships were equipped with as many as three spare boats. With a total of only four boats, the crew of the *Essex* would have scant margin for error. That was disturbing. Even the green hands knew that one day their lives could depend on the condition of these fragile cockleshells.

Pollard purchased the whaleboat, then sailed the *Essex* into the cove that served as Maio's harbor, where pointed hills of bone-white salt—procured from salt ponds in the interior of the island—added a sense of desolation to the scene. The *Essex* anchored beside another Nantucket whaleship, the *Atlantic*, which was off-loading more than three hundred barrels of oil for shipment back to the island. Whereas Captain Barzillai Coffin and his crew could boast of the seven or so whales they'd killed since leaving Nantucket on the Fourth of July, the men of the *Essex* were still putting their ship back together after the knockdown in the Gulf Stream and had yet to sight a whale.

White beans were the medium of exchange on Maio, and with a cask of beans aboard, Pollard took a whaleboat in to procure some hogs. Nickerson was at the aft oar. The harbor was without any docks or piers, and in the high surf, bringing a whaleboat into shore was exceedingly tricky. Even though they approached the beach at the best possible part of the harbor, Pollard and his men ran into trouble. 'Our boat was instantly capsized and overset in the surf,' Nickerson

56

recalled, 'and thrown upon the beach bottom upwards. The lads did not much mind this for none were hurt, but they were greatly amused to see the captain get so fine a ducking.'

Pollard traded one and a half barrels of beans for thirty hogs, whose squeals and grunts and filth turned the deck of the *Essex* into a barnyard. The impressionable Nickerson was disturbed by the condition of these animals. He called them 'almost skeletons,' and noted that their bones threatened to pierce through their skin as they walked about the ship.

*   *   *

Not until the *Essex* had crossed the equator and reached thirty degrees south latitude— approximately halfway between Rio de Janeiro and Buenos Aires—did the lookout sight the first whale of the voyage. It required sharp eyes to spot a whale's spout: a faint puff of white on the distant horizon lasting only a few seconds. But that was all it took for the lookout to bellow, 'There she blows!' or just 'B-l-o-o-o-w-s!'

After more than three whaleless months at sea, the officer on deck shouted back in excitement, 'Where away?' The lookout's subsequent commentary not only directed the helmsman toward the whales but also worked the crew into an ever increasing frenzy. If he saw a whale leap into the air, the lookout cried, 'There she breaches!' If he caught a glimpse of the whale's horizontal tail, he shouted, 'There goes flukes!' Any indication of spray or foam elicited the cry 'There's white water!' If he saw another spout, it was back to 'B-l-o-o-o-w-s!'

Under the direction of the captain and the mates, the men began to prepare the whaleboats. Tubs of harpoon line were placed into them; the sheaths were taken off the heads of the harpoons, or irons, which were hastily sharpened one last time. 'All was life and bustle,' remembered one former whaleman. Pollard's was the single boat kept on the starboard side. Chase's was on the aft larboard, or port, quarter. Joy's was just forward of Chase's and known as the waist boat.

Once within a mile of the shoal of whales, the ship was brought to a near standstill by backing the mainsail. The mate climbed into the stern of his whaleboat and the boatsteerer took his position in the bow as the four oarsmen remained on deck and lowered the boat into the water with a pair of block-and-tackle systems known as the falls. Once the boat was floating in the water beside the ship, the oarsmen—either sliding down the falls or climbing down the side of the ship—joined the mate and boatsteerer. An experienced crew could launch a rigged whaleboat from the davits in under a minute. Once all three whaleboats were away, it was up to the three shipkeepers to tend to the *Essex*.

At this early stage in the attack, the mate or captain stood at the steering oar in the stern of the whaleboat while the boatsteerer manned the forward-most, or harpooner's oar. Aft of the boatsteerer was the bow oarsman, usually the most experienced foremast hand in the boat. Once the whale had been harpooned, it would be his job to lead the crew in pulling in the whale line. Next was the midships oarsman, who worked the longest and

58

heaviest of the lateral oars—up to eighteen feet long and forty-five pounds. Next was the tub oarsman. He managed the two tubs of whale line. It was his job to wet the line with a small bucket like container, called a piggin, once the whale was harpooned. This wetting prevented the line from burning from the friction as it ran out around the loggerhead, an upright post mounted on the stern of the boat. Aft of the tub oarsman was the after oarsman. He was usually the lightest of the crew, and it was his job to make sure the whale line didn't tangle as it was hauled back into the boat.

Three of the oars were mounted on the starboard side of the boat and two were on the port side. If the mate shouted, 'Pull three,' only those men whose oars were on the starboard side began to row. 'Pull two' directed the tub oarsman and bow oarsman, whose oars were on the port side, to row. 'Avast' meant to stop rowing, while 'stern all' told them to begin rowing backward until sternway had been established. 'Give way all' was the order with which the chase began, telling the men to start pulling together, the after oarsman setting the stroke that the other four followed. With all five men pulling at the oars and the mate or captain urging them on, the whaleboat flew like a slender missile over the wave tops.

The competition among the boat-crews on a whaleship was always spirited. To be the fastest gave the six men bragging rights over the rest of the ship's crew. The pecking order of the *Essex* was about to be decided.

With nearly a mile between the ship and the whales, the three crews had plenty of space to test their speed. 'This trial more than any other during our voyage,' Nickerson remembered, 'was the subject of much debate and excitement among our crews; for neither was willing to yield the palm to the other.'

As the unsuspecting whales moved along at between three and four knots, the three whaleboats bore down on them at five or six knots. Even though all shared in the success of any single boat, no one wanted to be passed by the others; boat-crews were known to foul one another deliberately as they raced side by side behind the giant flukes of a sperm whale.

Sperm whales are typically underwater for ten to twenty minutes, although dives of up to ninety minutes have been reported. The whaleman's rule of thumb was that, before diving, a whale blew once for each minute it would spend underwater. Whalemen also knew that while underwater the whale continued at the same speed and in the same direction as it had been traveling before the dive. Thus, an experienced whaleman could calculate with remarkable precision where a submerged whale was likely to reappear.

Nickerson was the after oarsman on Chase's boat, placing him just forward of the first mate at the steering oar. Chase was the only man in the boat who could actually see the whale up ahead. While each mate or captain had his own style, they all coaxed and cajoled their crews with words that evoked the savagery, excitement, and the almost erotic bloodlust associated with pursuing one of the largest mammals on the planet. Adding to the tension was the need to remain as quiet as possible so as not to alarm or 'gully' the whale. William Comstock recorded the whispered words of a

Nantucket mate:

> Do for heaven's sake spring. The boat don't move. You're all asleep; see, see! There she lies; skote, skote! I love you, my dear fellows, yes, yes, I do; I'll do anything for you, I'll give you my heart's blood to drink; only take me up to this whale only this time, for this once, pull. Oh, St. Peter, St. Jerome, St. Stephen, St. James, St. John, the devil on two sticks; carry me up; O, let me tickle him, let me feel of his ribs. There, there, go on; O, O, O, most on, most on. Stand up, Starbuck [the harpooner]. Don't hold your iron that way; put one hand over the end of the pole. Now, now, look out. Dart, dart.

As it turned out, Chase's crew proved the fastest that day, and soon they were within harpooning distance of the whale. Now the attention turned to the boatsteerer, who had just spent more than a mile rowing as hard as he possibly could. His hands were sore, and the muscles in his arms were trembling with exhaustion. All the while he had been forced to keep his back turned to a creature that was now within a few feet, or possibly inches, of him, its tail—more than twelve feet across—working up and down within easy reach of his head. He could hear it—the hollow wet roar of the whale's lungs pumping air in and out of its sixty-ton body.

But for Chase's novice harpooner, the twenty-year-old Benjamin Lawrence, the mate himself was as frightening as any whale. Having been a boatsteerer on the *Essex*'s previous voyage, Chase had definite ideas on how a whale should be harpooned and maintained a continual patter of barely audible, expletive-laced advice. Lawrence tucked the end of his oar handle under the boat's gunnel, then braced his leg against the thigh thwart and took up the harpoon. There it was, the whale's black body, glistening in the sun. The blowhole was on the front left side of the head, and the spout enveloped Lawrence in a foul-smelling mist that stung his skin.

By hurling the harpoon he would transform this gigantic, passive creature into an angry, panicked monster that could easily dispatch him into the hereafter with a single swipe of that massive tail. Or, even worse, the whale might turn around and come at them with its tooth-studded jaw opened wide. New boatsteerers had been known to faint dead away when first presented with the terrifying prospect of attaching themselves to an infuriated sperm whale.

As Lawrence stood at the tossing bow, waves breaking around him, he knew that the mate was analyzing every one of his movements. If he let Chase down now, there would be hell to pay.

'Give it to him!' Chase bawled. 'Give it to him!'

Lawrence hadn't moved when there was a sudden splintering crack and crunch of cedar boards, and he and the other five men were airborne. A second whale had come up from beneath them, giving their boat a tremendous whack with its tail and pitching them into the sky. The entire side of the whaleboat was stove in, and the men, some of whom could not swim, clung to the wreck. 'I presume the monster was as much frightened as ourselves,' Nickerson commented, 'for he disappeared almost instantly after a slight flourish of his huge tail.' To their amazement, no one was injured.

Pollard and Joy abandoned the hunt and returned to pick up Chase's crew. It was a dispiriting way to end the day, especially since they were once again down a whaleboat, a loss that, in Nickerson's words, 'seemed to threaten the destruction of our voyage.'

*   *   *

Several days after Chase's boat was repaired, the lookout once again sighted whales. The boats were dispatched, a harpoon was hurled—successfully— and the whaleline went whizzing out until it was finally snubbed at the loggerhead, launching the boat and crew on the voyage's first 'Nantucket sleigh ride,' as it would come to be called.

Merchant seamen spoke derisively about the slow speeds of the average bluff-bowed whaleship, but the truth of the matter was that no other sailors in the early nineteenth century experienced the speeds of Nantucket whalemen. And, instead of doing it in the safe confines of a large, three-masted ship, the Nantucketer traveled in a twenty-five-foot boat crammed with half-a-dozen men, rope, and freshly sharpened harpoons and lances. The boat rocked from side to side and bounced up and down as the whale dragged it along at speeds that would have left the fleetest naval frigate wallowing in its wake. When it came to sheer velocity over the water, a Nantucketer—pinned to the flank of a whale that was pulling him miles and miles from a whaleship that was already hundreds of miles from land—was the fastest seaman in the world, traveling at fifteen (some claimed as many as twenty) bone-jarring knots.

The harpoon did not kill the whale. It was simply the means by which a whaleboat crew attached itself to its prey. After letting the creature tire itself out—by sounding to great depths or simply tearing along the water's surface—the men began to haul themselves, inch by inch, to within stabbing distance of the whale. By this point the boatsteerer and the mate had traded places, a miraculous feat in its own right on a craft as small and tender as a whaleboat. Not only did these two men have to contend with the violent slapping of the boat through the waves—which could be so severe that nails started from the planks in the bow and stern—but they had to stay clear of the whale line, quivering like a piano wire down the centerline of the boat. Eventually, however, the boatsteerer made it aft to the steering oar and the mate, who was always given the honor of the kill, took up his position in the bow.

If the whale was proving too spirited, the mate would hobble it by taking up a boat-spade and hacking away at the tendons in the tail. Then he'd take up the eleven- to twelve-foot-long killing lance, its petal-shaped blade designed for piercing a whale's vital organs. But finding 'the life' of a giant swimming mammal encased in a thick layer of blubber was not easy. Sometimes the mate would be forced to stab it as many as fifteen times, probing for a group of coiled arteries in the vicinity of the lungs with a violent churning motion that soon surrounded the whaleboat in a rushing river of bright red blood.

When the lance finally found its mark, the whale would begin to choke on its own blood, its spout transformed into a fifteen- to twenty-foot geyser of gore that prompted the mate to shout, 'Chimney's afire!' As the blood rained down on them, the men took up the oars and backed furiously away, then paused to watch as the whale went into what was known as its flurry. Beating the water with its tail, snapping at the air with its jaws—even as it regurgitated large chunks of fish and squid—the creature began to swim in an ever tightening circle. Then, just as abruptly as the attack had begun with the first thrust of the harpoon, it ended. The whale fell motionless and silent, a giant black corpse floating fin-up in a slick of its own blood and vomit.

This may have been the first time Thomas Nickerson had ever helped kill a warm-blooded animal. Back on Nantucket, where the largest wild quadruped was the Norway rat, there were no deer or even rabbits to hunt. And as any hunter knows, killing takes some getting used to. Even though this brutal and bloody display was the supposed dream of every young man from Nantucket, the sentiments of an eighteen-year-old green hand, Enoch Cloud, who kept a journal during his voyage on a whaleship, are telling: 'It is painful to witness the death of the smallest of God's created beings, much more, one in which life is so vigorously maintained as the Whale! And when I saw this, the largest and most terrible of all created animals bleeding, quivering, dying a victim to the cunning of man, my feelings were indeed peculiar!'

* * *

65

The dead whale was usually towed back to the ship headfirst. Even with all five men rowing—the mate at the steering oar sometimes lending a hand to the after oarsman—a boat towing a whale could go no faster than one mile per hour. It was dark by the time Chase and his men reached the ship.

Now it was time to butcher the body. The crew secured the whale to the *Essex*'s starboard side, with the head toward the stern. Then they lowered the cutting stage—a narrow plank upon which the mates balanced as they cut up the body. Although the stripping of a whale's blubber has been compared to the peeling of an orange, it was a little less refined than that.

First the mates hacked a hole in the whale's side, just above the fin, into which was inserted a giant hook suspended from the mast. Then the immense power of the ship's windlass was brought to bear, heeling the ship over on its side as the block-and-tackle system attached to the hook creaked with strain. Next the mates cut out the start of a five-foot-wide strip of the blubber adjacent to the hook. Pulled by the tackle attached to the windlass, the strip was gradually torn from the whale's carcass, slowly spinning it around, until a twenty-foot-long strip, dripping with blood and oil, was suspended from the rigging. This 'blanket piece' was severed from the whale and lowered into the blubber room below decks to be cut into more manageable pieces. Back at the corpse, the blubber-ripping continued.

Once the whale had been completely stripped of blubber, it was decapitated. A sperm whale's head accounts for close to a third of its length. The upper part of the head contains the case, a cavity filled with up to five hundred gallons of spermaceti, a clear, high-quality oil that partially solidifies on exposure to air. After the ship's system of blocks and tackles hauled the head up onto the deck, the men cut a hole into the top of the case and used buckets to remove the oil. One or two men might then be ordered to climb into the case to make sure all the spermaceti had been retrieved. Spillage was inevitable, and soon the decks were a slippery mess of oil and blood. Before cutting loose the whale's mutilated corpse, the mates probed its intestinal tract with a lance, searching for an opaque, ash-colored substance called ambergris. Thought to be the result of indigestion or constipation on the part of the whale, ambergris is a fatty substance used to make perfume and was worth more than its weight in gold.

By now, the two immense, four-barreled iron try-pots were full of pieces of blubber. To hasten the trying-out process, the blubber was chopped into foot-square hunks, then cut through into inch-thick slabs that resembled the fanned pages of a book and were known as bible leaves. A whale's blubber bears no similarity to the fat reserves of terrestrial animals. Rather than soft and flabby, it is tough, almost impenetrable, requiring the whalemen to resharpen their cutting tools constantly.

Wood was used to start the fires beneath the try-pots, but once the boiling process had begun, the crispy pieces of blubber floating on the surface of the pot—known as scraps or cracklings—were skimmed off and tossed into the fire for fuel. The flames that melted down the whale's blubber were thus fed by the whale itself. While this was a highly efficient use of materials, it produced a thick pall of black smoke with an unforgettable stench. 'The smell of the burning cracklings is too horribly nauseous for description,' remembered one whaleman. 'It is as though all the odors in the world were gathered together and being shaken up.'

At night the deck of the *Essex* looked like something out of Dante's *Inferno*. 'A trying-out scene has something peculiarly wild and savage in it,' stated a green hand from Kentucky, 'a kind of indescribable uncouthness, which renders it difficult to describe with anything like accuracy. There is a murderous appearance about the blood-stained decks, and the huge masses of flesh and blubber lying here and there, and a ferocity in the looks of the men, heightened by the red, fierce glare of the fires.' It was a scene that perfectly suited Melville's sinister artistic purposes in *Moby-Dick*. '[The] darkness was licked up by the fierce flames,' Ishmael tells us, 'which at intervals forked forth from the sooty flues, and illuminated every lofty rope in the rigging, as with the famed Greek fire. The burning ship drove on, as if remorselessly commissioned to some vengeful act.'

Trying out a whale could take as long as three days. Special try watches were set, lasting between five and six hours, and affording the men scant sleep. Experienced whalemen knew enough to sleep in their trying-out clothes (usually an old short-sleeved shirt and a worn pair of woolen drawers), postponing any attempts at cleaning themselves until the casks of oil had been stored in the hold and the ship had been thoroughly scrubbed down. Nickerson and his friends, however, were so revolted by the noisome mixture of oil, blood, and smoke covering their skin and clothes that they changed after every watch. By the time the first whale had been tried out, they had ruined nearly every piece of clothing stored in their sea chests.

This forced them to purchase additional clothing from the ship's slop chest—the nautical equivalent of the company store—at outrageous prices. Nickerson estimated that if the *Essex* ever made it back to Nantucket, he and his fellow green hands would owe the ship's owners close to 90 percent of their total earnings from the voyage. Instead of warning the teenagers about the potential perils of dipping into the slop chest, the ship's officers were content to let them learn the economics of whaling life the hard way. Nickerson's judgment: 'This should not have been.'

*   *   *

One night, not far from the Falkland Islands, the men were up in the rigging, reefing the topsails, when they heard a scream: a sharp, shrill shriek of terror coming from alongside the ship. Someone had apparently fallen overboard.

The officer of the watch was about to give the order to heave to when a second scream was heard. And then, perhaps with a nervous laugh, someone realized that it wasn't a man but a penguin, bobbing beside the ship, piercing the night with its all-too-human cries. Penguins! They must be nearing Antarctica.

The next day the wind vanished, leaving the *Essex* to languish in a complete calm. Seals played about the ship, 'plunging and swimming as though they desired our attention,' Nickerson remembered. There were several varieties of penguins, along with gulls and gannets pinwheeling in the sky—a sure sign that the *Essex* was approaching land.

While the seals and birds may have provided a distraction, morale about the *Essex* had reached a nadir. So far it had been a slow and unprofitable slog toward Cape Horn. With the knockdown several days out from Nantucket setting the unfortunate tone of the voyage, they had been more than four months at sea and had only a single whale to show for it. If the voyage continued in this fashion, the *Essex* would have to be out a good deal longer than two years if she were to return with a full cargo of oil. With the temperatures dropping and the legendary dangers of the Horn looming ahead of them, tensions aboard the *Essex* were reaching the breaking point.

Richard Henry Dana experienced firsthand how the morale of a ship's crew could deteriorate to the extent that even the slightest incident might be perceived as a horrendous, unbearable injustice:

> [A] thousand little things, daily and almost hourly occurring, which no one who has not himself been on a long and tedious voyage can conceive of or properly appreciate—little wars and rumors of wars,—reports of things said in the cabin,—misunderstanding of words and looks,—apparent abuses,—brought us into a state in which everything seemed to go wrong.

Aboard the *Essex*, the crew's discontent focused

on the issue of food. At no time were the differences that existed between the officers and the men more pronounced than at mealtimes. In the cabin, the officers ate much as they did back home on Nantucket—on plates, with forks, knives, and spoons, and with plenty of vegetables (as long as they lasted) to add to the ship's fare of salt beef and salt pork. If there was fresh meat available—as from those thirty Maio hogs—the officers were the ones who enjoyed most of it. As an alternative to hardtack (biscuits with the consistency of dried plaster), the steward regularly provided the officers with freshly baked bread.

The men in the forecastle and steerage enjoyed an entirely different dining experience. Instead of sitting at a table to eat, they sat on their sea chests around a large wooden tub, known as a kid, containing a hunk of pork or beef. Referred to as horse or junk, the meat was so salty that when the cook placed it in a barrel of saltwater for a day (to render it soft enough to chew), the meat's salt content was actually lowered. The sailors were required to supply their own utensils, usually a sheath knife and a spoon, plus a tin cup for tea or coffee.

Rather than the heaping portions provided to the officers, those before the mast were given only a negligible amount of this less-than-nutritious fare, their daily diet of hardtack and salt beef occasionally augmented with a little 'duff,' a flour pudding or dumpling boiled in a cloth bag. It has been estimated that sailors in the latter part of the nineteenth century were consuming around 3,800 calories a day. It is unlikely that the men in the forecastle of a whaler in 1819 consumed even close

71

to that amount. Complained one green hand on a Nantucket whaler, 'Alas, alas, the day that I came a-whaling. For what profiteth a man if he gain the whole world but in the meantime starveth to death?'

One day soon after passing the Falkland Islands, the men went below to find in the kid a ration of meat even paltrier than usual. An impromptu meeting was held. It was decided that no one would touch the meat until the kid had been shown to Captain Pollard and a complaint officially filed. The sailors took their stations on the forward portion of the deck while one of the men, the tub of beef on his shoulder, made his way aft toward the cabin gangway. Nickerson, who had been assigned to tar the netting of the main staysail, was well above the deck and had a good view of the ensuing confrontation.

The kid was no sooner set down than Captain Pollard came up onto the quarterdeck. Pollard glanced at the tub of beef, and Nickerson watched as his complexion seemed to shift from red, to blue, to almost black. Food was a difficult and sensitive issue for Captain Pollard. As he knew better than anyone, the *Essex* had been woefully under-provisioned by the parsimonious owners. If there was any hope of providing for the men in the several years ahead, he had to limit their provisions now. He may not have felt good about it, but he had no alternative.

In bringing the kid aft, the men had dared to violate the sacred space of the quarterdeck, normally reserved for the officers. Even if the crew's anger might be justified, this was a challenge to the ship's authority that no self-respecting captain could tolerate. It was a critical moment for a commander who desperately needed to shake his crew out of a corrosive and potentially disastrous malaise.

Casting aside his normal reticence, Pollard roared out, 'Who brought this kid aft? Come here, you damned scoundrels, and tell me!'

No one dared speak. The men sheepishly made their way toward the quarterdeck as a group, each trying to hide himself behind the others. It was just the display of timidity this first-time captain needed.

Pollard paced the quarterdeck in a fury, working a quid of tobacco in his mouth and spitting on the deck, all the while muttering, 'You'll throw your kid in my face, you damned scoundrels, will you?'

Finally, he made his way to the forward part of the quarterdeck, pulled off his jacket and hat, and stamped on them. 'You scoundrels,' he snarled, 'have not I given you all the ship could afford? Have not I treated you like men? Have you had plenty to eat and drink? What in hell do you want more? Do you wish me to coax you to eat? Or shall I chew your food for you?'

The men stood there dumbfounded. Pollard's eyes strayed up into the rigging where Nickerson sat with his tar brush. Pointing a finger at him, the captain bellowed, 'Come down here, you young rascal. I'll kill the whole bunch of you together and then bang up northwest and go home.'

Not having any idea what the captain meant by 'banging up northwest,' Nickerson slunk down to the deck, fully expecting to be, if not killed, at least flogged. But much to everyone's relief, Pollard dismissed all hands, saying, 'If I hear any more

73

from you about provisions, I'll tie the whole of you up together and whip it out of you.'

As the crew dispersed, Pollard could be heard growling what became known among the men as his 'soliloquy,' which they parodied in a bit of doggerel that Nickerson still remembered fifty-seven years later:

Thirty hogs in the Isle of May
Duff every other day
Butter and cheese as much as you could sway
And now you want more beef, damn you.

Pollard's behavior was fairly typical of Nantucket whaling captains, who were famous for oscillating wildly between tight-lipped reserve and incandescent rage. Pollard was, according to Nickerson, 'generally very kind where he could be so . . . [This] display of violence was only one of his freaks and passed off with the setting sun. The next morning found him as kind as before.'

Yet everything aboard the *Essex* had changed. Captain Pollard had proved he had the backbone to put the men in their place. From that day forward, no one ever complained about provisions.

CHAPTER FOUR

THE LEES OF FIRE

At eight in the morning on November 25, 1819, the lookout cried, 'Land ho!' In the distance, what appeared to be an island of rock towered high

74

above the water. Without hesitation, Captain Pollard pronounced it to be Staten Island, off the eastern tip of Cape Horn. The crew was staring at this legendary sphinxlike sight when suddenly it dissolved in the hazy air. It had been nothing but a fog bank.

The dangers of the Horn were proverbial. In 1788 Captain William Bligh and the crew of the *Bounty* had attempted to round this menacing promontory. After a solid month of sleet-filled headwinds and horrendous seas that threatened to break up the ship, Bligh decided that the only sensible way to reach the Pacific was to go the other way, so he turned the *Bounty* around and headed for Africa's Cape of Good Hope. Twenty-five years later, during the War of 1812, a much larger vessel, also named the *Essex*, an American naval frigate commanded by Captain David Porter, rounded the Horn. Porter and his men would eventually become famous for their heroics against a superior British force in the Pacific, but Cape Horn put a fright into the otherwise fearless mariner. '[O]ur sufferings (short as has been our passage) have been so great that I would advise those bound into the Pacific, never to attempt the passage of Cape Horn, if they can get there by another route.'

The whalemen of Nantucket had a different attitude toward the Horn. They'd been rounding it regularly ever since 1791, when Captain Paul Worth steered the *Beaver*, a whaleship about the size of the *Essex*, into the Pacific. Pollard and Chase had done it at least three times; for Pollard it may have been his fourth or even fifth time. Still, Cape Horn was nothing any captain took for

75

granted, certainly not one who, like Pollard, had almost lost his ship in the relatively benign Gulf Stream.

Soon after watching the mirage island vanish before them, the men of the *Essex* saw something so terrible that they could only hope their eyes were deceiving them once again. But it was all too real: from the southwest a line of ink black clouds was hurtling in their direction. In an instant the squall slammed into the ship with the force of a cannon shot. In the shrieking darkness, the crew labored to shorten sail. Under a close-reefed maintopsail and storm staysails, the *Essex* performed surprisingly well in the mountainous seas. '[T]he ship rode over them as buoyantly as a seagull,' Nickerson claimed, 'without taking onboard one bucket of water.'

But now, with the wind out of the southwest, there was the danger of being driven against the jagged rocks of the Horn. The days became weeks as the ship struggled against the wind and waves in near-freezing temperatures. In these high latitudes the light never entirely left the night sky. Without the usual sequence of light and dark, the passage stretched into a dreary, seemingly unending test of a whaleman's sanity.

It took more than a month for the *Essex* to round Cape Horn. Not until January of the new year, 1820, did the lookout sight the island of St. Mary's, a gathering spot for whalers off the coast of Chile. To the south of the island in the bay of Arauco they found several Nantucket vessels, including the *Chili*, the same ship with which they had left the island five months earlier.

The news from the west coast of South America

was not good. For one thing, the political situation in Chile and Peru was extremely volatile. In recent years towns up and down the coast had been ravaged by fighting between the Patriots, who hoped to wrest control of South America from Spain, and the Royalists, whose interests were still linked to the mother country. Although the Patriot forces, assisted by the swashbuckling British naval hero Lord Cochrane, appeared in the ascendancy, fighting was still going on, particularly in Peru. Caution was the watchword when provisioning on this coast.

For most vessels it had been a miserable whaling season. While the scarcity of whales kept up the price of oil back home on Nantucket, these were tough times for whalemen in the Pacific. After driving his crew to fill his ship, the *Independence*, Captain George Swain had returned to Nantucket in November and predicted, 'No other ship will ever fill with sperm oil in the South Seas.' Obed Macy feared Captain Swain might be right: 'Some new place must be found where the whales are more numerous,' he told his journal, 'or the business will not be worth pursuing.' Praying that they might elude these grim forecasts, the crew of the *Essex* headed out to sea.

After several luckless months off the Chilean coast, punctuated by a provisioning stop at Talcahuano, the *Essex* began to meet with some success off Peru. In just two months, Pollard and his men boiled down 450 barrels of oil, the equivalent of about eleven whales. This meant that they were killing, on average, a whale every five days, a pace that soon exhausted the crew.

The weather only added to their labors. High

winds and rugged seas made every aspect of whaling doubly onerous. Instead of providing a stable platform on which to cut up the blubber and boil the oil, the *Essex* pitched back and forth in the waves. The large seas made it next to impossible to lower and raise the whaleboats safely. 'Our boats were very much injured in hoisting them from the water,' Nickerson remembered, 'and were on more than one occasion dashed in pieces by the heavy rolling of the ship.' The much-abused boats were constantly in a state of repair.

As the number of casks of oil in the hold increased, the green hands became accustomed to the brutal business of whaling. The repetitious nature of the work—a whaler was, after all, a factory ship—tended to desensitize the men to the awesome wonder of the whale. Instead of seeing their prey as a fifty- to sixty-ton creature whose brain was close to six times the size of their own (and, what perhaps should have been even more impressive in the all-male world of the fishery, whose penis was as long as they were tall), the whalemen preferred to think of it as what one commentator called 'a self-propelled tub of high-income lard.' Whales were described by the amount of oil they would produce (as in a fifty-barrel whale), and although the whalemen took careful note of the mammal's habits, they made no attempt to regard it as anything more than a commodity whose constituent parts (head, blubber, ambergris, etc.) were of value to them. The rest of it—the tons of meat, bone, and guts—was simply thrown away, creating festering rafts of offal that attracted birds, fish, and, of course, sharks. Just as the skinned corpses of buffaloes would soon dot the prairies of the American West, so did the headless gray remains of sperm whales litter the Pacific Ocean in the early nineteenth century.

Even the most repugnant aspects of whaling became easier for the green hands to take as they grew to appreciate that each was just part of a process, like mining for gold or growing crops, designed to make them money. That was why veteran whalemen had a special fondness for trying out the blubber, the final step in the transformation of a living, breathing sperm whale into cold, hard cash. 'It is horrible,' the writer Charles Nordhoff admitted. 'Yet old whalemen delight in it. The fetid smoke is incense to their nostrils. The filthy oil seems to them a glorious representative of prospective dollars and delights.'

It was more than just the money. Each whale, each cask of oil, brought the Nantucketer closer to returning home to his loved ones. And it was when they were trying out the whale that the whalemen typically grew the most nostalgic for home. 'Wives and children are remembered with new affection at such moments,' claimed William H. Macy, 'and each feels nearer home and friends at each recurring sound of the light-driven bung, and the inspiring cry, "Away cask!" Truly is it remarked by old whalemen that the most delightful parts of the voyage are "Boiling" and arriving home.'

It was during this busy and exhausting two-month stretch off Peru that the crew of the *Essex* received what was for a whaleman the ultimate motivator: letters from home.

Toward the end of May, the *Essex* spoke, or hailed, the Aurora, the brand-new ship fitted out by Gideon Folger and Sons for Daniel Russell,

79

formerly the captain of the *Essex*. The Aurora had left Nantucket on the day after Christmas, bringing with her news that was only five months old—a blink of an eye in the time frame of a whaleman. When the *Aurora* left Nantucket, the price of whale oil was at an all-time high; people were still talking about the fire in Rhoda Harris's schoolroom in the black section of town, known as New Guinea; and they were catching codfish (two hundred to a boat) off the Nantucket village of Siasconset.

But of most interest to the men was the pouch of mail, along with several newspapers, that Daniel Russell handed over to Captain Pollard. After the officers had selected their letters, the bag was sent forward to the crew. 'It was amusing to watch those of our lads who had been disappointed and found no letters for them,' Nickerson recalled. 'They would follow us around the decks and whilst we were reading our letters would seat themselves beside us, as though our letters could be of service to them.' Despairing of finding out anything about their own families, the unlucky ones sought solace in what Nickerson called 'the careless folds of a newspaper.' For his part, Nickerson would reread the newspapers so many times that he would soon have their contents memorized.

The meeting between the *Aurora* and the *Essex* provided Pollard with the chance to speak with his former commander, the thirty-four-year-old Daniel Russell. The *Aurora* was a much larger, state-of-the-art ship and would return to Nantucket two years later, full of oil. Later it would be said that when Captain Russell had left the *Essex* to assume command of the *Aurora*, he had taken his old ship's luck with him.

80

*   *   *

One of the topics Pollard and Russell discussed was the recent discovery of a new whaling ground. As if to refute Captain Swain's dour prediction that the Pacific Ocean had been fished out of sperm whales, Captain George Washington Gardner of the *Globe* had headed farther out to sea in 1818 than any other Nantucket whaleship had so far dared to go. More than a thousand miles off the coast of Peru he hit the mother lode, an expanse of ocean full of sperm whales. He returned home to Nantucket in May of 1820 with more than two thousand barrels of oil.

Gardner's discovery became known as the Offshore Ground. During the spring and summer of 1820, it was the talk of the whale fishery. Understanding that whales appeared in the Offshore Ground in November, Pollard resolved to make one final provisioning stop in South America, where he'd secure plenty of fruits, vegetables, and water; then, after touching at the Galapagos Islands, where he would pick up a load of giant tortoises (which were prized for their meat), he would head out for this distant section of ocean.

Sometime in September the *Essex* called at Atacames, a little village of approximately three hundred Spaniards and Indians in Ecuador, just north of the equator. Anchored beside them they found a ghost ship, the whaler *George* from London, England. Every member of the *George*'s crew, save for Captain Benneford and two others, had come down with a life-threatening case of scurvy after a long time at sea. Their condition was

81

so serious that Benneford rented a house on shore and transformed it into a hospital for his men. Here was ample evidence of the dangers of venturing for extended periods out into the open Pacific.

Although poor, Atacames (called Tacames by the whalemen) was a beautiful town that for some sailors seemed a kind of Garden of Eden. 'I could not but admire the exuberant growth of everything belonging to the vegetable kingdom,' recalled Francis Olmsted, whose ship put in at Atacames in the 1830s. 'The most delicious pineapples spread out before us, while the coconut tree, the plaintain and the banana waved their broad leaves gracefully in the breeze. Here were oranges, limes and other fruits lying scattered around in neglected profusion. The fig trees had also begun to put forth, and the indigo plant grew spontaneously like the most common weed.'

There were, however, monsters lurking in the dense jungle surrounding the town, including jaguars. To guard against such predators, as well as against mosquitoes and sand fleas, the villagers lived in thatch-roofed bamboo huts raised up on stakes as much as twenty feet above the ground.

Atacames was known for its game birds. Soon after the Nantucket whaleship *Lucy Adams* also dropped anchor, Pollard set out with her captain, thirty-seven-year-old Shubael Hussey, on what Nickerson described as a turkey-hunting expedition. In preparation for this all-day affair, the cooks of the two vessels baked pies and other delicacies for the hunting party to take with them into the wilderness.

The hunters lacked a way to flush out the game.

'I being the youngest boy onboard,' Nickerson remembered, 'was chosen to make up the company in place of a hunter's dog.' And so they were off, 'over the meadows and through the woods toward the hunting grounds.'

About three hours out, they heard 'the most dismal howling that can be imagined.' Doing their best to ignore the cries, the two captains pushed on until it became clear that they were rapidly approaching the source of the disturbing sound. What could it be, Nickerson wondered, a blood-thirsty jaguar? But no one said a word. Finally, the two noble whale hunters stopped and 'looked at each other a few moments as though they wished to say something which each was ashamed to open first.' As if on cue, they turned around and began walking back to town, casually remarking that it was too hot an afternoon to hunt and that they would return on a cooler day.

But there was no fooling their surrogate hunting dog. '[They were] afraid some beast of prey would devour them,' Nickerson wrote, 'and that I could not find my way back, being too young to tell their anxious wives what became of them.' On a subsequent voyage to the region, Nickerson would discover the source of the sounds that had struck such terror in the hearts of these two whaling captains: a harmless bird smaller than a chickadee.

Something happened in Atacames that profoundly influenced the morale of the crew. Henry Dewitt, one of the *Essex*'s African American sailors, deserted.

Dewitt's act came as no great surprise. Sailors fled from whaleships all the time. Once a green hand realized how little money he was likely to make at the end of a voyage, he had no incentive to stay on if he had better options. However, the timing of the desertion could not have been worse for Captain Pollard. Since each whaleboat required a six-man crew, this now left only two shipkeepers whenever whales were being hunted. Two men could not safely manage a square-rigged ship the size of the *Essex*. If a storm should kick up, they would find it almost impossible to shorten sail. Yet Pollard, in a hurry to reach the Offshore Ground by November, had no alternative but to set out to sea shorthanded. Down a crew member and a whaleboat, the *Essex* was about to head out farther off the coast of South America than she had ever sailed before.

On October 2, the *Essex* set a course for the Galapagos Islands, approximately six hundred miles off the coast of Ecuador. Referred to as the 'Galleypaguses' by some seamen, these islands were also known as the Encantadas, Spanish for 'enchanted' or 'bewitched.' The strong and unpredictable currents that boiled in and around these volcanic outcroppings sometimes created the illusion that the islands were actually moving.

Even before the discovery of the Offshore Ground, the Galapagos had been a popular provisioning stop for whalers. Safely removed from the mainland, they provided a welcome refuge from the political turmoil in South America. They were also located in a region frequented by sperm whales. As early as 1793, just two years after the *Beaver* first rounded the Horn, Captain James Colnett, on a British exploratory voyage to investigate the potential for whaling in the Pacific, visited the Galapagos. What he found was part sperm-whale boudoir, part nursery. He and his crew witnessed something almost never seen by man: sperm whales copulating—the bull swimming upside down and beneath the female. They also spied vast numbers of baby whales, 'not larger than a small porpoise.' Colnett wrote, 'I am disposed to believe that we were now at the general rendezvous of the spermaceti whales from the coasts of Mexico, Peru, and the Gulf of Panama, who come here to calve.' He noted that of all the whales they killed, they found only one male.

Colnett's observations are in keeping with the results of the latest research on the sperm whales of the Galapagos. One of the world's premier sperm-whale experts, Hal Whitehead, began observing whales in this area in 1985. Using a cruising sailboat equipped with sophisticated technological gadgetry, Whitehead has monitored whales in the same waters plied by the *Essex* 180 years ago. He has found that the typical pod of whales, which ranges between three and twenty or so individuals, is comprised almost exclusively of interrelated adult females and immature whales. Adult males made up only 2 percent of the whales he observed.

The females work cooperatively in taking care of their young. The calves are passed from whale to whale so that an adult is always standing guard when the mother is feeding on squid thousands of feet below the ocean's surface. As an older whale raises its flukes at the start of a long dive, the calf will swim to another nearby adult.

Young males leave the family unit at around six years of age and make their way to the cooler waters of the high latitudes. Here they live singly or with other males, not returning to the warm waters of their birth until their late twenties. Even then, a male's return is fairly fitful and inconclusive; he spends only eight or so hours with any one group, sometimes mating but never establishing any strong attachments, before making his way back to the high latitudes. He may live for sixty or seventy years.

The sperm whales' network of female-based family units resembled, to a remarkable extent, the community the whalemen had left back home on Nantucket. In both societies the males were itinerants. In their dedication to killing sperm whales the Nantucketers had developed a system of social relationships that mimicked those of their prey.

*   *   *

During their six-day passage to the Galapagos, the men of the *Essex* killed two whales, bringing their total amount of oil to seven hundred barrels—about halfway to filling the ship. They had been out just over a year, and if they should experience some good luck in the Offshore Ground, there was a chance they might be returning to Nantucket within the next year and a half. But by the time they reached Hood Island, the easternmost of the Galapagos group, their prime concern had shifted from killing whales to keeping their vessel afloat. The *Essex* had developed a leak.

Surrounded by the bone-white beaches of Stephen's Bay, which almost seemed to glow at night, the officers supervised the *Essex*'s repair. In the well-protected anchorage, the *Essex* was 'hove down'—heeled over on her side to expose the problem area. Six years later, Captain Seth Coffin would use the same procedure in repairing a leak in the *Aurora*, the ship originally commanded by Daniel Russell on her maiden voyage. Coffin was disturbed to find that the bottom of this far-from-old vessel was 'eaten to a honeycomb' and attempted to stanch the leak with a mixture of chalk and slush, a greasy material used to lubricate the ship's spars. The much older *Essex* may have had similar problems below the waterline.

Nickerson's attention was soon directed to Hood Island. 'The rocks appear very much burned,' he remembered, 'and where there is soil it wears mostly the appearance of very dry snuff.' Since Hood's surface was covered with loose gravel and boulders, the simple act of walking was difficult, and the volcanic rocks rang metallically underfoot.

Herman Melville was profoundly affected by the Galapagos in the 1840s, ultimately writing a series of sketches entitled 'The Encantadas.' For Melville, there was something terrifyingly nonhuman about these islands. He described them as a place where 'change never comes' and spoke of their 'emphatic uninhabitableness':

Cut by the Equator, they know not autumn and they know not spring; while already reduced to the lees of fire, ruin itself can work little more upon them. The showers refresh the deserts, but in these isles, rain never falls. Like split Syrian gourds left withering in the sun, they are cracked by an everlasting drought beneath a torrid sky. 'Have mercy upon me,' the wailing spirit of the Encantadas seems to cry, 'and send Lazarus that he may dip the tip of his finger in water and cool my tongue, for I am tormented in this flame.'

To sea travelers, one great attraction of the Galapagos was their tortoises. The naturalist Charles Darwin visited these islands in 1835 aboard the *Beagle* and noted that the tortoises on each island, like his famous finches, varied markedly from one another—the tortoises in the coloring and shape of their shells. The creatures were interesting in another way to U.S. Navy captain David Porter. His frigate *Essex* visited the islands in 1813 and carried off a vast number of tortoises—an estimated four tons—to feed his crew on their voyage to the Marquesas.

By the time the whaleship *Essex* ventured to these islands seven years later, sailors had devised a well-established procedure for what they called turpining. Equipped with canvas harnesses, the seamen fanned out over the island, often following the deeply rutted tortoise tracks that crisscrossed the rocky surface, hoping these would lead them to their prey. The tortoises averaged about eighty pounds, but it wasn't unusual to find one that weighed four hundred pounds or more. If a sailor came across a tortoise that was too big for one person to carry, he'd call for help by crying out, 'Townho!'—a corruption of the Wampanoag whaling word 'townor.' In most cases, however, it was just one man per tortoise. After flipping the tortoise on its back and pinning it down with a large rock, which kept the creature from retracting its feet, the whaleman secured the ends of his canvas harness to the tortoise's legs, then swung the animal onto his back. Walking for several miles over the uneven surface of Hood Island in 105-degree temperatures with an eighty-pound tortoise strapped to one's back was not easy, particularly since each man was expected to bring back three tortoises a day to the ship. As far as Nickerson was concerned, turpining was the most difficult and exhausting form of work he'd ever known, especially given the tortoise's 'constant uneasiness' while strapped to a seaman's sweat-soaked back.

During their stay at Hood Island, Benjamin Lawrence, Owen Chase's boatsteerer, ran into trouble. He found a tortoise and set out in what he thought was the direction of the ship, belatedly realizing he'd gone in precisely the opposite direction. Eventually, he abandoned his tortoise and made his way down to the burning sands of the beach and began to backtrack toward the ship.

By the middle of the afternoon, the *Essex* was still not in sight and Lawrence was feeling the torments of severe thirst. He came across another tortoise and proceeded to cut off the reptile's snakelike head. The blood spurting from the neck was a startlingly cool 62 degrees in the 110-degree sun. After drinking his fill, Lawrence left the dead tortoise on the beach and resumed his search for the ship. He found it at dusk, but dreading what Nickerson termed 'the laugh which would be turned upon him if he returned to the boat empty handed,' he headed back into the island's interior in search of a tortoise. It was thoroughly dark by the time Lawrence, tortoise-laden, staggered down to the beach and was greeted by the men who had been sent out to search for him.

In the next four days the crew collected 180

tortoises on Hood. Then the *Essex* headed for nearby Charles Island. The short cruise gave Nickerson the opportunity to observe the creatures, which were for the most part stacked like boulders in the hold, although some of them were left to wander the ship's deck. One of the reasons Galapagos tortoises were so valued by the whalemen was that they could live for more than a year without any food or water. Not only was the tortoise's meat still plump and tasty after that long period, but it also yielded as much as eight to ten pounds of fat, which Nickerson described as 'clear and pure as the best of yellow butter and of a rich flavor.'

Some sailors insisted that the tortoises felt no pangs of hunger during their time on a whaleship, but Nickerson was not so sure. As the voyage progressed he noticed that they were constantly licking everything they encountered on the ship's deck. The tortoises' gradual starvation ended only when they were slaughtered for food.

On Charles Island the whalemen had created a crude post office—a simple box or cask sheltered by a giant tortoise shell, in which mail could be left for transportation back to Nantucket. While on Charles during the War of 1812, Captain David Porter had used to his tactical advantage information gleaned from letters left by British whaling captains. For the men of the *Essex*, the Charles Island mail drop offered an opportunity to reply to the letters they had received via the *Aurora*. They also collected another hundred tortoises. Nickerson claimed that these tortoises, which proved disappointingly scarce, were the sweetest-tasting of the Galapagos.

It was on Charles Island that they procured a six-hundred-pound monster of a tortoise. It took six men to carry it to the beach on crossed poles. No one knew how old a tortoise of this size might be, but on nearby Albemarle Island there was 'Port Royal Tom,' a giant tortoise whose shell had been carved with countless names and dates, the oldest going back to 1791. (Tom was reported still to be alive as late as 1881.)

Nickerson, who exhibited a Darwinesque interest in the natural world, made careful note of the many other creatures inhabiting Charles Island, including green tortoises, pelicans, and two kinds of iguanas. During his last day on the island, however, Nickerson was shaken by an event more in keeping with Melville's vision of the Galapagos than with Darwin's.

On the morning of October 22, Thomas Chappel, a boatsteerer from Plymouth, England, decided to play a prank. Not telling anyone else on the *Essex* what he was up to, the mischievous Chappel (who was, according to Nickerson, 'fond of fun at whatever expense') brought a tinderbox ashore with him. As the others searched the island for tortoises, Chappel secretly set a fire in the underbrush. It was the height of the dry season, and the fire soon burned out of control, surrounding the tortoise hunters and cutting off their route back to the ship. With no other alternative, they were forced to run through a gauntlet of flame. Although they singed their clothes and hair, no serious injuries resulted—at least not to the men of the *Essex*.

By the time they returned to the ship, almost the entire island was ablaze. The men were indignant that one of their own had committed such a stupid and careless act. But it was Pollard who was the most upset. '[T]he Captain's wrath knew no bounds,' Nickerson remembered, 'swearing vengeance upon the head of the incendiary should he be discovered.' Fearing a certain whipping, Chappel did not reveal his role in the conflagration until much later. Nickerson believed that the fire killed thousands upon thousands of tortoises, birds, lizards, and snakes.

The *Essex* had left a lasting impression on the island. When Nickerson returned to Charles years later, it was still a blackened wasteland. 'Wherever the fire raged neither trees, shrubbery, nor grass have since appeared,' he reported. Charles would be one of the first islands in the Galapagos to lose its tortoise population. Although the crew of the *Essex* had already done its part in diminishing the world's sperm-whale population, it was here on this tiny volcanic island that they contributed to the eradication of a species.

When they weighed anchor the next morning, Charles remained an inferno. That night, after a day of sailing west along the equator, they could still see it burning against the horizon. Backlit by the red glow of a dying island, the twenty men of the *Essex* ventured into the farthest reaches of the Pacific, looking for another whale to kill.

CHAPTER FIVE

THE ATTACK

Even today, in an age of instantaneous communication and high-speed transportation, the scale of the Pacific is difficult to grasp. Sailing due west from Panama, it is 11,000 miles to the Malay Peninsula—almost four times the distance Columbus sailed to the New World—and it is 9,600 miles from the Bering Strait to Antarctica. The Pacific is also deep. Hidden beneath its blue surface are some of the planet's most spectacular mountain ranges, with canyons that plunge more than six miles into the watery blackness. Geologically, the volcano-rimmed Pacific is the most active part of the world. Islands rise up; islands disappear. Herman Melville called this sixty-four-million-square-mile ocean the 'tide-beating heart of the earth.'

By November 16, 1820, the *Essex* had sailed more than a thousand miles west of the Galapagos, following the equator as if it were an invisible lifeline leading the ship ever farther into the largest ocean in the world. Nantucket whalemen were familiar with at least part of the Pacific. Over the last three decades the coast of South America had become their own backyard. They also knew the western edge of the Pacific quite well. By the early part of the century, English whalers, most of them captained by Nantucketers, were regularly rounding the Cape of Good Hope and taking whales in the vicinity of Australia and New

93

Zealand. In 1815, Hezekiah Coffin, the father of Pollard's young cousin Owen, had died during a provisioning stop in the fever-plagued islands off Timor, between Java and New Guinea.

Lying between the island of Timor and the west coast of South America is the Central Pacific, what Owen Chase called 'an almost untraversed ocean.' The longitudes and latitudes of islands with names such as Ohevahoa, Marokinee, Owyhee, and Mowee might be listed in Captain Pollard's navigational guide, but beyond that they were—save for blood-chilling rumors of native butchery and cannibalism—a virtual blank.

All this was about to change. Unknown to Pollard, only a few weeks earlier, on September 29, the Nantucket whaleships *Equator* and *Balaena* stopped at the Hawaiian island of Oahu for the first time. In 1823, Richard Macy would be the first Nantucketer to provision his ship at the Society Islands, now known as French Polynesia. But as far as Pollard and his men knew in November of 1820, they were at the edge of an unknown world filled with unimaginable dangers. And if they were to avoid the fate of the ship they'd encountered at Atacames, whose men had almost died of scurvy before they could reach the South American coast for provisions, there was no time for far-flung exploration. It had taken them more than a month to venture out this far, and it would take at least that to return. They had, at most, only a few months of whaling left before they must think about returning to South America and eventually to Nantucket.

So far, the whales they had sighted in this remote expanse of ocean had proved frustratingly elusive. 'Nothing occurred worthy of note during this passage,' Nickerson remembered, 'with the exception of occasionally chasing a wild shoal of whales to no purpose.' Tensions mounted among the *Essex*'s officers. The situation prompted Owen Chase to make an adjustment aboard his whaleboat. When he and his boat-crew did finally approach a whale, on November 16, it was he, Chase reported, not his boatsteerer, Benjamin Lawrence, who held the harpoon.

This was a radical and, for Lawrence, humiliating turn of events. A mate took over the harpoon only after he had lost all confidence in his boatsteerer's ability to fasten to a whale. William Comstock told of two instances when mates became so disgusted with their boatsteerers' unsuccessful attempts to harpoon whales that they ordered them aft and took the iron themselves. One mate, Comstock wrote, screamed, 'Who are you? What are you? Miserable trash, scum of Nantucket, a whimpering boy from the chimney corner. By Neptune I think you are afraid of a whale.' When the boatsteerer finally burst into tears, the mate ripped the harpoon from his hands and ordered him to take the steering oar.

With Chase at the bow and Lawrence relegated to the steering oar, the first mate's boat approached a patch of water where, Chase predicted, a whale would surface. Chase was, in his own words, 'standing in the fore part, with the harpoon in my hand, well braced, expecting every instant to catch sight of one of the shoal which we were in, that I might strike.' Unfortunately, a whale surfaced directly under their boat, hurling Chase and his crew into the air. Just as had occurred after their first attempt at killing a whale, off the Falkland Islands, Chase and his men found themselves clinging to a wrecked whaleboat.

Given the shortage of spare boats aboard the *Essex*, caution on the part of the officers might have been expected, but caution, at least when it came to pursuing whales, was not part of the first mate's makeup. Taking to heart the old adage 'A dead whale or a stove boat,' Chase reveled in the risk and danger of whaling. 'The profession is one of great ambition,' he would boast in his narrative, 'and full of honorable excitement: a tame man is never known amongst them.'

* * *

Four days later, on November 20, more than 1,500 nautical miles west of the Galapagos and just 40 miles south of the equator, the lookout saw spouts. It was about eight in the morning of a bright clear day. Only a slight breeze was blowing. It was a perfect day for killing whales.

Once they had sailed to within a half mile of the shoal, the two shipkeepers headed the *Essex* into the wind with the maintopsail aback, and the three boats were lowered. The whales, unaware that they were being pursued, sounded.

Chase directed his men to row to a specific spot, where they waited 'in anxious expectation,' scanning the water for the dark shape of a surfacing sperm whale. Once again, Chase tells us, he was the one with the harpoon, and sure enough, a small whale emerged just ahead of them and spouted. The first mate readied to hurl the harpoon and, for the second time in as many days of whaling, ran into trouble.

Chase had ordered Lawrence, the ex-harpooner, to steer the boat in close to the whale. Lawrence did so, so close that as soon as the harpoon sliced into it, the panicked animal whacked the already battered craft with its tail, opening up a hole in the boat's side. As water poured in, Chase cut the harpoon line with a hatchet and ordered the men to stuff their coats and shirts into the jagged opening. While one man bailed, they rowed back to the ship. Then they pulled the boat up onto the *Essex*'s deck.

By this time, both Pollard's and Joy's crews had fastened to whales. Angered that he had once again been knocked out of the hunt, Chase began working on his damaged boat with a fury, hoping to get the craft operable while whales were still to be taken. Although he could have outfitted and lowered the extra boat (the one they had bargained for in the Cape Verde Islands, now lashed to the rack over the quarterdeck), Chase felt it would be faster to repair the damaged boat temporarily by stretching some canvas across the hole. As he nailed the edges of the canvas to the boat, his after oarsman, Thomas Nickerson—all of fifteen years old—took over the helm of the *Essex* and steered the ship toward Pollard and Joy, whose whales had dragged them several miles to leeward. It was then that Nickerson saw something off the port bow.

It was a whale—a huge sperm whale, the largest they'd seen so far—a male about eighty-five feet long, they estimated, and approximately eighty tons. It was less than a hundred yards away, so close that they could see that its giant blunt head was etched with scars, and that it was pointed toward the ship. But this whale wasn't just large. It was acting strangely. Instead of fleeing in panic, it was floating quietly on the surface of the water, puffing occasionally through its blowhole, as if it were watching them. After spouting two or three times, the whale dove, then surfaced less than thirty-five yards from the ship.

Even with the whale just a stone's throw from the *Essex*, Chase did not see it as a threat. 'His appearance and attitude gave us at first no alarm,' he wrote. But suddenly the whale began to move. Its twenty-foot-wide tail pumped up and down. Slowly at first, with a slight side-to-side waggle, it picked up speed until the water crested around its massive barrel-shaped head. It was aimed at the *Essex*'s port side. In an instant, the whale was only a few yards away—'coming down for us,' Chase remembered, 'with great celerity.'

In desperate hopes of avoiding a direct hit, Chase shouted to Nickerson, 'Put the helm hard up!' Several other crew members cried out warnings. 'Scarcely had the sound of the voices reached my ears,' Nickerson remembered, 'when it was followed by a tremendous crash.' The whale rammed the ship just forward of the forechains.

The *Essex* shook as if she had struck a rock. Every man was knocked off his feet. Galapagos tortoises went skittering across the deck. 'We looked at each other with perfect amazement,' Chase recalled, 'deprived almost of the power of speech.'

As they pulled themselves up off the deck, Chase and his men had good reason to be amazed. Never before, in the entire history of the Nantucket whale fishery, had a whale been known to attack a ship. In

1807 the whaleship *Union* had accidentally plowed into a sperm whale at night and sunk, but something very different was happening here.

After the impact, the whale passed underneath the ship, bumping the bottom so hard that it knocked off the false keel—a formidable six-by-twelve-inch timber. The whale surfaced at the *Essex*'s starboard quarter. The creature appeared, Chase remembered, 'stunned with the violence of the blow' and floated beside the ship, its tail only a few feet from the stern.

Instinctively, Chase grabbed a lance. All it would take was one perfectly aimed throw and the first mate might slay the whale that had dared to attack a ship. This giant creature would yield more oil than two, maybe even three, normal-sized whales. If Pollard and Joy also proved successful that day, they would be boiling down at least 150 barrels of oil in the next week—more than 10 percent of the *Essex*'s total capacity. They might be heading back to Nantucket in a matter of weeks instead of months.

Chase motioned to stab the bull—still lying hull-to-hull with the *Essex*. Then he hesitated. The whale's flukes, he noticed, were perilously close to the ship's rudder. If provoked, the whale might smash the delicate steering device with its tail. They were too far from land, Chase decided, to risk damaging the rudder.

For the first mate, it was a highly uncharacteristic display of caution. 'But could [Chase] have foreseen all that so soon followed,' Nickerson wrote, 'he would probably have chosen the lesser evil and have saved the ship by killing the whale even at the expense of losing the rudder.'

*   *   *

A sperm whale is uniquely equipped to survive a head-on collision with a ship. Stretching for a third of its length between the front of the whale's battering ram-shaped head and its vital organs is an oil-filled cavity perfectly adapted to cushioning the impact of a collision. In less than a minute, this eighty-ton bull was once again showing signs of life.

Shaking off its woozy lethargy, the whale veered off to leeward, swimming approximately six hundred yards away. There it began snapping its jaws and thrashing the water with its tail, 'as if distracted,' Chase wrote, 'with rage and fury.' The whale then swam to windward, crossing the *Essex*'s bow at a high rate of speed. Several hundred yards ahead of the ship, the whale stopped and turned in the *Essex*'s direction. Fearful that the ship might be taking on water, Chase had, by this point, ordered the men to rig the pumps. '[W]hile my attention was thus engaged,' the first mate remembered, 'I was aroused with the cry of a man at the hatchway, "Here he is—he is making for us again."' Chase turned and saw a vision of 'fury and vengeance' that would haunt him in the long days ahead.

With its huge scarred head halfway out of the water and its tail beating the ocean into a white-water wake more than forty feet across, the whale approached the ship at twice its original speed—at least six knots. Chase, hoping 'to cross the line of his approach before he could get up to us, and thus avoid what I knew, if he should strike us again, would prove our inevitable destruction,' cried out to Nickerson, 'Hard up!' But it was too late for a

100

change of course. With a tremendous cracking and splintering of oak, the whale struck the ship just beneath the anchor secured at the cathead on the port bow. This time the men were prepared for the hit. Still, the force of the collision caused the whalemen's heads to jounce on their muscled necks as the ship lurched to a halt on the slablike forehead of the whale. The creature's tail continued to work up and down, pushing the 238-ton ship backward until—as had happened after the knockdown in the Gulf Stream—water surged up over the transom.

One of the men who had been belowdecks ran up onto the deck shouting, 'The ship is filling with water!' A quick glance down the hatchway revealed that the water was already above the lower deck, where the oil and provisions were stored.

No longer going backward, the *Essex* was now going down. The whale, having humbled its strange adversary, disengaged itself from the shattered timbers of the copper-sheathed hull and swam off to leeward, never to be seen again.

*   *   *

The ship was sinking bow-first. The forecastle, where the black sailors slept, was the first of the living quarters to flood, the men's sea chests and mattresses floating on the rising tide. Next the water surged aft into the blubber room, then into steerage, where Nickerson and the other Nantucketers slept. Soon even the mates' and captain's cabins were awash.

As the belowdecks creaked and gurgled, the black steward, William Bond, on his own initiative, returned several times to the rapidly filling aft cabins to retrieve Pollard's and Chase's trunks and—with great foresight—the navigational equipment. Meanwhile Chase and the rest of the crew cut the lashing off the spare whaleboat and carried it to the waist of the ship.

The *Essex* began to list dangerously to port. Bond made one last plunge below. Chase and the others carried the whaleboat to the edge of the deck, now only a few inches above the ocean's surface. When the trunks and other equipment had been loaded aboard, everyone, including Bond, scrambled into the boat, the tottering masts and yards looming above them. They were no more than two boat lengths away when the *Essex*, with an appalling slosh and groan, capsized behind them.

Just at that moment, two miles to leeward, Obed Hendricks, Pollard's boatsteerer, casually glanced over his shoulder. He couldn't believe what he saw. From that distance it looked as if the *Essex* had been hit by a sudden squall, the sails flying in all directions as the ship fell onto her beam-ends.

'Look, look,' he cried, 'what ails the ship? She is upsetting!'

But when the men turned to look, there was nothing to see. '[A] general cry of horror and despair burst from the lips of every man,' Chase wrote, 'as their looks were directed for [the ship], in vain, over every part of the ocean.' The *Essex* had vanished below the horizon.

The two boat-crews immediately released their whales and began rowing back toward the place the *Essex* should have been—all the time speculating frantically about what had happened to the ship. It never occurred to any of them that, in Nickerson's words, 'a whale [had] done the work.' Soon enough, they could see the ship's hull 'floating upon her side and presenting the appearance of a rock.'

As Pollard and Joy approached, the eight men crowded into Chase's boat continued to stare silently at the ship. '[E]very countenance was marked with the paleness of despair,' Chase recalled. 'Not a word was spoken for several minutes by any of us; all appeared to be bound in a spell of stupid consternation.'

From the point at which the whale first attacked, to the escape from the capsizing ship, no more than ten minutes had elapsed. In only a portion of that time, spurred by panic, eight of the crew had launched an unrigged whaleboat from the rack above the quarterdeck, a process that would have normally taken at least ten minutes and required the effort of the entire ship's crew. Now, here they were, with only the clothes on their backs, huddled in the whaleboat. It was not yet ten in the morning.

It was then that Chase fully appreciated the service that William Bond had rendered them. He had salvaged two compasses, two copies of Nathaniel Bowditch's *New American Practical Navigator*, and two quadrants. Chase later called this equipment 'the probable instruments of our salvation . . . Without them,' he added, 'all would have been dark and hopeless.'

For his part, Thomas Nickerson was swept by a sense of grief, not for himself, but for the ship. The giant black craft that he had come to know so intimately had been dealt a deathblow. 'Here lay our beautiful ship, a floating and dismal wreck,' Nickerson lamented, 'which but a few minutes before appeared in all her glory, the pride and boast of her captain and officers, and almost idolized by her crew.'

Soon the other two whaleboats came within hailing distance. But no one said a word. Pollard's boat was the first to reach them. The men stopped rowing about thirty feet away. Pollard stood at the steering oar, staring at the capsized hulk that had once been his formidable command, unable to speak. He dropped down onto the seat of his whaleboat, so overcome with astonishment, dread, and confusion that Chase 'could scarcely recognize his countenance.' Finally Pollard asked, 'My God, Mr. Chase, what is the matter?'

Chase's reply: 'We have been stove by a whale.'

*　　　*　　　*

Even by the colossal standards of a sperm whale, an eighty-five-foot bull is huge. Today, male sperm whales, which are on average three to four times bulkier than females, never grow past sixty-five feet. Sperm whale expert Hal Whitehead has his doubts that the *Essex* whale could have been as large as Chase and Nickerson claimed it was. However, the logs of Nantucket whalemen are filled with references to bulls that, given the amount of oil they yielded, must have been on the order of the *Essex* whale. It is an established fact that whalemen in both the nineteenth and twentieth centuries killed male sperm whales in disproportionate numbers: not only were they longer than the females but the males' oil-rich spermaceti organs accounted for a larger portion of that length. In 1820, before a century and a half of

104

selective killing had rid the world of large bulls, it may have indeed been possible to encounter an eighty-five-foot sperm whale. Perhaps the most convincing evidence resides in the hallowed halls of the Nantucket Whaling Museum. There, leaning against the wall, is an eighteen-foot jaw taken from a bull that was estimated to have been at least eighty feet long.

The sperm whale has the largest brain of any animal that has ever lived on earth, dwarfing even that of the mighty blue whale. The large size of the sperm whale's brain may be related to its highly sophisticated ability to generate and process sound. Just beneath its blowhole, a sperm whale has what the whalemen referred to as a monkey's muzzle, a cartilaginous clapper system that scientists believe to be the source of the clicking sounds it uses to 'see' the world through echolocation. Whales also use clicking signals to communicate over distances of up to five miles. Females tend to employ a Morse code-like series of clicks, known as a coda, and male sperm whales make slower, louder clicks called clangs. It has been speculated that males use clangs to announce themselves to eligible females and to warn off competing males.

Whalemen often heard sperm whales through the hulls of their ships. The sound-steady clicks at roughly half-second intervals—bore such a startling similarity to the tapping of a hammer that the whalemen dubbed the sperm whale 'the carpenter fish.' On the morning of November 20, 1820, sperm whales were not the only creatures filling the ocean with clicking sounds; there was also Owen Chase, busily nailing a piece of canvas to the bottom of an upturned whaleboat. With every blow of his hammer against the side of the damaged boat, Chase was unwittingly transmitting sounds down through the wooden skin of the whaleship out into the ocean. Whether or not the bull perceived these sounds as coming from another whale, Chase's hammering appears to have attracted the creature's attention.

Chase maintained that when the whale first struck the ship, it was going about three knots, the velocity of a whale at normal cruising speed. Whitehead, whose research vessel was once bumped into by a pregnant whale, speculates that the bull might have even initially run into the *Essex* by mistake.

Whatever prompted the encounter, the whale was clearly not prepared for something as solid and heavy as a whaleship, which at 238 tons weighed approximately three times more than it did. The *Essex* might have been an old, work-worn whaleship, but she had been built to take her share of abuse. She was constructed almost entirely of white oak, one of the toughest and strongest of woods. Her ribs had been hewn from immense timbers, at least a foot square. Over that, laid fore and aft, were oak planks four inches thick. On top of the planks was a sheathing of yellow pine, more than half an inch thick. Extending down from the waterline (the point of impact, according to Nickerson) was a layer of copper. The bull had slammed into a solid wooden wall.

What had begun as an experimental, perhaps unintentional jab with its head soon escalated into an all-out attack.

Like male elephants, bull sperm whales tend to be loners, moving from group to group of females and juveniles and challenging whatever males they meet along the way. The violence of these encounters is legendary. One whaleman described what happened when a bull sperm whale tried to move in on another bull's group:

> When the approaching bull attempted to join the herd, he was attacked by one of the established bulls, which rolled over on its back and attacked with its jaw . . . Large pieces of blubber and flesh were taken out. Both bulls then withdrew and again charged at full tilt. They locked jaws and wrestled, each seemingly to try to break the other's jaw. Great pieces of flesh again were torn from the animals' heads. Next they either withdrew or broke their holds, and then charged each other again. The fight was even more strenuous this time, and little could be seen because of the boiling spray. The charge and withdrawal were repeated two or three times before the water quieted, and then for a few seconds the two could be seen lying head to head. The smaller bull then swam slowly away and did not attempt to rejoin the cows . . . A whaleboat was dispatched, and the larger bull was captured. The jaw had been broken and was hanging by the flesh. Many teeth were broken and there were extensive head wounds.

Instead of fighting with its jaws and tail—the way whales commonly dispatched whaleboats—the *Essex* whale rammed the ship with its head, something that, Chase insisted, 'has never been heard of amongst the oldest and most experienced whalers.' But what most impressed the first mate was the remarkably astute way in which the bull employed its God-given battering ram. Both times the whale had approached the vessel from a direction 'calculated to do us the most injury, by being made ahead, and thereby combining the speed of the two objects for the shock.' Yet, even though it had come at the *Essex* from ahead, the whale had avoided striking the ship directly head-on, where the ship's heavily reinforced stem, the vertical timber at the leading edge of the bow, might have delivered a mortal gash.

Chase estimated that the whale was traveling at six knots when it struck the *Essex* the second time and that the ship was traveling at three knots. To bring the *Essex* to a complete standstill, the whale, whose mass was roughly a third of the ship's, would have to be moving at more than three times the speed of the ship, at least nine knots. One naval architect's calculations project that if the *Essex* had been a new ship, her oak planking would have withstood even this tremendous blow. Since the whale did punch a hole in the bow, the *Essex*'s twenty-one-year-old planking must have been significantly weakened by rot or marine growth.

Chase was convinced that the *Essex* and her crew had been the victims of 'decided, calculating mischief' on the part of the whale. For a Nantucketer, it was a shocking thought. If other sperm whales should start ramming ships, it would be only a matter of time before the island's whaling fleet was reduced to so much flotsam and jetsam.

Chase began to wonder what 'unaccountable destiny or design' had been at work. It almost

108

seemed as if something—could it have been God?—had possessed the beast for its own strange, unfathomable purpose. Whatever or whoever might be behind it, Chase was convinced that 'anything but chance' had sunk the *Essex.*

*   *   *

After listening to the first mate's account of the sinking, Pollard attempted to take command of the dire situation. Their first priority, he announced, was to get as much food and water out of the wreck as possible. To do that, they needed to cut away the masts so that the still partially floating hull could right. The men climbed onto the ship and began to hack away at the spars and rigging with hatchets from the whaleboats. As noon approached, Captain Pollard shoved off in his boat to take an observation with his quadrant. They were at latitude 0°40' south, longitude 119°0' west, just about as far from land as it was possible to be anywhere on earth.

Forty-five minutes later, the masts had been reduced to twenty-foot stumps and the *Essex* was floating partly upright again, at a forty-five-degree angle. Although most of the provisions were unreachable in the lower hold, there were two large casks of bread between decks in the waist of the ship. And since the casks were on the *Essex*'s upper side, the men could hope that they were still dry.

Through the holes they chopped into the deck they were able to extract six hundred pounds of hardtack: Elsewhere they broke through the planks to find casks of freshwater—more, in fact, than they could safely hold in their whaleboats. They

109

also scavenged tools and equipment, including two pounds of boat nails, a musket, two pistols, and a small canister of powder. Several Galapagos tortoises swam to the whaleboats from the wreck, as did two skinny hogs. Then it began to blow.

In need of shelter from the mounting wind and waves, yet fearful the *Essex* might at any moment break up and sink like a stone, Pollard ordered that they tie up to the ship but leave at least a hundred yards of line between it and themselves. Like a string of ducklings trailing their mother, they spent the night in the lee of the ship.

*   *   *

The ship shuddered with each wave. Chase lay sleepless in his boat, staring at the wreck and reliving the catastrophe over and over again in his mind. Some of the men slept and others 'wasted the night in unavailing murmurs,' Chase wrote. Once, he admitted, he found himself breaking into tears.

Part of him was guilt-wracked, knowing that if he had only hurled the lance, it might have all turned out differently. (When it came time to write his own account of the attack, Chase would neglect to mention that he had the chance to lance the whale—an omission Nickerson made sure to correct in his narrative.) But the more Chase thought about it, the more he realized that no one could have expected a whale to attack a ship, and not just once but twice. Instead of acting as a whale was supposed to—as a creature 'never before suspected of premeditated violence, and proverbial for its inoffensiveness'—this big bull had been

110

possessed by what Chase finally took to be a very human concern for the other whales. 'He came directly from the shoal which we had just before entered,' the first mate wrote, 'and in which we had struck three of his companions, as if fired with revenge for their sufferings.'

As they bobbed in the lee of the wreck, the men of the *Essex* were of no mind to debate the whale's motives. Their overwhelming question was how twenty men in three boats could get out of a plight like this alive.

CHAPTER SIX

THE PLAN

All night the wind blew out of the southeast. Waves beat against the stricken hull, dislodging spars and casks and splintering timbers. Jagged debris might at any time pierce the frail sides of the three whaleboats tied up to leeward of the ship, so each officer posted a man in the bow of his boat and commanded him to keep a sharp lookout for floating objects bearing down on them and to shove those objects aside before they could do damage. It was terrifying duty—straining to see what threat would next emerge from the darkness.

When the sun lit the eastern horizon, the men rose up blinking from the bilges of the boats, most of them having had little sleep. '[W]e began to think of doing something,' Chase recalled, 'what, we did not know.'

The three boat-crews returned to the wreck, and

111

for most of the morning the men wandered about the wave-washed deck 'in a sort of vacant idleness.' The officers instructed them to search for any additional provisions that might have floated up from the depths of the hold during the night. Except for a few more Galapagos tortoises, of which they already had as many as could be safely carried in the whaleboats, they found nothing of use.

The obvious next step was to make preparations for leaving the wreck. But this was a prospect that none of the men wanted to contemplate, no matter how 'cheerless and desolate' their current circumstances might be. 'Our thoughts . . . hung about the ship, wrecked and sunken as she was,' Chase remembered, 'and we could scarcely discard from our minds the idea of her continuing protection.'

Eventually some of the men began stripping the sails off the ship to make sails for the three whaleboats. Luckily Chase's trunk contained the necessary needles and twine, and the men set to work. Others were directed to build masts for the whaleboats from the ship's spars. Once the crew had been given specific tasks to accomplish, the change in morale was swift. Nickerson noticed 'more cheerful faces than we dared to expect.'

As the men worked—equipping each boat with two short masts, two sprit sails, and a small sail up forward known as a jib—a lookout remained posted on the stump of the *Essex*'s foremast, gazing out across the ocean for a sail. At noon, Chase took an observation and determined that the prevailing southeasterly winds and westerly current had driven the *Essex* and her crew almost fifty miles to

112

the northwest of where they'd been the day before—*away* from the distant coast of South America. For the first mate, this troubling information made clear 'the necessity of not wasting our time, and of endeavoring to seek some relief wherever God might direct us.'

The wind increased throughout the day, making it difficult to work in the whaleboats, especially when waves broke across them, drenching the men. The officers realized that some further modifications were necessary to increase the vessels' seaworthiness. Using rough cedar boards from the wreck, the men built up the sides of each boat by more than half afoot. This simple alteration—done almost as an afterthought—proved crucial. '[T]he boats must otherwise have taken in so much water,' Chase wrote, 'that all the efforts of twenty such weak, starving men as we afterwards came to be, would not have sufficed to keep [them from swamping].'

It was also now clear that they had to work out some method of shielding their provisions of bread from the salt spray. Each end of the whaleboat contained a cupboardlike space called a cuddy. After wrapping the bread in several layers of canvas, they placed it in the boat's aft cuddy, as far as they could from the waves breaking at the bow. Having it in the aft cuddy also made it easy for the officer at the steering oar to monitor the bread's distribution to the rest of the crew.

When darkness began to come on, they reluctantly put aside their hammers, nails, needles, and twine and once again tied up the whaleboats in the lee of the wreck. It was still blowing hard, and all twenty men dreaded what Chase called 'the horrors of another tempestuous night.' It wasn't just the discomfort of attempting to sleep in a tiny rocking boat but also the prospect of an entire night with nothing to distract them from their fears.

The same men who had worked so cheerfully at modifying the whaleboats were suddenly bludgeoned by despair. '[T]he miseries of their situation came upon them with such force,' Chase remembered, 'as to produce spells of extreme debility, approaching almost to fainting.' Even though it had been almost two days since their last meal, they found it impossible to eat. Their throats parched by anxiety, they indulged instead in frequent drinks of water.

Chase lay down in the bottom of his boat and began to pray. But his supplication provided little consolation: 'Sometimes . . . a light hope would dawn, but then, to feel such an utter dependence on . . . chance alone for aid and rescue, would chase it again from my mind.' Rather than contemplating the possible means of their deliverance, Chase found himself once again reliving the circumstances that had brought them to this point, especially 'the mysterious and mortal attack of the animal.'

By seven o'clock the next morning, the ship's deck had broken almost entirely from the hull. Like a whale dying in a slow-motion flurry, the *Essex* in dissolution made for a grim and disturbing sight, her joints and seams working violently in the waves. She was bleeding from the burst casks within her hull, surrounding the men in a reeking slick of whale oil—a yellowish slime that coated the boats' sides and slopped over the gunwales with the waves. The boats became slippery and dangerous to move around in. The fluid that only a few days before had been their fortune, their obsession, was now their torment.

Chase decided that something must be done. He rowed over to Pollard and declared that it was time for them to sail 'towards the nearest land.' The captain stalled, insisting that they scavenge the wreck one last time for provisions they might have overlooked. Only after he had the opportunity for another observation at noon, he said, would he discuss what to do next.

Pollard's noon observation revealed that they had drifted nineteen miles to the north, taking them across the equator during the night. Now, with their sails ready and Pollard's navigational calculations complete, it was time for what Chase termed a 'council.' So, with his two mates joining him in his whaleboat, Pollard spread out before them their two copies of Bowditch's Navigator and its list of the latitudes and longitudes of 'Friendly and other Islands in the Pacific Ocean' and began the discussion of what they should do.

Since their sail-equipped whaleboats could travel only with the wind, their options were quite limited. Backtracking their way to the Galapagos and beyond that to South America, a trip of more than two thousand miles, meant bucking both the southeasterly trade winds and a strong west-flowing current. Pollard deemed it impossible. Sailing to the west, however, was another matter. The closest islands in this direction were the Marquesas, about 1,200 miles away. Unfortunately, the *Essex* men had heard that their native inhabitants had a reputation for cannibalism. Several travelers to the Marquesas, including Captain David Porter of the

U.S. frigate *Essex*, who visited these islands during the War of 1812, had published reports of the frequent wars among the natives. '[I]n times of famine,' insisted another visitor, 'the men butcher their wives, and children, and aged parents.' Georg von Langsdorff, whose ship touched at the Marquesas in 1804, claimed that the natives found human flesh so delicious 'that those who have once eaten it can with difficulty abstain from it.' Langsdorff, along with several others, remarked on the great size and strength of the Marquesan men. There were also reports of ritualized homosexual activity among the natives, which, unlike the rumors of cannibalism, have been confirmed by modern-day anthropologists. The officers agreed that the Marquesas must be avoided.

Several hundred miles to the south of the Marquesas were the islands of the Tuamotu Archipelago. These, too, had a dark and disturbing reputation among American sailors. To the west of the Tuamotus were the Society Islands, about two thousand miles away. Although he had no trustworthy information to go on, Pollard was under the impression that the Society Islands were a safer option than the Marquesas. With a little luck, these islands might be reached in less than thirty days. There were also the Hawaiian Islands, more than 2,500 miles to the northwest, but Pollard was fearful of the storms that frequented this region of the Pacific in the late fall. He stated his conclusion: They should sail for the Society Islands.

Chase and Joy disagreed. They pointed out that, except for vague rumors, they were 'entirely ignorant' of the Society Islands. '[I]f [the islands were] inhabited,' the first mate wrote, 'we presumed they were by savages, from whom we had as much to fear, as from the elements, or even death itself.' Nature had already betrayed them once—with the vicious attack on them by their rightful prey, the normally benign sperm whale. In the absence of any strong evidence to the contrary, Chase and Joy were disposed to believe that the people of the Society Islands practiced, like the Marquesans, an even more horrific inversion of the natural order: the eating of human flesh.

Chase and Joy proposed what they felt was a better alternative. Although the easterly slant of the trade winds precluded sailing directly for the coast of South America, there was another possibility. If they sailed south for about 1,500 miles to latitude 26° south, they would enter a band of variable breezes which they could then ride to Chile or Peru. They figured their boats could cover a degree of latitude—sixty nautical miles—a day. That would put them in the variables in twenty-six days; thirty days later and they would be on the coast of South America. With enough bread and water to last about sixty days, it all seemed—at least to Chase and Joy—very feasible. And besides, somewhere along the way they might be spotted by another whaleship. The two mates lightly described their proposal as 'going up the coast.'

Just as he had after the knockdown in the Gulf Stream, Pollard succumbed to them. 'Not wishing to oppose where there was two against one,' Nickerson remembered, 'the captain reluctantly yielded to their arguments.' When writing of this 'fatal error' later, the *Essex*'s cabin boy asked, 'How many warm hearts have ceased to beat in

117

consequence of it?'

*   *   *

Today, the Nantucketers' lack of knowledge of the Pacific, an ocean in which they had been sailing for several decades, seems incredible. Since before the turn of the century, China traders from the nearby ports of New York, Boston, and Salem had been making frequent stops at not only the Marquesas but also the Hawaiian Islands on their way to Canton. While rumors of cannibalism in the Marquesas were widespread, there was plenty of readily accessible information to the contrary.

Several months before the *Essex*'s departure from Nantucket in 1819, when both Pollard and Chase were on-island, an article appeared in the April 28 issue of the *New Bedford Mercury* with the latest news from the Marquesas. According to the *Lion's* Captain Townsend, who had recently returned from Canton with three natives from the island of Nukahivah, all had been peaceful on these islands ever since Captain David Porter had visited them during the War of 1812. '[T]he benign influence of his name still remained with the natives, who live in great harmony and social intercourse,' the *Mercury* recorded. 'The hostile tribes learnt war no more; and the Typees [formerly known for their cannibalism] were frequent visitors of the Lion, while she lay at that island.' Unfortunately, Pollard and his officers appear not to have read the report.

Their ignorance of the Society Islands, in particular Tahiti, is even more extraordinary. Since 1797, there had been a thriving English mission on

118

the island. Tahiti's huge royal mission chapel, 712 feet long and 54 feet wide, was bigger than any Quaker meetinghouse on Nantucket. As Melville noted in his copy of Chase's *Narrative*,

> All the sufferings of these miserable men of the *Essex* might, in all human probability, have been avoided, had they, immediately after leaving the wreck, steered straight for Tahiti, from which they were not very distant at the time, & to which, there was a fair Trade wind. But they dreaded cannibals, & strange to tell knew not that . . . it was entirely safe for the Mariner to touch at Tahiti.—But they chose to stem a headwind, & make a passage of several thousand miles (an unavoidably roundabout one too) in order to gain a civilized harbor on the coast of South America.

The men of the *Essex* were the victims of their particular moment in the history of the whale fishery. The Offshore Ground had been discovered only the year before. In another few years whaleships would go so far from the coast of South America that they would be compelled to provision in the islands of the Central Pacific, making the opening up of the Marquesas and the Society Islands to the west an accomplished fact. But in November 1820, these islands were outside the bounds of what they considered to be reliable knowledge.

Nantucketers were suspicious of anything beyond their immediate experience. Their far-reaching success in whaling was founded not on radical technological advances or bold gambles but on a profound conservatism. Gradually building on the achievements of the generations before them, they had expanded their whaling empire in a most deliberate and painstaking manner. If new information didn't come to them from the lips of another Nantucketer, it was suspect.

By spurning the Society Islands and sailing for South America, the *Essex* officers chose to take their chances with an element they did know well: the sea. 'The whaling business is peculiarly an ocean life,' Obed Macy wrote. 'The sea, to mariners generally, is but a highway over which they travel to foreign markets; but to the whaler it is his field of labor, it is the home of his business.' Or, as Melville would write in the 'Nantucket' chapter of *Moby-Dick*: 'The Nantucketer, he alone resides and rests on the sea; he alone, in Bible language, goes down to it in ships; to and fro ploughing it as his own special plantation. *There* is his home; *there* lies his business, which a Noah's flood would not interrupt, though it overwhelmed all the millions in China.'

For these Nantucketers the prospect of a long-distance voyage in twenty-five-foot boats was certainly daunting, but it was a challenge for which they were prepared. Their vessels, after all, were not cumbersome, run-of-the-mill lifeboats; these were whaleboats, high-performance craft that had been designed for the open ocean. Made of light, half-inch-thick cedar planks, a whaleboat possessed the buoyancy required to ride over rather than through the waves. 'I would not have exchanged [my boat], old and crazy as she was,' Chase claimed, 'for even a ship's launch,' the sturdy type of craft in which, three decades earlier, Captain Bligh had sailed more than four thousand miles after the *Bounty* mutiny.

The perils of whaling had given the Nantucketers a high tolerance for danger and suffering. They had been tossed in the air by the flukes of a whale; they had spent hours clinging to the battered remnants of a capsized whaleboat in a cold and choppy sea. 'We are so much accustomed to the continual recurrence of such scenes as these,' Chase wrote, 'that we become familiarized to them, and consequently always feel that confidence and self-possession, which teaches us every expedient in danger, and inures the body, as well as the mind, to fatigue, privation, and peril, in frequent cases exceeding belief.' Only a Nantucketer in November 1820 possessed the necessary combination of arrogance, ignorance, and xenophobia to shun a beckoning (albeit unknown) island and choose instead an open-sea voyage of several thousand miles.

*　　　*　　　*

Pollard had known better, but instead of pulling rank and insisting that his officers carry out his proposal to sail for the Society Islands, he embraced a more democratic style of command. Modern survival psychologists have determined that this 'social'—as opposed to 'authoritarian'— form of leadership is ill-suited to the early stages of a disaster, when decisions must be made quickly and firmly. Only later, as the ordeal drags on and it is necessary to maintain morale, do social leadership skills become important.

121

Whalemen in the nineteenth century had a clear understanding of these two approaches. The captain was expected to be the authoritarian, what Nantucketers called a fishy man. A fishy man loved to kill whales and lacked the tendency toward self-doubt and self-examination that could get in the way of making a quick decision. To be called 'fishy to the backbone' was the ultimate compliment a Nantucketer could receive and meant that he was destined to become, if he wasn't already, a captain.

Mates, however, were expected to temper their fishiness with a more personal, even outgoing, approach. After breaking in the green hands at the onset of the voyage—when they gained their well-deserved reputations as 'spit-fires'—mates worked to instill a sense of cooperation among the men. This required them to remain sensitive to the crew's changeable moods and to keep the lines of communication open.

Nantucketers recognized that the positions of captain and first mate required contrasting personalities. Not all mates had the necessary edge to become captains, and there were many future captains who did not have the patience to be successful mates. There was a saying on the island: '[I] t is a pity to spoil a good mate by making him a master.'

Pollard's behavior, after both the knockdown and the whale attack, indicates that he lacked the resolve to overrule his two younger and less experienced officers. In his deference to others, Pollard was conducting himself less like a captain and more like the veteran mate described by the Nantucketer William H. Macy: '[H]e had no lungs to blow his own trumpet, and sometimes distrusted

122

his own powers, though generally found equal to any emergency after it arose. This want of confidence sometimes led him to hesitate, where a more impulsive or less thoughtful man would act at once. In the course of his career he had seen many 'fishy" young men lifted over his head.'

Shipowners hoped to combine a fishy, hard-driving captain with an approachable and steady mate. But in the labor-starved frenzy of Nantucket in 1819, the *Essex* had ended up with a captain who had the instincts and soul of a mate, and a mate who had the ambition and fire of a captain. Instead of giving an order and sticking with it, Pollard indulged his mate-like tendency to listen to others. This provided Chase—who had no qualms about speaking up—with the opportunity to impose his own will. For better or worse, the men of the *Essex* were sailing toward a destiny that would be determined, in large part, not by their unassertive captain but by their forceful and fishy mate.

*   *   *

Now that they had devised a plan, it was time to split up the crew among the three whaleboats. Since Chase's boat was in the worst shape, his crew remained at just six, while the other boats were obliged to carry seven men each.

At the beginning of the voyage, the officers' prime consideration when choosing a man for a boat-crew had been whether or not he was a Nantucketer. In the aftermath of a disaster, ties of family and friendship are, if anything, even more strongly felt, and it is apparent that the Nantucketers' clannishness, now intensified,

123

strongly influenced the makeup of the three crews. So did rank. Of the twenty crew members, nine were Nantucketers, five were white off-islanders, and six were African Americans. As captain, Pollard was given the most Nantucketers—five out of the seven men in his boat. Chase managed to get two, along with two white Cape Codders and a black. Second mate Matthew Joy, however, the *Essex*'s most junior officer, found himself without a single Nantucketer; instead he was given four of the six blacks.

Feeling personally responsible for the welfare of the young Nantucketers aboard the *Essex*, Pollard made sure that his boat contained his eighteen-year-old cousin, Owen Coffin, and Coffin's two boyhood friends, Charles Ramsdell and Barzillai Ray. Thomas Nickerson's position as Chase's after oarsman meant that he was not included in this group but must manage as best he could on the leakiest of the three boats. From a Nantucketer's perspective, however, Chase's boat was preferable to Joy's.

Although originally from Nantucket, Joy's family had moved to the recently established whaling port of Hudson, New York. Chase reported that Joy had been suffering from an undiagnosed illness, possibly tuberculosis, well before the sinking. Seriously ill and not a full-fledged Nantucketer, Joy was given only coofs. If the success of a group in a survival situation is dependent on strong, active leadership, Joy's six crew members were put at an immediate disadvantage. The Nantucketers had done their best to take care of their own.

All twenty men were nominally under the command of Captain Pollard, but each boat-crew remained an autonomous entity that might at any moment become separated from the others. Each boat was given two hundred pounds of hardtack, sixty-five gallons of water, and two Galapagos tortoises. To ensure that discipline would be maintained even under the most arduous circumstances, Pollard gave each mate a pistol and some powder, keeping a musket for himself.

At 12:30—less than a half hour after the officers had convened their council—they set out in a strong breeze, their schooner-rigged whaleboats, according to Nickerson, 'a very handsome show on this our first start.' The men's spirits were the lowest they'd ever been. With the *Essex* receding rapidly behind them, they were beginning to appreciate what Nickerson called 'the slender thread upon which our lives were hung.'

All were affected by leaving their ship for the last time. Even the stoic Chase could not help but wonder at how 'we looked upon our shattered and sunken vessel with such an excessive fondness and regret . . . [I]t seemed as if abandoning her we had parted with all hope.' The men exchanged frightened glances, even as they continued to search out the disappearing wreck, 'as though,' Nickerson said, 'it were possible that she could relieve us from the fate that seemed to await us.'

By four o'clock that afternoon, they had lost sight of the *Essex*. Almost immediately, the men's morale began to improve. Nickerson sensed that, no longer haunted by the vision of the disabled ship, '[we had been] relieved from a spell by which we had been bound.' He went so far as to claim that 'now that our minds were made up for the worst, half the struggle was over.' With no turning

125

back, they had only one recourse—to hold to their plan.

CHAPTER SEVEN

AT SEA

As darkness approached at the end of the first day, the wind built steadily, kicking up a steep, irregular chop. The *Essex* whaleboats were hybrids—built for rowing but now adapted to sail—and the men were still learning how they handled. Instead of a rudder, each boat was equipped with a steering oar. This eighteen-foot lever enabled a rowed whaleboat to spin around in its own length, but it was not so effective in guiding a sailboat, and required the helmsman to stand at the cumbersome oar. At this early stage in the voyage, the whaleboats were dangerously overloaded. Instead of five hundred pounds of whaling equipment, each boat contained close to a thousand pounds of bread, water, and tortoises, and waves broke over the built-up gunnels and soaked the men. The boats were also without centerboards or skegs to help them track through the water, forcing the helmsmen to tug and push their steering oars as their little, deeply laden boats corkscrewed in the turbulent seas.

Each boat-crew was divided into two watches. While half the men attempted to rest—curling up with the Galapagos tortoises in the bilge or leaning uncomfortably against the seats—the others steered, tended the sails, and bailed. They also

126

attempted to keep an eye on the other boats, which would sometimes disappear entirely from view when they dipped down into the trough of a wave.

At the start it had been decided that every effort would be made to keep the three boats together. Together they could help if one of them ran into trouble; together they could keep one anothers' spirits up. '[U]naided, and unencouraged by each other,' Chase observed, 'there were with us many whose weak minds, I am confident, would have sunk under the dismal retrospections of the past catastrophe, and who did not possess either sense or firmness enough to contemplate our approaching destiny, without the cheering of some more determined countenance than their own.'

There was also a more practical reason for staying together: there was not enough navigational equipment to go around. Pollard and Chase each had a compass, a quadrant, and a copy of Bowditch's Navigator, but Joy had nothing. If his boat-crew should become separated from the other two, they would be unable to find their way across the ocean.

Night came on. Although moon and starlight still made it possible to detect the ghostly paleness of the whaleboats' sails, the men's field of vision shrank dramatically in the darkness even as their perception of sounds was heightened. The whaleboats' clinker, or lapstrake, construction (with planks overlapping, resembling the clapboards of a house) made them much noisier than a smooth-bottomed boat, and the fussy, fluted sound of water licking up against their boats' lapped sides would accompany them for the duration of the voyage.

Even at night the crews were able to maintain a lively three-way conversation among the boats. The subject on everyone's mind was of course the 'means and prospects of our deliverance.' It was agreed that their best chance of survival lay in happening upon a whaleship. The *Essex* had sunk about three hundred miles north of the Offshore Ground. They still had about five days of sailing before they entered the Ground, where, they desperately hoped, they would come across a whaler.

A circumstance in their favor was that, unlike merchant vessels, whaleships almost always had a lookout posted at the masthead, so in whaling territory they had a better chance of being seen. Against them was the immensity of the Offshore Ground. It encompassed an enormous amount of ocean—more than twice the area of the state of Texas, a rectangle about three hundred miles north to south and almost two thousand miles from east to west. There were at least seven whaleships on the Offshore Ground at this time. But even if there were double that number, the odds were poor that three whaleboats sailing along a straight line through the Ground (which might take only four or five days to cross) would be spotted by a ship.

One possibility was to extend their time in the Offshore Ground and actively search for whalers. But that was a gamble. If they searched the region and didn't find a ship, they would jeopardize their chances of reaching South America before their food supplies ran out. As it was, they would be entering the western extreme of the Ground and would have a difficult time heading east against the southeasterly trades.

There was another factor influencing their decision to continue on with the original plan. After having fallen victim to such a seemingly random and inexplicable attack, the men felt an overpowering need to reclaim at least some control of their own destiny. Being sighted by a whaleship would, according to Chase, not 'depend on our own exertions, but on chance alone.' Reaching South America, on the other hand, depended 'on our own labors.' From Chase's perspective, this made all the difference and demanded that they not 'lose sight, for one moment, of the strong probabilities which, under Divine Providence, there were of our reaching land by the route we had prescribed to ourselves.'

The plan had one iron requirement: they had to make their provisions last two months. Each man would get six ounces of hardtack and half a pint of water a day. Hardtack was a simple dried bread made out of flour and water. Baked into a moisture-free rock to prevent spoilage, hardtack had to be broken into small pieces or soaked in water before it was eaten, if a sailor didn't want to crack a tooth.

The daily ration was equivalent to six slices of bread, and it provided about five hundred calories. Chase estimated that this amounted to less than a third of the nourishment required by 'an ordinary man.' Modern dietary analysis indicates that for a five-foot, eight-inch person weighing 145 pounds, these provisions met about a quarter of his daily energy needs. True, the men of the *Essex* had more than just bread; they had tortoises. Each tortoise was a pod of fresh meat, fat, and blood that was capable of providing as many as 4,500 calories per

129

man—the equivalent of nine days of hardtack. Yet, even augmented by the tortoises, their daily rations amounted to a starvation diet. If they did succeed in reaching South America in sixty days, each man knew he would be little more than a breathing skeleton.

But as they would soon discover, their greatest concern was not food but rather water. The human body, which is 70 percent water, requires a bare minimum of a pint a day to remove its waste products. The men of the *Essex* would have to make do with half that daily amount. If they experienced any hot weather, the deficit would only increase.

That first night of their journey, Chase, Pollard, and Joy distributed the rations of bread and water to their boat-crews. It was two days after the sinking now, and the men's interest in food had finally returned; the bread was quickly eaten. There was something else they craved: tobacco. A whaleman almost always had a quid of tobacco in his mouth, going through more than seventy pounds of it in a single voyage. In addition to all their other woes, the crew of the *Essex* had to contend with the jittery withdrawal symptoms associated with nicotine addiction.

After the meager meal, the men not on watch went to sleep. 'Nature became at last worn out with the watchings and anxieties of the two preceding nights,' Chase recalled, 'and sleep came insensibly upon us.' But as his men fell into what he judged to be a dreamless stupor, Chase found himself in the middle of a waking nightmare.

Unable to sleep for the third night in a row, he continued to dwell obsessively on the circumstances of the ship's sinking. He could not get the creature out of his mind: '[T]he horrid aspect and revenge of the whale, wholly engrossed my reflections.' In his desperate attempts to find some explanation for how a normally passive creature could suddenly become a predator, Chase was plagued by what psychologists call a 'tormenting memory'—a common response to disasters. Forced to relive the trauma over and over again, the survivor finds larger, hidden forces operating through the incident. The philosopher William James felt this compulsion first-hand some years later. After the San Francisco earthquake of 1906, he wrote: 'I realize now how inevitable were men's earlier mythological versions [of disaster] and how artificial and against the grain of our spontaneous perceiving are the later habits which science educates us.'

For most disaster victims, the repeated flashbacks of a tormenting memory have a therapeutic value, gradually weaning the sufferer from anxieties that might otherwise interfere with his ability to survive. There are some, however, who cannot rid themselves of the memory. Melville, building upon Chase's account, would make his Captain Ahab a man who never emerged from the psychic depths in which Chase had writhed these three nights. Just as Chase was convinced that the whale that attacked the *Essex* exhibited 'decided, calculating mischief,' so was Ahab haunted by a sense of the white whale's 'outrageous strength, with an inscrutable malice sinewing it.' Locked in his own private chamber of horrors, Ahab resolved that his only escape was through hunting down and killing Moby Dick:

'How can the prisoner reach outside except by thrusting through the wall? To me, the white whale is that wall, shoved near to me.' Chase, on a tiny boat a thousand miles from land, did not have the possibility of revenge. Ahab was fighting a symbol; Chase and his shipmates were fighting for their lives.

*   *   *

The next morning, the men were greatly relieved to discover that after a night of high winds all three boats were still close together. The wind built throughout the day, requiring them to shorten sail. The boats' schooner rigs could be easily adapted to the changing conditions, and after the sails were reefed, Chase reported, the men 'did not apprehend any very great danger from the then violence of the wind.' The high seas, however, continued to afflict them. Constantly wet from the salt spray, they had begun to develop painful sores on their skin that the violent bouncing of the boats only exacerbated.

In his sea chest, Chase found an assortment of useful items: a jackknife, a whetstone, three small fish hooks, a cake of soap, a suit of clothes, a pencil, and ten sheets of writing paper. As first mate, Chase had been responsible for keeping the *Essex*'s log, and using the pencil and paper he now attempted to start 'a sort of sea journal'—despite the horrendous conditions. 'It was with much difficulty . . . that I could keep any sort of record,' Chase remembered, 'owing to the incessant rocking and unsteadiness of the boat and the continual dashing of spray of the sea over us.'

Chase's journal-keeping satisfied more than an official obligation; it also fulfilled a personal need. The act of self-expression—through writing a journal or letters—often enables a survivor to distance himself from his fears. After beginning his informal log, Chase would never again suffer another sleepless night tortured by his memory of the whale.

There were other daily rituals. Every morning they shaved with the same knife Chase used to sharpen his pencil. Benjamin Lawrence spent a portion of each day twisting stray strands of rope into an ever lengthening piece of twine. The boatsteerer vowed that if he should ever get out of the whaleboat alive, he would save the string as a memorial to the ordeal.

At noon they paused to take an observation. Determining the angle of the sun with a quadrant was not easy on a tiny, wave-tossed boat. Their best estimate put them at latitude 0°58' south. It was an encouraging indication. They had not only crossed back over the equator but had traveled approximately seventy-one nautical miles since leaving the wreck the day before, putting them ahead of their daily target of sixty miles. In the afternoon the wind moderated, enabling them to shake out the reefs in their sails and dry their wet clothes in the sun.

That day Pollard decided to abandon 'the idea altogether of keeping any correct longitudinal reckoning.' To maintain an accurate estimate of a vessel's position, it is necessary to keep track of both its north-to-south position, or latitude, and its east-to-west position, or longitude. A noon observation with a quadrant indicates only a craft's

133

latitude. If a navigator in 1820 had a chronometer—an exceptionally accurate timepiece adapted to the rigors of being stored on a ship—he could compare the time of his noon sight with the time in Greenwich, England, and calculate his longitude. But chronometers at this time were expensive and not yet widely used on Nantucket whaleships.

The alternative was to perform what was called a lunar observation, or simply a lunar. This was an extremely complicated process that involved as many as three hours of calculations before the vessel's longitude could be determined—an impossibility on a whaleboat. Besides, according to Nickerson, Pollard had not yet learned how to work a lunar.

That left dead reckoning. The officers of every ship kept a careful record of its heading, as indicated by the compass, and its speed. Speed was determined by throwing a knotted length of line with a piece of wood at the end of it (called a log line) into the water and determining how much of it (that is, how many 'knots') ran out in a set period of time. A sandglass, known as a slowglass, was used to measure the time. The ship's speed and direction were recorded, and this information was transferred onto a chart, where the captain established the ship's estimated position.

Survivors of other maritime catastrophes—most notably the *Bounty*'s Captain Bligh—placed in similar situations managed to navigate successfully with dead reckoning. Soon after being abandoned in the middle of the Pacific in the ship's launch, Captain Bligh manufactured his own log line and trained his men to count the seconds as it was run out. Bligh's estimates of their latitude and longitude proved amazingly accurate, enabling him to find the distant island of Timor, one of history's greatest feats of navigation.

Chase explained that 'having no glass, nor log-line,' they decided that it was futile to maintain an estimate of their longitude. If Pollard's inability to work a lunar is any indication, he was not a particularly skilled navigator or an unusually unskilled one. There were many captains who were also navigating their vessels by dead reckoning and, like Pollard, never expected to find themselves in such a situation. By forgoing all estimates of their longitude, he and his men were now sailing blind, with no way to determine their distance from South America.

*   *   *

In the afternoon a school of porpoises surrounded the three boats and followed them until well after sunset. That night the wind built to almost a gale. Chase and his crew watched in horror as the planks of their old boat worked and twisted in the waves. The boat was in such terrible shape, Nickerson claimed, that he normally would not have felt safe sailing ten miles in it, let alone the thousands they had ahead of them.

By the morning of Friday, November 24, the third day in the boats, the waves were 'very large,' according to Chase, 'and increased, if possible, the extreme uncomfortableness of our situation.' Nickerson observed that if they'd been aboard the *Essex*, the wind would have seemed unexceptional, but now, he said, 'in our crippled state it answers the purpose of a gale, and keeps us constantly wet

135

and chilled through.' That day an immense wave broke over Chase's boat and almost filled it with water. The swamped boat threatened to roll over on its side as kegs, tortoises, and Chase's sea chest floated up from the bottom and knocked against the men. They bailed frantically, knowing that the next wave might sink them.

Once they'd brought the boat out of danger, they discovered that some of the hardtack—which they'd carefully wrapped in sailcloth—had been soaked by the seawater. They did their best to salvage as much of the damaged bread as possible. Over the course of the next few days, they would seize every chance to dry the dissolving lumps in the sun. While this saved the provisions from what Nickerson called 'utter ruin,' the bread remained infiltrated with salt, the worst possible thing for their already water-deprived bodies. 'The bread being our only dependence,' Nickerson remembered, '[this] gave . . . us on the whole a cheerless prospect'—a prospect that only worsened when they learned that a portion of the bread on Pollard's boat had also been damaged. A few days before, the officers had possessed cautious faith in 'the human means at our command'; now they recognized 'our utter dependence on that divine aid we so much the more stood in need of.'

At eight o'clock the next morning, the man assigned to bailing Chase's boat became alarmed. Try as he might, he couldn't keep ahead of the rising tide of water. Their boat, he alerted the rest of the crew, was sinking. Soon all six men were searching for the new leak, their hands probing desperately in the sloshing bilge, feeling the boat's sides for the gush of incoming water. It wasn't until

136

they'd torn up the floor that they discovered the problem: one of the planks in the bow had sprung from the hull, and water was pouring in. The leak was about six inches below the waterline, and if they were going to fix it, they needed to figure out some way to get at it from the outside.

The sprung board was on the starboard, or leeward, side, and Chase immediately 'hove about,' using the steering oar to turn the boat so that the wind was now coming over the other side. This put the leak on the windward, or 'high,' side; Chase hoped to heel the boat over enough so that the hole would rise up out of the water.

Noticing that Chase had suddenly veered away, Pollard brought his own boat around and headed for the first mate. After shortening sail, Pollard came alongside and asked what was wrong.

Now that the captain's boat was beside them, Chase ordered his own crew to move to the port side and as far aft as possible, canting the bow up into the air. Working from Pollard's boat, the first mate and captain attempted to steady the bow, realign the board, and hammer it into place. There was little room for error. The end of the board was already riddled with old nail holes, and it was critical that they drive in each new nail cleanly. Even though they were being bounced up and down by the waves, Chase and Pollard managed 'to drive in a few nails, and secured [the plank], much beyond our expectations.' Soon all three boats were once again sailing to the south.

'This little incident, although it may seem small,' Nickerson recalled, '[caused] amongst us the greatest excitement.' With a clear demonstration that their whaleboats might fall apart around them at any time, the men felt 'a great gloominess over the natural prospects of our deliverance.' They knew that the longer the ordeal lasted, the more the boats would suffer in 'the heavy and repeated racking of the swell.' All it took was the starting of a single nail, and one of these boats might be lost forever.

For the men in Chase's crew it had been an especially trying day. That evening Richard Peterson, the sole African American on their boat, led them in prayers and a few hymns. Nickerson remembered how the words and songs of the 'pious old colored man . . . drew our minds from our present miseries to seek deliverance from a higher power.' That comfort notwithstanding, by the morning of November 26, the tentative optimism with which the men had begun the boat voyage had eroded into despair.

For the last four days the windy and overcast weather had made it impossible to take an observation. Judging by the compass course they'd been forced to steer, their sails strapped in tight against the southeasterly trades, they knew they had been sailing parallel to, rather than toward, the coast of South America. They also knew that their boats, which were without centerboards, had a tendency to sideslip to leeward. Because of that slippage, they must now be well to the west of where they should have been. Despite having made significant progress south, they were no closer to their ultimate destination. The hopeful talk of being rescued by a passing whaleship had ceased. '[W]e looked forward,' Chase wrote, 'not without an extreme dread, and anxiety, to the gloomy and disheartening prospect before us.'

That afternoon the breeze dropped to a more comfortable level, allowing them to spread out their damaged bread to dry. Then the wind shifted, gradually backing into the north. For the first time since leaving the *Essex*, they were able to steer toward South America. Men began to talk about how far ahead of schedule they would be if the wind would only hold.

But it was not to last. The next day, the wind shifted back into the east and 'destroyed the fine prospect we had entertained of making a good run.' As if to mock them, the following day the wind veered even farther, to the east-southeast. Then it started to blow hard.

That night they shortened sail and 'began to entertain fears that we should be separated' in the darkness. To prevent just such an occurrence, the crew of the *Union*, the Nantucket ship that accidentally rammed into a whale in 1807, tied their boats together at night. But tethering interfered with sailing ability. The officers of the *Essex*—so intent on reaching the distant coast of South America—were reluctant to compromise their boats' speed. Instead of tying themselves together, they sailed in a kind of formation, with Chase in the lead, Pollard in the middle, and Joy taking up the rear. If they could remain within one hundred feet of one another, each could always see the other two whaleboats' white sails in the darkness.

*   *   *

At about eleven o'clock, Chase lay down in the bottom of his boat to sleep. He had just nodded off

139

when he was startled awake by a cry from one of his men. Captain Pollard, the man said, was calling out to them in the darkness. Chase sat up and listened. In the howling wind and breaking waves, he could hear Pollard shouting to Joy, whose boat was nearest to him. Chase tacked around and sailed for the other two boats, only dimly visible in the moonless dark, and asked what was wrong. Given what had happened to the *Essex* only a week before, the reply seemed like a sick joke.

Pollard told them that his boat had been attacked by a whale.

Instead of a sperm whale, it had been a smaller, but more aggressive, killer whale. These eight- to twelve-ton toothed whales feed on warm-blooded animals such as dolphins and seals. They hunt in packs and have even been known to attack and kill sperm whales. There have been documented cases in which killer whales, also known as orcas, have repeatedly rammed and sunk wooden sailing yachts.

Pollard explained that, entirely unprovoked, the whale had slammed its head against their boat and taken a sizable bite out of it. Then it proceeded to 'play about' the boat, batting it around with its head and tail as a cat might toy with a mouse, before it finally attacked once again, this time splitting the boat's stem. As the whale churned up the water around them, the men grabbed the two poles that held up the tips of the sails (known as sprit poles) and repeatedly punched the creature's sides. Chase arrived just as Pollard and his men succeeded in beating back the whale and sending it swimming away.

Pollard's boat had begun to swamp, so he

140

ordered his crew to transfer their provisions to the other boats. All night the three boats lay huddled together in the swells. Unable to see very far in the inky darkness, the men let their imaginations fill the void with their fears. Over the last week they had contended with stiff headwinds, spoiled provisions, and leaky boats. To be attacked by yet another whale was the crowning blow: '[I]t seemed to us as if fate was wholly relentless, in pursuing us with such a cruel complication of disasters.' They searched the water's black surface, convinced that the whale would reappear. 'We were not without our fears that the fish might renew his attack, some time during the night, upon one of the other boats, and unexpectedly destroy us.' Without their ship to protect them, the hunters had become the prey.

*　　　*　　　*

The next morning they accomplished a quick repair of Pollard's boat by nailing thin strips of wood along the interior of the broken section. Once again, they were on their way, this time in a strong southeasterly breeze. That day the men in Chase's boat began to experience overpowering sensations of thirst—a lust for water that made it impossible to think about anything else. Despite the dryness of their mouths, they talked compulsively about their cravings. Only gradually did they realize the cause of their distress.

The day before, they had started eating the saltwater-damaged bread. The bread, which they had carefully dried in the sun, now contained all the salt of seawater but not, of course, the water. Already severely dehydrated, the men were, in

141

effect, pouring gasoline on the fire of their thirsts— forcing their kidneys to extract additional fluid from their bodies to excrete the salt. They were beginning to suffer from a condition known as hypernatremia, in which an excessive amount of sodium can bring on convulsions.

'The privation of water is justly ranked among the most dreadful of the miseries of our life,' Chase recorded. '[T]he violence of raving thirst has no parallel in the catalogue of human calamities.' Chase claimed that it was on this day, November 28—the sixth since leaving the wreck—that 'our extreme sufferings here first commenced.'

Even after they realized that the bread was responsible for their agony, the men in the first mate's boat resolved to continue eating the damaged provisions. The bread would spoil if it wasn't eaten soon, and their plan was contingent on a full sixty days of provisions. 'Our determination was, to suffer as long as human patience and endurance would hold out,' Chase wrote, 'having only in view, the relief that would be afforded us, when the quantity of wet provisions should be exhausted.'

The next day it became clear that the strain of sailing in the open ocean, day and night, for more than a week had taken its toll on the boats. The seams were gradually pulling apart, and all three craft now had to be bailed constantly. On board Chase's boat the situation was the most dire, but the first mate refused to give in. With his hammer in hand, he attended to even the most trivial repair. '[B]eing an active and ingenious man,' Nickerson recalled, the first mate let 'no opportunity pass whereby he [could] add a nail by way of

142

strengthening' the boat's ribs and planks. The incessant activity helped to divert Chase's men from the reality of their situation. They were in the worst of the three boats, but they had a leader who had dedicated himself to postponing its disintegration until it was beyond his final powers to prevent it.

That morning a school of iridescent dolphin fish appeared in the waters surrounding the boats and followed them for most of the day. Placing pieces of a white rag on one of Chase's fish hooks, they attempted, in Nickerson's words, 'to use all our persuasive powers . . . to induce them to come aboard.' The fish proved 'as tenacious of their existence as ourselves' and refused to bite.

By the following day, the men's hunger had become almost as difficult to bear as their thirst. The weather proved the best they'd seen since leaving the *Essex* eight days before, and Chase proposed that they attempt to allay 'the ravenous gnawings upon our stomachs' by eating one of the tortoises. All the men readily agreed, and at one o'clock that afternoon, Chase's dissection began. First they flipped the tortoise on its back. As his men held its beak and claws; Chase slit the creature's throat, cutting the arteries and veins on either side of the vertebrae in the neck. Nickerson claimed that 'all seemed quite impatient of the opportunity to drink the blood as it came oozing from the wound of the sacrificed animal,' eager to consume it before it coagulated.

They collected the blood in the same tin cup from which they drank their water rations. Despite their shrieking thirst, some of the men could not make themselves drink the blood. For this part,

Chase 'took it like a medicine to relieve the extreme dryness of my palate.'

All of them, however, were willing to eat. Chase inserted his knife into the leathery skin beside the neck and worked his way around the shell's edge, cutting with a sawing motion until he could lift out the meat and guts. With the help of the tinderbox stored in the whaleboat's small keg of emergency equipment, they kindled a fire in the shell and cooked the terrapin, 'entrails and all.'

After ten days of eating only bread, the men greedily attacked the tortoise, their teeth ripping the succulent flesh as warm juice ran down their salt-encrusted faces. Their bodies' instinctive need for nutrition led them irresistibly to the tortoise's vitamin-rich heart and liver. Chase dubbed it 'an unspeakably fine repast.'

Their hunger was so voracious that once they began to eat, they found it difficult to stop. An average-sized tortoise would have provided each man with about three pounds of meat, one pound of fat, and at least half a cup of blood, together worth more than 4,500 calories—equivalent to a large Thanksgiving dinner. This would have been a tremendous amount of food to introduce into the shrunken stomach of a person who had only eaten a total of four pounds of bread over the last ten days. The men's dehydrated condition would have also made it difficult for their stomachs to generate the digestive juices required to handle the large amount of food. But neither Chase nor Nickerson speaks of saving any of the cooked tortoise for a later day. For these starved men, this was one gratification no one was willing to delay. '[O]our bodies were considerably recruited,' Chase wrote,

144

'and I felt my spirits now much higher than they had been at anytime before.' Instead of limiting each whaleboat to two live tortoises, they now realized, they should have butchered and cooked the meat of every animal they found on the wreck.

For the first time in several days, the sky was clear enough for a noon observation. Pollard's sight indicated that they were approaching latitude 8° south. Since leaving the wreck on November 22, they had traveled almost five hundred miles, putting them slightly ahead of schedule—at least in terms of distance sailed over the water. That evening, with the bones and charred carapace of the tortoise littering the boat's bilge, Richard Peterson once again led the men in prayer.

*   *   *

For the next three days, the weather remained mild and clear. The wind shifted to the north, allowing them to shape their course toward Peru. Their stomachs full, they dared to believe that 'our situation was not at that moment . . . so comfortless as we had been led at first to consider.' Nickerson noticed 'a degree of repose and carelessness, scarcely to be looked for amid persons in our forlorn and hopeless situation.'

Only one thing lay between them and 'a momentary forgetfulness of our actual situation'—a ferocious, unbearable thirst. Chase reported that even after consuming the tortoise and its blood, they still yearned for a long, cool drink of water: '[H]ad it not been for the pains which that gave us, we should have tasted, during this spell of fine weather, a species of enjoyment.'

145

On Sunday, December 3, they ate the last of their damaged bread. For the men in Chase's boat, it was a turning point. At first they didn't notice the change, but with each succeeding day of eating unspoiled hardtack, 'the moisture began to collect in our mouths and the parching fever of the palate imperceptibly left it.' They were still seriously dehydrated, and becoming only more so, but no longer were they introducing excessive amounts of salt into their bodies.

That evening, after the men in Chase's boat had conducted what Nickerson called 'our usual prayer meeting,' clouds moved in, cutting them off from the starlight. At around ten o'clock, Chase and Pollard lost track of Joy's boat. Its disappearance was so sudden that Nickerson feared 'something had destroyed them.' Almost immediately, Chase hove to and raised a lantern to the masthead as the rest of his crew scanned the darkness for some sign of the second mate's boat. About a quarter of a mile to leeward, they spotted a small light flickering in the gloom. It proved to be Joy's answering signal. All three boats were once again accounted for.

Two nights later, it was Chase's turn to become separated from the others. Instead of lighting a lantern, the first mate fired his pistol. Soon after, Pollard and Joy appeared out of the darkness to windward. That night the officers agreed that if they should ever become separated again, no action would be taken to reassemble the convoy. Too much time was being lost trying to keep the boats together. Besides, if one of the boats either capsized or became unrepairable, there was little the other crews could do. All three boats were already overloaded, and to add any more men would result in the eventual deaths of all of them. The prospect of beating away the helpless crew of another boat with their oars was awful to contemplate, even if they all realized that each boat should go it alone.

However, so strong was what Chase called 'the extraordinary interest which we felt in each other's company' that none of them would consider voluntarily separating. This 'desperate instinct' persisted to such a point that, even in the midst of conditions that made simply staying afloat a full-time occupation, they 'continued to cling to each other with a strong and involuntary impulse.'

On December 8, the seventeenth day, the wind increased to a full gale. Forty- to fifty-knot gusts lashed the men with rain. It was the most wind they'd experienced so far, and after gradually shortening sail all night, each boat-crew found it necessary to lower its masts. The waves were huge, the giant crests atomized into foam by the shrieking wind. Despite the horrendous conditions, the men attempted to collect rainwater in the folds of their sails. They soon discovered that the sailcloth was even more permeated with salt than their damaged provisions had been, and the water proved as salty as seawater.

The boats became unmanageable in the immense waves. 'The sea rose to a fearful height,' Chase remembered, 'and every wave that came looked as if it must be the last that would be necessary for our destruction.' There was nothing for the men to do but lie down in the bottoms of their fragile vessels and 'await the approaching issue with firmness and resignation.'

Gale-force winds in the open ocean can create waves of up to forty feet. But the mountainous size of the waves actually worked to the men's advantage. The whaleboats flicked over the crests, then wallowed in the troughs, temporarily protected from the wind. The vertical walls of water looming on either side were a terrifying sight, but not once did a wave crash down and swamp a boat.

The intense darkness of the night was, according to Nickerson, 'past conception to those who have not witnessed the same.' Making the blackness all the more horrible were flashes of lightning that seemed to envelop the boats in crackling sheets of fire.

By noon of the following day, the wind had moderated enough that the men dared to poke their heads above the raised gunwales of the boats. Incredibly, all three boats were still within sight of one another. 'To an overruling Providence alone must be attributed our salvation from the horrors of that terrible night,' Chase wrote. 'It can be accounted for in no other way: that a speck of substance, like that which we were, before the driving terrors of the tempest, could have been conducted safely through it.'

None of the men had slept all night. All of them had expected to die. When Chase ordered his crew to raise the masts and set sail, they resisted. 'My companions . . . were dispirited and broken down to such a degree,' the first mate remembered, 'as to appear to want some more powerful stimulus than the fears of death to enable them to do their duty.'

But Chase was unrelenting. 'By great exertions,' he induced them to restep the masts and set a double-reefed mainsail and jib, even though dawn had not yet arrived. All three boats were back to sailing again when 'the sun rose and showed the disconsolate faces of our companions once more to each other.'

As they sailed to the south, the large waves left over from the storm pummeled the boats, opening up their seams even wider. The constant bailing had become 'an extremely irksome and laborious task' for these starved and dehydrated men. Their noon observation on Saturday, December 9, put them at latitude 17°40' south. In their seventeen days at sea, they had stayed ahead—just barely—of their target of a degree of latitude a day, traveling close to 1,100 nautical miles. However, because of the easterly direction of the winds, they were now farther from South America than when they'd started.

They had close to three thousand miles left to go if they were to reach their destination. They were starving and thirsty. Their boats were barely holding together. But there was a way out.

On December 9, well into their third week in the open boats, they drew abreast of the Society Islands. If they had headed west, sailing along latitude 17° south, they would have reached Tahiti, perhaps in as little as a week. There were islands in the Tuamotu Archipelago that they might have sighted in less than half that time. They would have also been sailing *with* the wind and waves, easing the strain on the boats.

However, despite the numerous setbacks they had already faced, despite the extremity of their sufferings, Pollard, Chase, and Joy pushed on with the original plan. Nickerson could not understand

149

why. 'I can only say there was gross ignorance or a great oversight somewhere, which cost many . . . fine seamen their lives.' The men's sufferings only narrowed and intensified their focus. It was 'up the coast' or nothing.

CHAPTER EIGHT

CENTERING DOWN

Four years earlier, in 1816, the French ship *Medusa* was wrecked on a shoal well off the coast of west Africa. The vessel was transporting settlers to the colony of Senegal, and it soon became apparent that there were not enough boats to go around. The crew constructed a crude raft from the ship's timbers. Initially the captain and the rest of the officers, who had all taken to the boats, started towing the raft. Before long, however, they decided to cut the tow rope and abandon the passengers to their fate. With only a few casks of wine to share among more than 150 people, the raft quickly became a chaotic hell ship. Vicious fighting broke out between a faction of alcohol-crazed soldiers and some more level-headed but equally desperate settlers. Two weeks later, when the brig *Argus* sighted the raft, only fifteen people were left alive.

The story of the *Medusa* became a worldwide sensation. Two of the survivors penned an account that inspired a monumental painting by Théodore Géricault. In 1818 the narrative was translated into English and became a best-seller. Whether or not they had heard of the *Medusa*, the men of the *Essex*

150

were all too aware of what might happen if sufficient discipline was not maintained.

At eleven o'clock on the night of December 9, the seventeenth night since leaving the wreck, Pollard's boat vanished in the darkness. The men on the other two boats cried out for their lost companions, but there was no response. Chase and Joy discussed what to do next. Both were well aware of what they *should* do. As had been agreed the last time one of the boats had become separated, they were to keep on sailing and make no attempt to find the missing crew. 'We, however, concluded on this occasion to make a small effort,' Chase remembered, 'which, if it did not immediately prove the means of restoring the lost boat, we would discontinue, and again make sail.'

So Chase and Joy lowered their sails and waited. The minutes stretched on, and Chase loaded his pistol and fired. Nothing. After a full hour of bobbing in the dark, the two boat-crews reluctantly set sail, assuming they would never again see their captain and his men.

Early the next morning, someone saw a sail, two miles to the leeward. Chase and Joy immediately altered course, and soon all three crews were reunited. Once again, their destinies were, in Chase's words, 'involuntarily linked together.'

It was on this day, the eighteenth since leaving the wreck, that the men's thirst and hunger reached a new, agonizing level. Even the stoic Chase was tempted 'to violate our resolution, and satisfy, for once, the hard yearnings of nature from our stock.' Raiding their stores, however, would be a death sentence: '[A] little reflection served to convince us of the imprudence and unmanliness of the

151

measure, and it was abandoned with a sort of melancholy effort of satisfaction.'

Just to make sure that no one was tempted to steal any of the bread, Chase transferred the provisions to his sea chest. Whenever he slept, he made sure to have an arm or a leg draped across it. He also kept the loaded pistol at his side. For a man from the Quaker island of Nantucket, it was an unusual display of force. Nickerson's impression was that 'nothing but violence to his person' would have induced the first mate to surrender the provisions. Chase decided that if anyone should object to his method of rationing, he would immediately divide up the hardtack into equal portions and distribute it among the men. If it came down to giving up his own stock, he was 'resolved to make the consequences of it fatal.'

That afternoon, a school of flying fish surrounded the three whaleboats. Four of the fish hit the sails of Chase's boat. One fell at the first mate's feet and, instinctively, he devoured it whole, scales and all. As the rest of the crew scrambled for the other three fish, Chase found himself inclined to laugh for the first time since the sinking of the *Essex* at 'the ludicrous and almost desperate efforts of my five companions, who each sought to get a fish.' The first mate might insist on the disciplined sharing of the bread and water, but a different standard prevailed when it came to windfalls such as flying fish—then, it was every man for himself.

The next day the wind dropped to almost nothing, and Chase proposed that they eat their second tortoise. As had happened eleven days earlier, the 'luxuriant repast . . . invigorated our bodies, and gave a fresh flow to our spirits.' Over the next three days, the wind remained light. The temperature climbed and the men languished beneath a cloudless sky. '[H]aving no way of screening ourselves from [the sun's] piercing rays,' Nickerson wrote, 'our suffering became most intolerable as our short allowance of water was barely enough to support life.'

On Wednesday, December 13, the wind sprang out of an unexpected direction—the north—bringing with it 'a most welcome and unlocked for relief.' It was now possible to steer directly for South America. Their noon observation revealed that they had barely reached latitude 21° south, putting them at least five degrees (or three hundred nautical miles) from the band of light variable winds that they hoped would propel them east. But the officers chose to believe that they had 'run out of the trade-winds, and had got into the variables, and should, in all probability, reach the land many days sooner than we expected.'

When the northerly breeze vanished the following day, they were devastated: 'But alas! Our anticipations were but a dream, from which we shortly experienced a cruel awaking.' The men's gloomy reflections grew even darker as the calm persisted for three more days, baking them beneath a blinding, unyielding sun: 'The extreme oppression of the weather, the sudden and unexpected prostration of our hopes, and the consequent dejection of our spirits, set us again to thinking, and filled our souls with fearful and melancholy forebodings.'

By December 14, the twenty-third day since leaving the *Essex*, they were rapidly approaching their deadline for reaching the variables. But they were stuck in a calm, with hundreds of miles still to go to the south. If they were to have any hope of reaching the coast alive, their provisions would have to last them considerably longer than sixty days. Chase announced to his men that he was cutting their rations of hardtack in half, to only three ounces a day. He studied his crew carefully, looking for any signs of resistance. 'No objections were made to this arrangement,' Chase reported. '[A]ll submitted, or seemed to do so, with an admirable fortitude and forbearance.'

Even though their supply of water was in even greater danger of running out, Chase had no alternative but to maintain their daily ration at half a pint. '[Our] thirst had become now incessantly more intolerable than our hunger,' he wrote, 'and the quantity then allowed was barely sufficient to keep the mouth in a state of moisture, for about one third of the time.'

In 1906, W J. McGee, Director of the St. Louis Public Museum, published one of the most detailed and graphic descriptions of the ravages of extreme dehydration ever recorded. McGee's account was based on the experiences of Pablo Valencia, a forty-year-old sailor-turned-prospector, who survived almost seven days in the Arizona desert without water. The only liquid Valencia drank during his ordeal was the few drops of moisture he was able to extract from a scorpion and his own urine, which he collected each day in his canteen.

The men of the *Essex* were driven to similar extremes. 'In vain was every expedient tried to relieve the raging fever of the throat,' Chase recalled. They knew that drinking saltwater would only worsen their condition, but this did not stop

154

some of them from attempting to hold small quantities of it in their mouths, hoping that they might absorb some of the moisture. It only increased their thirst. Like Valencia, they drank their urine. 'Our suffering during these calm days,' Chase wrote, 'almost exceeded human belief.'

The *Essex* survivors had entered what McGee describes as the 'cotton-mouth' phase of thirst. Saliva becomes thick and foul-tasting; the tongue clings irritatingly to the teeth and the roof of the mouth. Even though speech is difficult sufferers are often moved to complain ceaselessly about their thirst until their voices become so cracked and hoarse that they can speak no more. A lump seems to form in the throat, causing the sufferer to swallow repeatedly in a vain attempt to dislodge it. Severe pain is felt in the head and neck. The face feels full due to the shrinking of the skin. Hearing is affected, and many people begin to hallucinate.

Still to come for the *Essex* crew were the agonies of a mouth that has ceased to generate saliva. The tongue hardens into what McGee describes as 'a senseless weight, swinging on the still-soft root and striking foreignly against the teeth.' Speech becomes impossible, although sufferers are known to moan and bellow. Next is the 'blood sweats' phase, involving 'a progressive mummification of the initially living body.' The tongue swells to such proportions that it squeezes past the jaws. The eyelids crack and the eyeballs begin to weep tears of blood. The throat is so swollen that breathing becomes difficult, creating an incongruous yet terrifying sensation of drowning. Finally, as the power of the sun inexorably draws the remaining moisture from the body, there is 'living death,' the

155

state into which Pablo Valencia had entered when McGee discovered him on a desert trail, crawling on his hands and knees:

[H]is lips had disappeared as if amputated, leaving low edges of blackened tissue; his teeth and gums projected like those of a skinned animal, but the flesh was black and dry as a hank of jerky; his nose was withered and shrunken to half its length, and the nostril-lining showing black; his eyes were set in a winkless stare, with surrounding skin so contracted as to expose the conjunctiva, itself black as the gums . . . ; his skin [had] generally turned a ghastly purplish yet ashen gray, with great livid blotches and streaks; his lower legs and feet, with forearms and hands, were torn and scratched by contact with thorns and sharp rocks, yet even the freshest cuts were so many scratches in dry leather, without trace of blood.

Thanks to their daily half pint of water, the men of the *Essex* had not yet reached this point—but they were deteriorating rapidly. As the sun beat down out of an empty blue sky, the heat became so intolerable that three of the men in Chase's boat decided to hang over the gunwale and cool their blistered bodies in the sea. Almost as soon as the first man dropped over the side, he shouted with excitement. The bottom of their boat was covered with what he described as small clams. He quickly pulled one off and ate it, pronouncing it a 'most delicious and agreeable food.'

Actually not clams, these were gooseneck

barnacles. Unlike the whitish, cone-shaped barnacles commonly seen on dock pilings and ships, goosenecks are stalked barnacles, with a dark brown shell surrounding a fleshy, pinkish-white neck. A medieval myth claimed that once these barnacles grew to a sufficient size, they would transform themselves into geese and fly away. Today the Coast Guard uses the size of the gooseneck barnacles growing on the bottom of a derelict craft to determine how long the vessel has been at sea. They can grow to half a foot in length, but the barnacles on Chase's whaleboat were probably not much more than a few inches long.

Soon all six men were plucking the crustaceans off the boat's bottom and popping them into their mouths 'like a set of gluttons.' Gooseneck barnacles have long been considered a delicacy in Morocco, Portugal, and Spain, and are farmed commercially today in the state of Washington. Connoisseurs, who eat the tubelike neck only after peeling off the outer skin, compare the taste to crab, lobster, or shrimp. The *Essex* men, not as discriminating, consumed everything but the shells.

'[A]fter having satisfied the immediate craving of the stomach,' Chase wrote, 'we gathered large quantities and laid them up in the boat.' But getting the men back aboard proved a problem. They were too weak to pull themselves over the gunwale. Luckily, the three men who couldn't swim had elected to remain on the boat and were able to haul the others in. They had intended to save the uneaten goosenecks for another day. But after less than a half hour of staring at the delectable morsels, they surrendered to temptation and ate them all.

157

Except for flying fish, gooseneck barnacles would be the only marine life the *Essex* crew would manage to harvest from the open ocean. Indeed, these twenty whalemen were singularly unsuccessful in catching the fish that castaways normally depend on for survival. Part of the problem was that their search for the band of variable winds had taken them into a notoriously sterile region of the Pacific.

For an ocean to support life, it must contain the nutrients necessary for the production of phytoplankton, the organism at the base of the ocean's food chain. These nutrients come from two places: the land, through rivers and streams, and from the organic material on the ocean floor. The region into which the *Essex* crew had now ventured was so far removed from South America that the only source of nutrients was at the bottom of the sea.

Cold water is denser than warm water, and when the surface waters of the ocean cool in the winter months, they are replaced by the warmer water underneath, creating a mixing action that brings the nutrient-rich waters at the bottom up to the surface. In the subtropical region, however, the temperature is fairly constant throughout the year. As a result, the ocean remains permanently divided into a warm upper layer and a cold lower layer, effectively sealing off the bottom nutrients from the surface.

Over the next few decades seamen became well aware that the waters in this portion of the Pacific were almost devoid of fish and birds. In the middle of the nineteenth century Matthew Fontaine Maury compiled a definitive set of wind and current charts based largely on information provided by whalemen. In his chart of the Pacific is a vast oval-shaped area, stretching from the lower portion of the Offshore Ground to the southern tip of Chile, called the 'Desolate Region.' Here, Maury indicates, '[m]ariners report few signs of life in sea or air.' The three *Essex* whaleboats were now in the heart of the Desolate Region. Like Pablo Valencia, they had journeyed into their very own valley of death.

*   *   *

The calm continued into December 15, the twenty-fourth day of the ordeal. Despite the windless conditions, Chase's boat was taking on even more water than usual. Their search for the leak once again prompted them to pull up the floorboards in the bow. This time they discovered that a plank next to the keel, at the very bottom of the boat, had pulled loose. If they had been on the deck of the *Essex*, they would have simply flipped the boat over and renailed the plank. But now, in the middle of the ocean, they had no way of reaching the underside of the boat. Even Chase, whom Nickerson described as their boat's 'doctor,' could not figure out away to repair it.

After a few moments' consideration, the twenty-one-year-old boatsteerer Benjamin Lawrence ventured a proposal. He would tie a rope around his waist and dive underwater with the boat's hatchet in his hand. As Chase hammered in a nail from the inside of the boat, Lawrence would hold the hatchet against the outside of the plank. When the tip of the nail hit the metal face of the hatchet,

159

it would curl up like a fishhook and be driven back into the boat. The last blows of Chase's hammer would set the head of the nail while drawing the planks tightly together. This was known as clenching a nail and was usually performed with a tool known as a backing iron. For now, the hatchet would have to do.

On the *Essex*, Lawrence's abilities as a boatsteerer had been called into question, and he had been forced to surrender the harpoon to his demanding first mate. This time, however, it was Lawrence to whom Chase and the rest of the boat-crew looked for guidance. Chase readily agreed to the plan, and soon Lawrence was in the water, pressing the hatchet up against the bottom of the boat. Just as he had predicted, the sprung plank was drawn in snug. Even Chase had to admit that it 'answered the purpose much beyond our expectations.'

The oppressive conditions continued through the next day and 'bore upon our health and spirits with an amazing force and severity.' Some of the men experienced thirst-induced delusions. 'The most disagreeable excitements were produced by it,' Chase commented, 'which added to the disconsolate endurance of the calm, called loudly for some mitigating expedient—some sort of relief to our prolonged sufferings.' The need for action intensified when the noon observation revealed that they had drifted ten miles backward in the last twenty-four hours.

All around them, the unruffled ocean reached out to the curved horizon like the bottom of a shiny blue bowl. Their parched mouths made talking, let alone singing hymns, difficult. The prayer meetings, along with their progress, ceased. That Sunday they sat silently in their boats, desperate for deliverance, knowing that back on Nantucket thousands of people were sitting on the wooden benches of the North and South Meeting Houses, waiting for God's will to be revealed.

At worship, a Quaker sought to 'center down,' shutting out all worldly cares in his attempt to find the divine spirit. When a person was moved to speak, he chanted in a peculiar way—a kind of half-singing, half-sobbing that could break into more natural speech. Although only a few of the *Essex* crew were active Quakers, all of the Nantucketers had, at one time or another, attended a meeting. The protocol and rhythms of a Friends meeting were part of their shared cultural heritage.

Up until this point, it had been the African Americans, specifically the sixty-year-old Richard Peterson, who had led the men in prayer. This was not uncommon at sea. White sailors often looked to blacks and their evangelical style of worship as sources of religious strength, especially in times of peril. In 1818, the captain of a ship about to go down in a North Atlantic gale beseeched the black cook, a member of New Bedford's Baptist church, to seek the Lord's help on the crew's behalf. The cook knelt down on the tossing deck and 'prayed most fervently for God to protect and save us from the dreadful, raging storm.' The ship survived.

But that afternoon, it was Pollard who was finally moved to speak beneath the punishing sun. His voice ravaged by dehydration, he proposed in a halting rasp that they attempt to row their way out of the calm. Each man would be given double rations during the day, and then that night they would row 'until we should get a breeze from some quarter or other.'

All readily agreed to the proposal. At last, after days of being stuck as if pinned to a place in the ocean, with nothing to distract them from their thirst and hunger, they had something to prepare for. They ate the bread and felt every sublimely refreshing drop of water seep into their cracked and shriveled mouths. They looked forward to the night ahead.

Under normal circumstances, rowing was a task that helped define each man's worth on a whaleship. Each crew took pride in its ability to row effortlessly, for hours at a time, and nothing made the men happier than passing another boat. But that night any flickering of those competitive fires was soon extinguished. Though in their teens and twenties, they rowed like old men—wincing and groaning with every stroke. For the last three weeks, their bodies had been consuming themselves. Without any natural padding to cushion their bones, they found the simple act of sitting to be a torture. Their arms had shrunk to sticks as their muscles withered, making it difficult to hold, let alone pull, the oars. As man after man collapsed in a slumped heap, it became impossible to continue.

'[W]e made but a very sorry progress,' Chase remembered. 'Hunger and thirst, and long inactivity, had so weakened us, that in three hours every man gave out, and we abandoned the further prosecution of the plan.' Air rattled in their desiccated throats and lungs as they lay panting in the boats. Despite the raging heat of their bodies, their thin papery skin was without a hint of perspiration. Gradually the noise of their breathing ebbed, and they were once again deafened by the forbidding silence of a windless and empty ocean.

The next morning they detected a change—a rustling of the water and a movement across their faces as, for the first time in five days, a light breeze poured out across the sea. Even though it was from precisely the wrong direction (southeast), the men welcomed it 'with almost frenzied feelings of gratitude and joy.'

By noon it was blowing a gale. The wind had veered into the east-southeast, and once again, they were forced to take in all sail and lower the masts. The next day the wind moderated, and soon their sails were pulling them along. Despite the improvement in the weather, that night proved to be, Chase recalled, 'one of the most distressing nights in the whole catalogue of our sufferings.'

They now knew that even if the wind did miraculously shift into the west, they no longer had enough water to last the thirty or more days it would take to sail to the coast of Chile. Their physical torments had reached a terrible crescendo. It was almost as if they were being poisoned by the combined effects of thirst and hunger. A glutinous and bitter saliva collected in their mouths that was 'intolerable beyond expression.' Their hair was falling out in clumps. Their skin was so burned and covered with sores that a splash of seawater felt like acid burning on their flesh. Strangest of all, as their eyes sunk into their skulls and their cheekbones projected, they all began to look alike, their identities obliterated by dehydration and starvation.

Throughout this long and dismal week, the men

had attempted to sustain themselves with a kind of mantra: '"patience and longsuffering" was the constant language of our lips,' Chase remembered, 'and a determination, strong as the resolves of the soul could make it, to cling to existence as long as hope and breath remained to us.' But by the night of December 19, almost precisely a month since the sinking of the *Essex*, several of the men had given up. Chase could see it in their 'lagging spirits and worn out frames'—'an utter indifference to their fate.' One more day, maybe two, and people would start to die.

The next morning began like so many others. Nickerson recalled how at around seven o'clock, they were 'sitting in the bottom of our little boat quite silent and dejected.' Nineteen year-old William Wright, from Cape Cod, stood up to stretch his legs. He glanced to leeward, then looked again.

'There is land!' he cried.

CHAPTER NINE

THE ISLAND

The men in Chase's boat stared eagerly ahead. Ravaged by hunger and thirst, half blinded by glare from the sea and sky, they had seen mirages before, and they feared this might prove to be another. But all of them could see the white sandy beach in the distance. 'It was no visionary delusion,' Nickerson wrote, 'but in reality "Land Ho."'

Even the most decrepit of Chase's men sprang to

164

life. 'We were all aroused in an instant,' the first mate remembered, 'as if electrified . . . A new and extraordinary impulse now took possession of us. We shook off the lethargy of our senses, and seemed to take another, and a fresh existence.' At first glance, the island bore an eerie resemblance to their native Nantucket: a low rise of sand topped with green. Chase called it 'a basking paradise before our longing eyes.' Nickerson immediately assumed that it marked 'the final end to [our] long confinement and sufferings,' and added, 'Never have my eyes rested on anything so pleasingly beautiful.'

It wasn't long before the men in the other two boats had seen the island. Spontaneous cheers rose from their cracked and swollen lips. 'It is not within the scope of human calculation,' Chase wrote, 'to divine what the feelings of our hearts were on this occasion. Alternate expectation, fear, gratitude, surprise, and exultation, each swayed our minds, and quickened our exertions.'

By eleven o'clock they were within a quarter mile of the island. They could now see that instead of sand, it was made mostly of rock, with thirty-foot vertical cliffs lining the shore. Beyond the cliffs, the interior of the island was amazingly flat, yet 'fresh and green with vegetation.' This boded well, they assured themselves, for the presence of ample supplies of water.

Pollard and Chase studied their copies of Bowditch's *Navigator*. Judging from the day's previous observation, they determined it must be Ducie Island at latitude 24°20" south, longitude 124°40" west. After a month at sea, after traveling approximately 1,500 nautical miles, they were farther from the coast of South America than when they had started.

The men's immediate concern was that the island might be inhabited. 'In our present state,' Nickerson wrote, 'we could have made but feeble resistance to an attack from natives.' Keeping about a hundred yards from shore, they began sailing around the island. 'We . . . frequently fi[red] a pistol,' Nickerson remembered, 'as we glided past some valley or nook in the woods to arouse its inhabitants should there be any within hearing. But neither friend nor foe appeared.'

The island was an irregular oblong, about six miles long and three miles wide, rimmed by a jagged ledge of rocks and coral. The three boat-crews gradually made their way to the north end, which put them in the lee of the southeasterly trades. At a bend in the shoreline they found the island's largest beach. '[T]his seemed the most promising position we had seen,' Nickerson wrote, 'to make an attempt to land with our boats.' But first Chase would lead a preliminary scouting party while the three boats stood offshore, just in case they 'should unexpectedly find savages in ambush.'

Chase, with musket in hand, and two others were dropped off on a large rock. By the time they'd waded ashore, they were already exhausted. 'Upon arriving at the beach,' the first mate recalled, 'it was necessary to take a little breath, and we laid down for a few minutes to rest our weak bodies.' They sat on the coarse coral sand, drinking in the sights and sounds of a stunningly beautiful island world. The cliffs behind them were festooned with flowers, shrubs, grasses, and vines. Birds flew about them, seemingly unconcerned by the men's

166

presence. After a month of deprivation and suffering, they were about to enjoy, Chase was convinced, 'a rich banquet of food and drink.' But first they had to find a source of water.

They split up, each one hobbling down the uneven beach in a different direction. In an inlet Chase was able to spear an eighteen-inch fish with the ramrod of his musket. He dragged the fish onto the shore and immediately sat down to eat. His two companions joined him, and in less than ten minutes the fish was consumed—'bones, and skin, and scales, and all.'

They now imagined they were strong enough to attempt a climb of the cliffs, which they figured to be the most probable source of water. But instead of rocks glistening with moisture, Chase found a dry, scrubby wall of dead coral. The shrubs and vines were not strong enough to support his weight, forcing him to grab the cutting edges of coral. Slashed and bruised, Chase realized he did not have the strength to reach the top.

The euphoria of only a few hours before gave way to the realization that this sterile outcropping of fossilized sea organisms might be without drinkable water. If this was true, every second they remained on the island reduced their already slim chances of survival. No matter how tempting it might be to spend at least one night on solid ground, Chase's first inclination was to set sail for South America immediately: 'I never for one moment lost sight of the main chance, which I conceived we still had, of either getting to the coast, or of meeting some vessel at sea.'

When he returned to the beach he discovered that one of the men had some promising news. He had found a cleft in a rock that exuded the slightest trickle of water just enough to wet his lips, but no more. Perhaps it was advisable to spend the night on the island and devote the next day to searching for water. Chase and his companions went out to the boats, and Chase told Pollard what he thought. They agreed to land.

They dragged the boats up onto a grassy area beneath a stand of trees. 'We then turned [the boats] bottom upwards,' Nickerson remembered, 'thus forming a protection from the night dews.' The men fanned out along the shore, and after collecting a few crabs and fish, they settled down beneath the boats, ate their catch, then stretched out their bony limbs for the first time in a month. Sleep soon followed. '[F]ree from all the anxieties of watching and labor,' Chase wrote, '[we] gave ourselves up to an unreserved forgetfulness and peace of mind.'

Morning came quickly and, with it, a return to the agonies of hunger and thirst. They were now so severely dehydrated that they had begun to lose the ability to speak. 'Relief,' Chase wrote, 'must come soon, or nature would sink.' They wandered the beach like ragged skeletons, pausing to lean against trees and rocks to catch their breath. They tried chewing the waxy green leaves of the shrubs that grew in the cliffs, but they were bitter to the taste. They found birds that made no attempt to escape when they plucked them from their nests. In the crevices of the rocks sprouted a grass that, when chewed, produced a temporary flow of moisture in their mouths. But nowhere did they find fresh water.

As soon as they strayed beyond the beach, they

168

discovered that the island was a scrap heap of fractured coral as sharp and piercing as shattered glass. Many of the men had no shoes, which made it impossible for them to explore any great distance from their encampment. They also feared that if they did venture out, they might not have the stamina to return before nightfall, thus exposing themselves 'to attacks of wild beasts, which might inhabit the island.' That evening they returned, Nickerson wrote, 'sorrowing and dejected to our little town of boats in the valley.'

But Pollard had a surprise for them. The captain and his steward, William Bond, had spent the day gathering crabs and birds, and by the time the men returned from their searches, Pollard and Bond were in the midst of roasting what Nickerson called 'a magnificent repast.' Prior to the sinking, food had been a source of dissension between Pollard and his men. Now it was what brought them together, and this time it was the master who was serving his crew. 'Here everyone seated himself upon the beautiful green grass,' Nickerson remembered, 'and perhaps no banquet was ever enjoyed with greater gusto or gave such universal satisfaction.'

Pollard had done everything he could that day to increase the health and morale of his men. Chase remained focused on the 'main chance': getting to South America and safety. Restless and impatient as always, he had become convinced that they were wasting their time on this island without water. 'In this state of affairs, we could not reconcile it to ourselves to remain longer at this place,' he wrote. '[A] day, an hour, lost to us unnecessarily here, might cost us our preservation.' That evening

169

Chase expressed his concerns to Pollard: 'I addressed the substance of these few reflections to the captain, who agreed with me in opinion, upon the necessity of taking some decisive steps in our present dilemma.'

While he agreed with his first mate in principle, Pollard attempted to defuse some of Chase's impetuousness. The captain pointed out that without a new supply of water, their chances of survival were next to nil. To push blindly ahead without exhausting every possibility of finding a spring would be a tragic mistake. 'After some considerable conversation on this subject,' Chase wrote, 'it was finally concluded to spend the succeeding day in the further search for water, and if none should be found, to quit the island the morning after.'

*　　　*　　　*

The men of the *Essex* did not know that they were within just a few hundred miles of saving themselves. Pollard and Chase were mistaken as to their whereabouts. This was not Ducie Island but rather Henderson Island, at virtually the same latitude but seventy miles to the west. Both islands are part of a group named for its most famous member, Pitcairn, an island whose history was inextricably linked with Nantucket. In 1808, a sealing captain from Nantucket named Mayhew Folger stumbled across Pitcairn (whose location was incorrectly recorded on all available navigational guides) and discovered the answer to a nineteen-year-old mystery: what had happened to Fletcher Christian and the *Bounty*.

After abandoning Captain Bligh in the ship's launch in 1789, the *Bounty* mutineers had wandered the Pacific. They picked up some native women and a few men in Tahiti, and eventually made their way to an uninhabited island in the southeastern extreme of Polynesia. In 1820, a small community of *Bounty* descendants was flourishing on Pitcairn. Just four hundred miles to the southwest, a few days' sail from Henderson, they would have provided the *Essex* crew with all the food and water they needed. But Pitcairn was not listed in their Bowditch's Navigator. Even if it had been, it's questionable whether they could have found it. As it was, they were off by almost a hundred miles when they tried to determine their current location.

Henderson Island began as a coral atoll about 370,000 years ago. Twenty thousand years later, volcanic activity associated with Pitcairn caused the land underneath the atoll to rise. Today, the cliffs of Henderson are between thirty and thirty-five feet high and enclose a dry fossil lagoon. Surrounded by a vast ocean, this uninhabited speck of coral might seem an unlikely source of anyone's salvation.

As much as sixty-five inches of rain falls on Henderson each year. This water does not all run off into the sea or evaporate into the air. Much of it seeps down through the thin soils and layers of fossilized coral to a depth of afoot or so above sea level. Here it flows into a horizontal layer of freshwater saturating the rock and sand. The freshwater, which is lighter than saltwater, floats on the surface of the sea in the shape of a dome or lens beneath the island. But, unless they could find

171

a spring, all this groundwater would be of no use to the men of the *Essex*.

They weren't the first to be enticed by Henderson and then cheated. Although they weren't aware of it, in the cliffs behind them was a cave in which lay eight human skeletons.

A medical examination performed on the bones in 1966 revealed that they were of Caucasian origin, which suggests that these unidentified people, like the *Essex* crew, had been shipwreck survivors. The examination also revealed that one of the skeletons had belonged to a child between three and five years old. All eight people had died of dehydration.

*   *   *

The next morning—December 22, the thirty-first since leaving the wreck—the men resumed their search for water. Some, like Nickerson, climbed into the cliffs; others investigated the rocks along the beach. Chase returned to where they had found evidence of fresh water two days before. The rock was about a quarter mile from their encampment and, with a hatchet and an old rusted chisel, he and two others made their way across the sand.

'The rock proved to be very soft,' Chase wrote, 'and in a very short time I had obtained a considerable hole, but, alas! without the least wished-for effect.' As the sun rose in the sky, Chase continued to peck away at the rock, hoping that by deepening the hole, he might establish a flow of water. '[B]ut all my hopes and efforts were unavailing,' he remembered, 'and at last I desisted from further labor, and sat down near it in utter despair.'

Then he noticed something curious. On the beach, in the direction of the boats, two men were lugging a container of some sort. He was amazed to see them begin to run. '[T]he idea suddenly darted across my mind,' Chase wrote, 'that they had found water, and were taking a keg to fill it.' Up in the cliffs, Nickerson had noticed the same display of 'extraordinary spirit and activity' and soon became part of a general rush for the beach.

The men had, in fact, found a spring bubbling up from a hole in a large flat rock. 'The sensation that I experienced was indeed strange, and such as I shall never forget,' Chase remembered. 'At one instant I felt an almost choking excess of joy, and at the next I wanted the relief of a flood of tears.'

By the time Chase reached the spring, men had already begun to drink, eagerly filling their mouths with the miraculous nectar. Mindful that in their dehydrated condition it was dangerous to drink too much water too quickly, Chase exhorted them to sip only small quantities and to wait several minutes between drinks. But their thirst proved overpowering, and some of the men had to be held back. Despite the officers' best efforts, several of the crew 'thoughtlessly swallowed large quantities of [water], until they could drink no more.' But the agonizing cramps Chase had warned against never came: '[I]t only served to make them a little stupid and indolent for the remainder of the day.'

Once everyone had been given a chance to drink, they began to marvel at their good fortune. The spring was so far below the tide line that it was exposed for just a half hour at dead low; at high tide it was as much as six feet underwater. They

173

had time to fill only two small kegs before the rock once again disappeared below the surf.

After collecting more fish and birds, they sat down for the evening meal. With a dependable source of water and a seemingly bountiful supply of food, they now thought it possible to hold out indefinitely on the island. At the very least, they could stay at Henderson until they had recovered their strength and repaired their worn-out whaleboats for a final attempt at reaching South America. That night they agreed to remain on the island for at least another four or five days before they decided 'whether it would be advisable to make any arrangement for a more permanent abode.' Their stomachs full and their thirst slaked, they quickly drifted off into what Chase described as 'a most comfortable and delicious sleep.'

At eleven o'clock the next morning, they returned to the spring. They arrived just as the tide fell below the rock. At first the water was somewhat brackish, raising fears that the spring was not as reliable a source of fresh water as they had first thought. But as the tide continued to retreat, the quality of the water steadily improved. After filling their casks with about twenty gallons, they set out in search of food.

Every spare moment of every day was, in Chase's words, 'employed in roving about for food.' The evening hours proved the most productive, for it was then that the plump white birds known as tropic birds, about the size of chickens, returned to shore to feed their young. Approaching stealthily, the men would 'pounce upon [the birds] with a stick and take them without difficulty.'

They were not the only ones who lay in wait for

174

the tropic birds each evening. There were also what Nickerson called the man-of-war hawks. But instead of killing the tropic birds, the hawks had what scientists call a kleptoparasitic relationship with them, pecking their backs and beating them with their wings until the tropic birds disgorged the fish that had been intended for their young. With the regurgitated food in their beaks, the hawks would fly away, 'leaving,' Nickerson observed, 'the young tropicbirds supperless.'

The following day, December 24, they detected an alarming change. Nickerson noticed that the birds, 'being so constantly harassed, began to forsake the island.' That evening some of the crew returned to camp complaining that they had not been able to find enough to eat. In just five days, these twenty voracious men had exhausted their portion of the island. 'Every accessible part of the mountain, contiguous to us, or within the reach of our weak enterprise,' Chase wrote, 'was already ransacked, for bird's eggs and grass, and was rifled of all that they contained.'

*   *   *

Deep in the Desolate Region, Henderson Island had never been rich in natural resources. Scientists believe that flora and fauna originally spread to the islands of the Pacific from the luxuriant margins of Southeast Asia, and Henderson is more than nine thousand miles from this source. Making it even more difficult for life to reach this isolated outcropping of coral is the direction of the prevailing winds and currents. Like the men of the *Essex*, birds and plant species had to fight their way upwind and upstream to reach Henderson. Moreover, the island is south of the Tropic of Capricorn, a relatively cool band of water that acts as a further barrier to the spread of tropical species. As a result, Henderson has always been a difficult place for man to live.

The human colonization of the Pacific Islands appears to have followed a pattern similar to the spread of plants and birds. Moving from one stepping-stone of an island to the next, people pushed out ever farther to the east and south. Archeological digs on Henderson have revealed that man first arrived on the island sometime between 800 and 1050 AD. These first inhabitants established a settlement on the same beach where the *Essex* crew hauled up their whaleboats. In the few places where the soil allowed for it, they grew sweet potatoes. They fished with hooks made out of imported pearl shells. They buried their dead in slab crypts. But by 1450, they were gone, no longer able to scratch out a living on what is considered today the 'last pristine elevated limestone island in the world.'

*   *   *

There was no Christmas feast for the *Essex* crew. That evening they 'found that a fruitless search for nourishment had not repaid us the labors of a whole day.' Only grass remained, and that was 'not much relished,' Chase wrote, 'without some other food.' They began to 'entertain serious apprehensions that we should not be able to live long here.'

In less than a week, the *Essex* crew had

176

accomplished what had taken their Polynesian predecessors at least four centuries. By December 26, their seventh day on Henderson and their thirty-fifth since leaving the wreck, they had resolved to abandon this used-up island. In Chase's words, their situation was 'worse than it would have been in our boats on the ocean; because, in the latter case we should be still making some progress towards the land, while our provisions lasted.' In preparation for their departure, they had already begun working on the whaleboats. 'We nailed our boats as well as it was possible to do,' Nickerson wrote, 'with the small quantity of boat nails in our possession, in order to prepare them to stand against the boisterous elements which we were again . . . to encounter.'

The coast of Chile was approximately three thousand miles away—about twice as far as they had already sailed. Upon studying their copies of Bowditch's Navigator, they realized that Easter Island, at latitude 27°9' south, longitude 109°35' west, was less than a third of that distance. Although they, once again, knew nothing about the island, they decided to sail for it, belatedly realizing that the potential terrors of an unknown island were nothing compared to the known terrors of an open boat in the open ocean.

Early in the day, 'all hands were called together,' Nickerson remembered, 'for a last talk previous to taking a final departure.' Pollard explained that they would be leaving the next day and that the boat-crews would remain the same as they'd been prior to their arrival on Henderson. It was then that three men came forward—Joy's boatsteerer Thomas Chappel and two teenagers from Cape

Cod, Seth Weeks and William Wright, from Pollard's and Chase's boats, respectively. Several times over the last few days these three white off-islanders had been observed 'reasoning upon the probabilities of their deliverance.' And the more they talked about it, the more they dreaded the prospect of climbing back into the whaleboats.

Chappel, the once spirited and mischievous Englishman who had set fire to Charles Island, could see that second mate Matthew Joy did not have long to live. As the rest of the crew gradually regained weight and strength during the week on Henderson, Joy, who had possessed a 'weak and sickly constitution' even before the sinking, had remained shockingly thin. Chappel knew that if Joy should die, he would become, by default, his whaleboat's leader—a prospect no reasonable man could relish, given what might lie ahead.

In preparing for a sea voyage that could result in the deaths of some, if not all, of the men assembled on the beach, the crew of the *Essex* were reenacting a scenario that had been played out countless times before on islands across the Pacific. The colonization of the Polynesian islands had depended on such scenarios. But instead of a last, desperate push to reach a known world, the early South Sea islanders had set out on voyages of discovery—sailing east and south into the giant blue void of the Pacific. During these long and uncertain passages, starvation inevitably took its toll. The biological anthropologist Stephen McGarvey has speculated that the people who survived these voyages tended to have a higher percentage of body fat before the voyage began and/or more efficient metabolisms, allowing them

178

to live longer on less food than their thinner companions. (McGarvey theorizes that this is why modern-day Polynesians suffer from a high incidence of obesity.)

The same factors that favored fat, metabolically efficient Polynesians were now at work among the crew of the *Essex*. Although they had all survived on the same rations during their month in the boats, this had not been the case prior to the sinking. As was customary aboard a whaleship, the food served in the forecastle (where the blacks lived) had been a grade below the miserable fare that had been served to the boatsteerers and young Nantucketers in steerage. The blacks were also, in all probability, in poorer health than the whites even before they sailed on the *Essex*. (The life expectancy of a black infant in 1900—the earliest date for which there are statistics—was only thirty-three years, more than fourteen years less than that of a white infant.) Now, thirty-eight days after the whale attack, it was plain to all that the African Americans, although not as weak as Joy, were faring more poorly than the rest of the crew.

At the other extreme were the Nantucketers. Besides being better fed, they had an additional source of strength: they were all from the same close-knit community. The younger Nantucketers had been friends since childhood, while the officers, especially Captain Pollard, demonstrated a fatherly concern for the teenagers' welfare. Whether enduring the torments of thirst and hunger on the boats or foraging for food on Henderson, the Nantucketers provided one another with support and encouragement that they did not offer the others.

179

They had all seen how the man-of-war hawks robbed the tropic birds of their food. As conditions deteriorated on the boats, one could only wonder who of these nine Nantucketers, six African Americans, and five white off-islanders would become the hawks and who would become the tropic birds. Chappel, Wright, and Weeks decided that they did not want to find out.

'The rest of us could make no objection to their plan,' Chase wrote, 'as it lessened the load of our boats, [and] allowed us their share of the provisions.' Even the first mate had to admit that 'the probability of their being able to sustain themselves on the island was much stronger than that of our reaching the mainland.' Pollard assured the three men that if he did make it back to South America, he would do everything in his power to see that they were rescued.

With downcast eyes and trembling lips, the three men drew away from the rest of the crew. They'd already picked a spot, well removed from the original encampment, on which to construct a crude shelter out of tree branches. It was time they started work. But their seventeen shipmates were reluctant to see them go, offering 'every little article that could be spared from the boats.' After accepting the gifts, Chappel and his two companions turned and started down the beach.

*   *   *

That evening Pollard wrote what he assumed would be his last letter home. It was addressed to his wife, Mary, the twenty-year-old ropemaker's daughter with whom he had spent the sum total of fifty-seven days of married life. He also wrote another, more public letter:

Account of the loss of the Ship *Essex* of Nantucket in North America, Ducies Island, December 20, 1820, commanded by Capt. Pollard, jun. which shipwreck happened on the 20th day of November, 1820 on the equator in long. 120°W done by a large whale striking her in the bow, which caused her to fill with water in about 10 minutes. We got what provisions and water the boats would carry, and left her on the 22nd of November, and arrived here this day with all hands, except one black man, who left the ship at Ticamus. We intend to leave tomorrow, which will be the 26th of December [actually December 27], 1820, for the continent. I shall leave with this a letter for my wife, and whoever finds, and will have the goodness to forward it will oblige an unfortunate man, and receive his sincere wishes.
George Pollard, Jun.

To the west of their encampment, they had found a large tree with the name of a ship—the *Elizabeth*—carved into it. They transformed the tree into a Galapagos-like post office, placing the letters in a small wooden box they nailed to the trunk.

On December 27 at ten o'clock in the morning, by which time the tide had risen far enough to allow the boats to float over the rocks that surrounded the island, they began to load up. In Pollard's boat were his boatsteerer, Obed

181

Hendricks, along with their fellow Nantucketers Barzillai Ray, Owen Coffin, and Charles Ramsdell, and the African American Samuel Reed. Owen Chase's crew was down to five: the Nantucketers Benjamin Lawrence and Thomas Nickerson, along with Richard Peterson, the elderly black from New York, and Isaac Cole, a young white off-islander. Joy's crew contained the white off-islander Joseph West and four blacks—Lawson Thomas, Charles Shorter, Isaiah Sheppard, and the steward William Bond. Not only were these men under the command of a seriously ill second mate, but Chappel's decision to remain on the island had left them without a boatsteerer to assist Joy in the management of the crew. But neither Pollard nor Chase was willing to part with a Nantucket-born boatsteerer.

Soon it was time for them to leave the island. But Chappel, Wright, and Weeks were nowhere to be found. '[T]hey had not come down,' Chase wrote, 'either to assist us to get off, nor to take any kind of leave of us.' The first mate walked down the beach to their dwelling and told them they were about to set sail. The men were, Chase observed, 'very much affected,' and one of them began to cry. 'They wished us to write to their relations, should Providence safely direct us again to our homes, and said but little else.' Seeing that they were 'ill at heart about taking any leave of us,' Chase bid them a hasty good-bye and left for the boats. 'They followed me with their eyes,' he wrote, 'until I was out of sight, and I never saw more of them.'

Before leaving the island, the men in the boats decided to backtrack a bit and sail to a beach they had seen during their original circuit of the island.

182

It had looked like a spot that 'might be productive of some unexpected good fortune,' possibly providing them with fresh provisions for the start of their journey. After dropping half a dozen men on shore to search for food, the rest of them spent the day fishing. They saw several sharks but were unable to catch anything save a few mackerel-sized fish. The shore party returned at about six o'clock that evening with some more birds, and they made final preparations to leave.

It had been more of a tease than a salvation, but Henderson Island had at least given them a fighting chance. Back on December 20, Chase had seen 'death itself staring us in the face.' Now, after more than a week of food and drink, their casks were full of fresh water. Their boats no longer leaked. In addition to hardtack, each crew had some fish and birds. There were also three fewer men to support. 'We again set sail,' Nickerson wrote, 'finally [leaving] this land which had been so providentially thrown in our way.'

CHAPTER TEN

THE WHISPER OF NECESSITY

Before they left Henderson Island, Chase loaded a flat stone and an armful of firewood into each boat. That first evening back on the water, as both the island and the sun slipped below the western horizon behind them, they put the stones to use as platforms for cooking fires. '[W]e kept our fires going,' Chase wrote, 'and cooked our fish and

183

birds, and felt our situation as comfortable as could be expected.'

For a month they had been driven south and even west; now they hoped to sail almost directly east to Easter Island. For this to happen they needed two weeks of westerly breezes. However, at latitude 24° south, they were still in the trades, where for more than 70 percent of the year the wind blows out of the southeast. But that night, as if in answer to their prayers, a strong breeze sprang up out of the northwest, and they steered straight for Easter.

If they were to keep track of their progress east, they needed to find a way to estimate their longitude—something they had not done during the first leg of the voyage. A month of sailing without knowing their east-to-west position had proved to them the necessity of at least attempting to determine it. Before leaving Henderson, they decided to maintain what Chase called 'a regular reckoning.' Their noon observation told them their latitude, and by doing as Captain Bligh had done before them—using an improvised log line to gauge their speed and their compass to determine their direction—they could calculate their longitude. The *Essex* boats were no longer sailing blind.

For three days the northwesterly breeze held. Then, on December 30, the wind shifted into the east-southeast, and for two days they were forced to steer a course well to the south of Easter Island. But by the first day of the new year, 1821, the wind had shifted to the north, and they were once again back on track.

On January 3 they sailed into what Nickerson

called 'hard weather.' Squalls blasted them from the southwest. 'The seas had become so rough,' Nickerson remembered, 'that we were fearful that each successive gust would swamp our boats . . . Every squall was attended with the most vivid flashes of lightning and awful thunder claps, which seemed to cause the very bosom of the deep to tremble and threw a cheerless aspect upon the face of the ocean.'

The next day, the capricious wind shifted to the east-northeast. With their sails trimmed in tight on the port tack, they steered as close to the wind as possible but were still unable to fetch Easter Island. Pollard and Chase came to the same distressing conclusion: they were now too far to the south to have any hope of reaching the island. They searched their *Navigator* copies for the next closest island 'where the wind would allow of our going.' About eight hundred miles off the Chilean coast are the islands of Juan Fernandez and Masafuera. Unfortunately there were more than 2,500 miles between them and these islands—farther than they had sailed since leaving the *Essex* forty-four days before.

On the same day that they abandoned all hope of reaching Easter Island, they ate the last of their fish and birds. It was back to their daily ration of a cup of water and three ounces of hardtack per man.

For the next two days, the wind deserted them. The sun beat down with the same withering force that had so oppressed them prior to their arrival at Henderson. The conditions were the hardest on Matthew Joy, whose bowels had ceased to function. Ever since leaving the island he had continued to deteriorate, and his glassy, distracted eyes had taken on the unmistakable look of death.

On January 7, a breeze rose up out of the north. Their noon observation revealed that they had slipped almost six degrees of latitude, or 360 nautical miles, to the south. But it was their progress to the east that most concerned them. They estimated that they were now only six hundred miles closer to the mainland than when they had left Henderson eleven days before.

The next day Matthew Joy made a request. The twenty-seven-year-old second mate asked if he might be moved to the captain's boat. The transfer was effected, Chase wrote, 'under the impression that he would be more comfortable there, and more attention and pains be bestowed in nursing and endeavoring to comfort him.' But all knew the real reason for the second mate's removal. Now that he was reaching the end, Joy, who had been on a boat with five coofs, wanted to die among his own people.

Joy came from an old Quaker family. Near the town hall on Nantucket his grandfather had owned a large house that was still referred to as the Reuben Joy homestead. In 1800, when Matthew was only seven years old, his parents moved the family to Hudson, New York, where Nantucketers had established a whaling port soon after the Revolution. Matthew remained a Friend until 1817, when he returned to his native island to wed nineteen-year-old Nancy Slade, a Congregationalist. As was customary in such cases, he was disowned that year by the Nantucket Monthly Meeting for 'marrying out.'

Joy was no longer a Quaker, but on January 10,

a hot, windless day in the Pacific, he demonstrated a Friend's sense of duty and devotion. For the last two days his boat-crew had been left leaderless; he now asked to be returned to them. His loyalty to his crew was in the end greater than his need for comfort from his fellow Nantucketers. The transfer was made, and by four o'clock that afternoon Matthew Joy was dead.

Nantucket's Quaker Graveyard was without worldly monuments of any kind, and many had compared its smooth, unmarred sweep to the anonymous surface of the sea. Like that graveyard thousands of miles away, the sea that morning was calm and smooth—not a breath of air ruffled the Pacific's slow, rhythmic swell. The three boats were brought together, and after sewing Joy up in his clothes, they tied a stone to his feet and 'consigned him in a solemn manner to the ocean.'

Even though they knew Joy had been ill for quite some time, his loss hit them hard. 'It was an incident,' Chase wrote, 'which threw a gloom over our feelings for many days.' The last two weeks had been particularly difficult for the men on the second mate's boat. Instead of drawing strength and inspiration from their leader, they had been required to expend valuable energy nursing him. Making it even harder was the absence of Joy's boatsteerer, Thomas Chappel. To fill the void, Pollard ordered his own boatsteerer, the twenty-one-year-old Obed Hendricks, to take command of the second mate's shaken and dispirited crew.

Soon after taking over the steering oar, Hendricks made a disturbing discovery. Joy's illness had apparently prevented him from closely monitoring the distribution of his boat's provisions.

187

As best as Hendricks could determine, there was only enough hardtack in his boat's cuddy to last two, maybe three more days.

*   *   *

Throughout the morning and afternoon of the following day—the fifty-second since the men had left the *Essex*—the wind built out of the northwest until by nightfall it was blowing a full gale. The men took in all sail and steered their boats before the wind. Even without a stitch of canvas set, the boats surfed wildly down the crests of the waves. 'Flashes of lightning were quick and vivid,' Chase wrote, 'and the rain came down in cataracts.' Instead of being terrified, the men were exhilarated to know that each fifty-knot gust was blowing them toward their destination. 'Although the danger was very great,' Nickerson remembered, 'yet none seemed to dread this so much as death by starvation, and I believe none would have exchanged this terrific gale for a more moderate head wind or a calm.'

Visibility was low that night in the driving rain. They had agreed that in the event they became separated, they would steer a course of east-southeast in the hope that they would be within sight of one another come daybreak. As usual, Chase was in the lead. Every minute or so, he turned his head to make sure he could see the other two boats. But at around eleven o'clock he glanced back and saw nothing. 'It was blowing and raining at this time as if the heavens were separating,' he wrote, 'and I knew not hardly at the moment what to do.' He decided to head up into the wind and hove to. After drifting for about an hour, 'expecting every moment that they would come up with [us],' Chase and his men resumed their agreed-upon course, hopeful that, as had happened before, they would sight the other boats in the morning.

'As soon as daylight appeared,' Nickerson wrote, 'every man in our boat raised [himself] searching the waters.' Grabbing the masts, and one another, for support, they stood up on the seats, craning their necks for a glimpse of their lost companions on the wave-fringed horizon. But they had disappeared. 'It was folly to repine at the circumstances,' Chase commented; 'it could neither be remedied, nor could sorrow secure their return; but it was impossible to prevent ourselves feeling all the poignancy and bitterness that characterizes the separation of men who have long suffered in each other's company, and whose interests and feelings fate had so closely linked together.'

They were at latitude 32°16' south, longitude 112°20' west, about six hundred miles south of Easter Island. Nineteen days from Henderson, with more than a thousand miles still left to go, Chase and his men were alone. 'For many days after this accident, our progress was attended with dull and melancholy reflections,' he wrote. 'We had lost the cheering of each other's faces, that, which strange as it is, we so much required in both our mental and bodily distresses.'

The squalls and rain continued through the next day. Chase decided to take an inventory of their remaining provisions. Thanks to his rigorous supervision, they still had a considerable store of bread left. But they had been fifty-four days at sea,

189

and there were more than 1,200 miles between them and the island of Juan Fernandez. 'Necessity began to whisper [to] us,' Chase wrote, 'that a still further reduction of our allowance must take place, or we must abandon altogether the hopes of reaching the land, and rely wholly on the chance of being taken up by a vessel.'

They were already on half provisions, eating only three ounces of bread a day. '[H]ow to reduce the daily quantity of food, with any regard to life itself, was a question of the utmost consequence.' Three ounces of hardtack provided them with only two hundred and fifty calories a day, less than 15 percent of their daily needs. Chase told his men that they had no choice but to cut these half rations once again—to only one and a half ounces of bread a day. This, he knew, 'must, in short time, reduce us to mere skeletons again.'

It was a terrifying dilemma, and Chase did not arrive at the decision easily. 'It required a great effort to bring matters to this dreadful alternative,' he wrote. '[E]ither . . . feed our bodies and our hopes a little longer, or in the agonies of hunger to seize upon and devour our provisions, and coolly await the approach of death.' Somewhere to the north of them, their companions were about to discover the consequences of taking the latter course.

*   *   *

The men in Pollard's and Hendricks's boats were just as gravely affected by the separation. They continued on, however, almost confident that they would once again meet up with Chase's boat. That

190

day, January 14, Obed Hendricks's boat ran out of provisions. For Hendricks and his five crew members—Joseph West, Lawson Thomas, Charles Shorter, Isaiah Sheppard, and William Bond—the question was whether Pollard would be willing to share his boat's provisions.

Having placed Hendricks in command of the second mate's boat only three days before, Pollard could not easily deny his former boatsteerer some of his own stock of food. And if he was willing to feed Hendricks, he would have to feed the other five. So Pollard and his men shared with them what little bread they had, knowing full well that in only a few more days there would be nothing left.

Chase's separation from Pollard and Hendricks saved the first mate from having to face this painful predicament. From the beginning, Chase had strictly, even obsessively, attended to the distribution of rations aboard his boat. To throw open his sea chest of provisions to Hendricks's men, all of them off-islanders who had begun the ordeal with the same amount of bread as his crew, would have been, from Chase's perspective, an act of collective suicide. Earlier in the ordeal the men had discussed the possibility of having to share their provisions if one of the crews should lose their stock. '[S]uch a course of conduct,' Chase wrote, 'was calculated to weaken the chances of a final deliverance for some, and might be the only means of consigning every soul of us to a horrid death of starvation.' For Chase, intent on getting himself and his boat-crew to safety, no matter what, the separation from Pollard's and Hendricks's boats could not have been better timed.

On the same day that Chase cut his crew's daily

191

ration of bread in half, the wind gradually died to nothing. The clouds thinned until the sun's rays once again became overwhelming. In desperation, Chase and his men tore the sails from the spars and hid beneath the salt-encrusted canvas. Swaddling themselves in the sails, they lay down in the bottom of the boat and 'abandoned her,' the first mate wrote, 'to the mercy of the waves.'

Despite the severity of the sun, the men did not complain of thirst. After a week of drinking their fill at Henderson Island, they had been rehydrated to the extent that food had replaced water as their most desperate need. In fact some of the men were now suffering from diarrhea—a common symptom of starvation—which Chase attributed to the 'relaxing effects of the water.' As he put it, 'we were fast wasting away.

While the body can rebound quite quickly from dehydration, it takes a frustratingly long time to recover from the effects of starvation. During World War II, the University of Minnesota's Laboratory of Physiological Hygiene conducted what scientists and relief workers still regard today as a benchmark study of starvation. Partly funded by religious groups, including the Society of Friends, the study was intended to help the Allies cope with released concentration-camp internees, prisoners of war, and refugees. The participants were all conscientious objectors who volunteered to lose 25 percent of their body weight over six months.

The experiment was supervised by Dr. Ancel Keys (for whom the K-ration was named). The volunteers lived a spare but comfortable existence at a stadium on the campus of the University of

Minnesota. Although meager, their carefully measured rations of potatoes, turnips, rutabagas, dark bread, and macaroni (similar to the kinds of foods refugees might scavenge during wartime) possessed a wide variety of vitamins and minerals. Yet, despite the clinically safe circumstances of the experiment, the volunteers suffered severe physiological and psychological distress.

As they lost weight, the men became lethargic in both body and spirit. They became increasingly irritable. Concentration became difficult. They were appalled at their lack of physical strength and coordination, and many suffered blackouts when they stood up quickly. Their limbs swelled. They lost their sexual desire and would indulge instead in a kind of 'stomach masturbation,' describing favorite meals to one another and poring over cookbooks for hours at a time. They complained of losing all sense of initiative and creativity. 'Many of the so-called American characteristics,' a chronicler of the experiment wrote, '—abounding energy, generosity, optimism—become intelligible as the expected behavior response of a well-fed people.'

For many of the men, the most difficult part of the experiment was the recovery period. Weeks after increasing their food intake, they still felt hunger cravings. In some cases, they actually lost weight during their first week off the starvation diet. If the findings of the Minnesota study apply, the *Essex* crew's week on Henderson did little to restore their bodies' reserves of muscle and fat. Now, three weeks later, the sailors were as close to starving to death as they'd ever been.

The symptoms the men suffered as their boats

lay becalmed on January 14, 1821, were similar to those experienced by the conscientious objectors in 1945. Chase reported that they barely had the strength 'to move about in our boats, and slowly perform the necessary labors appertaining to [them].' That evening, when they sat up from the bottom of the boat, they experienced the same kind of blackouts that afflicted the men at the University of Minnesota. 'Upon [our] attempting to rise again,' Chase wrote, 'the blood would rush into the head, and an intoxicating blindness come over us, almost to occasion our suddenly falling down again.'

Chase's sufferings were so severe that he forgot to lock the lid of his sea chest before falling asleep in the bottom of the boat. That night one of the crew awoke the first mate and informed him that Richard Peterson, the old black man from New York who had led them all in prayer, had stolen some bread.

Chase leaped up in a rage. 'I felt at the moment the highest indignation and resentment at such conduct in any of our crew,' he wrote, 'and immediately took my pistol in my hand, and charged him if he had taken any [bread], to give it up without the least hesitation, or I should instantly shoot him!' Peterson immediately returned the provisions, 'pleading,' Chase wrote, 'the hard necessity that urged him to do it.' Almost three times the age of anyone else in the boat, Peterson was reaching the end of his endurance, and he knew that without more bread, he would soon die.

Nonetheless, the first mate felt that an example had to be made. 'This was the first infraction,' he wrote, 'and the security of our lives, our hopes of

194

redemption from our sufferings, loudly called for a prompt and signal punishment.' But, as Nickerson observed, Peterson 'was a good old man, and nothing but the cravings of a starved appetite could have induced him to be guilty of so rash an attempt.' Chase finally decided to grant him mercy. 'I could not find it in my soul to extend towards him the least severity on this account,' he wrote, 'however much, according to the strict imposition which we felt upon ourselves it might demand.' Chase warned Peterson that if he attempted to steal again, it would cost him his life.

Light breezes persisted throughout the next day and into the following night. The tensions among Chase's crew had begun to ease, but their individual suffering continued unabated, their bodies wracked by a hunger that the daily ration of an ounce and a half of bread hardly began to alleviate. Still, the distribution of provisions remained the most important part of the day. Some of the men attempted to make their portion last as long as possible, nibbling it almost daintily and savoring each tiny morsel with what little saliva their mouths could generate. Others ate their ration virtually whole, hoping to provide their stomachs with at least some sensation of fullness. Afterward, all of them fastidiously licked the residue from their fingers.

That night the placid waters around Chase's boat suddenly erupted into pale foam as something enormous slammed into the stern. Clinging to the gunwales, the men rose up from the bottom of the boat and saw that a shark, nearly as large as the killer whale that had attacked Pollard's boat, was 'swimming about us in a most ravenous manner, making attempts every now and then upon different parts of the boat, as if he would devour the very wood.' The monster snapped at the steering oar, then tried to get its massive jaws around the boat's sternpost, as if possessed by the same gnawing hunger that was consuming all of them.

In the bottom of the boat was a lance just like the one Chase had been tempted to hurl at the whale that sank the *Essex*. If they could kill this giant shark, they'd have enough food to last them for several weeks. But when Chase attempted to stab the creature, he discovered that he did not have the strength even to dent its sandpaper-like skin. '[H]e was so much larger than an ordinary [shark],' Chase wrote, 'and manifested such a fearless malignity, as to make us afraid of him; and our utmost efforts, which were at first directed to kill him for prey, became in the end self-defense.' There was little the men could do as the shark pushed and slapped their whaleboat's thin sides. Eventually, the shark grew bored with them. 'Baffled . . . in all his hungry attempts upon us,' Chase wrote, 'he shortly made off.'

The next day a group of porpoises replaced the shark. For almost an hour Chase's men did everything they could to catch one of these playful creatures. Whenever a porpoise surfaced near the boat, they tried to stab it with the lance. But as had been true with the shark, they could not, in Nickerson's words, 'muster strength sufficient to pierce through their tough hide.' While a shark is a primitive killing machine, a porpoise is one of the most intelligent mammals on earth. The porpoises' mastery of their environment was now cruelly

196

obvious to this boatload of starving land-dwellers. '[T]hey soon left us,' Nickerson wrote, 'apparently in high glee[,] leaping from the water and . . . in full exercise of every enjoyment. Poor devils, how much they are now our superiors and yet not . . . know it.'

For the next two days, January 17 and 18, the calms returned. '[T]he distresses of a cheerless prospect and a burning hot sun were,' Chase wrote, 'once again visited upon our devoted heads.' As they approached their sixtieth day since leaving the *Essex*, even Chase had become convinced that it was their destiny to die. 'We began to think that Divine Providence had abandoned us at last,' the first mate wrote, 'and it was but an unavailing effort to endeavor to prolong a now tedious existence.' They could not help but wonder how they would die: 'Horrible were the feelings that took possession of us!—The contemplation of a death of agony and torment, refined by the most dreadful and distressing reflections, absolutely prostrated both body and soul.'

Chase called the night of January 18 'a despairing era in our sufferings.' Two months of deprivation and fear had reached an unbearable climax as they anticipated the horrors to come. '[O]ur minds were wrought up to the highest pitch of dread and apprehension for our fate,' Chase wrote, 'and all in them was dark, gloomy, and confused.'

At around eight o'clock, the darkness came to life with a familiar sound: the breathing of sperm whales. It was a black night, and the noise that had once signaled the thrill of the hunt now terrified them. '[W]e could distinctly hear the furious thrashing of their tails in the water,' Chase remembered, 'and our weak minds pictured out their appalling and hideous aspects.'

As the whales surfaced and dove around them, Richard Peterson 'took an immediate fright' and pleaded with his companions to row them to safety. But no one had the strength even to lift an oar. After three whales passed the stern in rapid succession, 'blowing and spouting at a terrible rate,' the pod disappeared.

When Peterson's panic had receded, he talked with Chase about his religious beliefs. Although he knew his own death was imminent, Peterson's faith in God remained undiminished. '[H]e reasoned very sensibly,' Chase wrote, 'and with much composure.' Peterson had a wife back in New York City, and he asked Chase to contact her if the first mate should ever reach home alive.

The next day, January 19, the wind blew so fiercely that they had to take in their sails and lie to. Lightning flashed and the rain poured down as the wind shifted through 'every point of the compass.' As their little craft tossed in the confused seas, Peterson lay between the seats of the boat, 'utterly dispirited and broken down.' That evening the wind finally settled into the east-northeast.

On January 20, exactly two months since the sinking of the *Essex*, Richard Peterson declared that it was his time to die. When Chase offered Peterson his daily ration of bread, he refused it, saying, 'It may be of service to someone but can be of none to me.' Soon after, he lost the power of speech.

Modern-day proponents of euthanasia have long endorsed the combined effects of starvation and dehydration as a painless and dignified way for a terminally ill patient to die. In the final stages, hunger pangs cease, as does the sensation of thirst. The patient slips into unconsciousness as the deterioration of his internal organs results in a peaceful death. This was apparently how Richard Peterson passed away. '[T]he breath appeared to be leaving his body without the least pain,' Chase reported, 'and at four o'clock he was gone.'

The next day, at latitude 35°07' south, longitude 105°46' west, a thousand miles from Juan Fernandez, Peterson's body joined Joy's in the vast burial ground of the sea.

CHAPTER ELEVEN

GAMES OF CHANCE

On January 20, 1821, eight days after losing sight of Chase's boat, Pollard's and Hendricks's men were coming to the end of their provisions. That day, Lawson Thomas, one of the blacks on Hendricks's boat, died. With barely a pound of hardtack left to share among ten men, Hendricks and his crew dared speak of a subject that had been on all their minds: whether they should eat, instead of bury, the body.

For as long as men had been sailing the world's oceans, famished sailors had been sustaining themselves on the remains of dead shipmates. By the early nineteenth century, cannibalism at sea was so widespread that survivors often felt compelled to inform their rescuers if they had *not* resorted to it since, according to one historian,

199

'suspicion of this practice among starving castaways was a routine reaction.' One of the most thoroughly documented cases of cannibalism occurred in the winter of 1710, when the *Nottingham Galley*, a British trading vessel under the command of Captain John Dean, wrecked on Boon Island, a tiny outcropping of rock just off the coast of Maine. Despite being within sight of the mainland, the men found themselves marooned with no provisions and no way of reaching help. When the ship's carpenter died in the third week, one of the crew suggested that they use their shipmate's body for food. Captain Dean initially found the proposal to be 'most grievous and shocking.' Then, as they stood over the carpenter's dead body, a discussion ensued. 'After abundance of mature thought and consultation about the lawfulness or sinfulness on the one hand, and the absolute necessity on the other,' Dean wrote, 'judgment, conscience, etc. were obliged to submit to the more prevailing arguments of our craving appetites.'

One hundred and eleven years later, in the middle of the Pacific, ten men of the *Essex* reached a similar conclusion. Two months after deciding to spurn the Society Islands because, in Pollard's words, 'we feared we should be devoured by cannibals,' they were about to eat one of their own shipmates.

First they had to butcher the body. On Nantucket there was a slaughterhouse at the foot of Old North Wharf where any island boy could watch a cow or sheep be transformed into marketable cuts of meat. On a whaleship it was the black members of the crew who prepared and cooked the food. In the case of the *Essex*, more than thirty hogs and dozens of tortoises had been butchered by the African American cook before the whale attack. And, of course, all twenty crew members had taken part in the cutting up of several dozen sperm whales. But this was not a whale or a hog or a tortoise. This was Lawson Thomas, a shipmate with whom they had shared two hellish months in an open boat. Whoever butchered Thomas's body had to contend not only with the cramped quarters of a twenty-five-foot boat but also with the chaos of his own emotions.

The crew of the *Nottingham Galley*, the ship that wrecked off Maine, had found it so difficult to begin the gruesome task of cutting up the carpenter's body that they pleaded with the reluctant Captain Dean to do it for them. '[T]heir incessant prayers and entreaties at last prevailed,' Dean wrote, 'and by night I had performed my labor.' Dean, like most sailors forced to resort to cannibalism, began by removing the most obvious signs of the corpse's humanity—the head, hands, feet, and skin—and consigned them to the sea.

If Hendricks and his men followed Dean's example, they next would have removed Thomas's heart, liver, and kidneys from the bloody basket of his ribs. Then they would have begun to hack the meat from the backbone, ribs, and pelvis. In any case, Pollard reported that after lighting a fire on the flat stone at the bottom of the boat, they roasted the organs and meat and began to eat.

Instead of easing their hunger pangs, their first taste of meat only intensified their atavistic urge to eat. The saliva flowed in their mouths as their long-dormant stomachs gurgled with digestive juices.

And the more they ate, the hungrier they became.

Anthropologists and archaeologists studying the phenomenon of cannibalism have estimated that the average human adult would provide about sixty-six pounds of edible meat. But Lawson Thomas's body was not average. Autopsies of starvation victims have revealed a dramatic atrophy of muscle tissue and a complete absence of fat replaced, in some instances, by a translucent gelatinous substance. Starvation and dehydration had also shrunk Thomas's internal organs, including the heart and liver. His body may have yielded as little as thirty pounds of lean, fibrous meat. On the following day, when the captain's store of bread ran out, Pollard and his men 'were glad to partake of the wretched fare with the other crew.'

Two days later, on January 23—the sixty-third day since leaving the wreck—yet another member of Hendricks's crew died and was eaten. And like Lawson Thomas before him, Charles Shorter was black.

It was likely that the African Americans had suffered from an inferior diet prior to the sinking. But there may have been yet another factor at work. A recent scientific study comparing the percentage of body fat among different ethnic groups claims that American blacks tend to have less body fat than their Caucasian counterparts. Once a starving body exhausts its reserves of fat, it begins consuming muscle, a process that soon results in the deterioration of the internal organs and, eventually, death. The blacks' initially lower amount of body fat meant that they had begun living off muscle tissue before the whites.

The importance of body fat in determining long-term survival under starvation conditions was shown among the members of the Donner Party, a group of settlers who became snowbound in the foothills of the Sierras during the winter of 1847. Despite their reputation as the weaker sex, the women tended to outlast the men, thanks in part to their higher percentage of body fat (approximately ten percent more than males). Now that people had begun to die among the *Essex* crew, it was no accident that the first to go (with the exception of the sickly Matthew Joy, who, in Chase's words, 'did not die of absolute starvation') were African American.

Of the whites, the *Essex*'s twenty-nine-year-old captain had an advantage. He was short, had a tendency toward corpulence prior to the ordeal, and being older had a lower metabolic rate. Of these twenty sailors, Pollard was the most likely to survive this ordeal of starvation. Yet, given the complex range of factors—psychological as well as physiological—influencing each man's health, it was impossible to predict with total precision who would live and who would die.

*   *   *

More than a hundred miles to the south, as their shipmates consumed their second body in four days, Owen Chase and his men drifted in a windless sea. A week of eating only one and a half ounces of bread a day had left them 'hardly able to crawl around the boat, and possessing but strength enough to convey our scanty morsel to our mouths.' Boils had begun to break out on their skin. On the morning of January 24, with another day of calms and broiling sun ahead of them, Chase was certain that some of his crew would not see nightfall. '[W]hat it was that buoyed me above all the terrors which surrounded us,' Chase wrote, 'God alone knows.'

That night, the first mate had a vivid dream. He had just sat down to a 'splendid and rich repast, where there was everything that the most dainty appetite could desire.' But just as he reached for his first taste of food, he 'awoke to the cold realities of my miserable situation.' Fired to a kind of madness by his dream, Chase began to gnaw on the leather sheathing of an oar only to find that he lacked the strength in his jaws to penetrate the stiff, salt-caked hide.

With the death of Peterson, Chase's crew had been whittled down to only three—Nantucketers Benjamin Lawrence and Thomas Nickerson, along with Isaac Cole from Rochester, Massachusetts. As their sufferings mounted, the men relied increasingly on the first mate. Chase reported that they 'press[ed] me continually with questions upon the probability of our reaching land again. I kept constantly rallying my spirits to enable me to afford them comfort.'

Chase had changed since the beginning of the ordeal. Instead of the harsh disciplinarian who had doled out rations with a gun by his side, he now spoke to the men in what Nickerson described as an almost cheerful voice. As their torments reached new heights, Chase recognized that it wasn't discipline his men needed but encouragement. For as they had all seen with Peterson, hope was all that stood between them and death.

Chase's ability to adjust his manner of leadership to the needs of his men begs comparison to one of the greatest and most revered leaders of all time, Sir Ernest Shackleton. Shackleton's feat of delivering all twenty-seven men of his Antarctic expedition to safety has been called 'the supreme epic of leadership in totally impossible circumstances.' In 1916, after seventeen months of fighting the cruelest conditions imaginable—which included a grueling trek across the pack ice, two voyages in tiny, whaleboat-size craft over a storm-tossed Southern Ocean, and a terrifying hike across the jagged peaks of South Georgia—Shackleton finally reached a whaling station and safety, then returned to rescue those he had left behind on Elephant Island.

Shackleton's sensitivity to the needs of his men was legendary. 'So great was his care of his people,' his associate Frank Worsley wrote, 'that, to rough men, it seemed at times to have a touch of the woman about it, even to the verge of fussiness.' But Shackleton was also capable of insisting on a Bligh-like discipline. On an earlier expedition, when one of the men felt his freedoms were being infringed upon, Shackleton quelled the insurrection by knocking the man to the ground. This combination of decisive, authoritative action and an ability to empathize with others is rarely found in a single leader. But Chase, at twenty-three (almost half Shackleton's age), had learned to move beyond the ruthless intensity of a fishy man and do everything in his power to lift his men from the depths of despair.

Nickerson called the first mate a 'remarkable

man' and recognized Chase's genius for identifying hope in a seemingly hopeless situation. Having already endured so much, Chase reasoned, they owed it to one another to cling as tenaciously to life as possible: 'I reasoned with them, and told them that we would not die sooner by keeping our hopes.' But it was more than a question of loyalty to one another. As far as Chase was concerned, God was also involved in this struggle for survival. '[T]he dreadful sacrifices and privations we [had] endured were to preserve us from death,' he assured them, 'and were not to be put in competition with the price which we set upon our lives.' In addition to saying it would be 'unmanly to repine at what neither admitted of alleviation nor cure,' Chase insisted that 'it was our solemn duty to recognize in our calamities an overruling divinity, by whose mercy we might be suddenly snatched from peril, and to rely upon him alone, "Who tempers the wind to the shorn lamb."' Although they had seen little evidence of the Lord's mercy in the last two months, Chase insisted that they 'bear up against all evils . . . and not weakly distrust the providence of the Almighty, by giving ourselves up to despair.'

For the next three days the wind continued out of the east, forcing them farther and farther south. '[I]t was impossible to silence the rebellious repinings of our nature,' Chase admitted. 'It was our cruel lot not to have had one bright anticipation realized—not one wish of our thirsting souls gratified.'

On January 26, the sixty-sixth day since leaving the wreck, their noon observation indicated that they had sunk to latitude 36° south, more than 600

206

nautical miles south of Henderson Island and 1,800 miles due west of Valparaiso, Chile. That day the searing sun gave way to a bitterly cold rain. Starvation had lowered their body temperatures by several degrees, and with few clothes to warm their thin bodies, they were now in danger of dying of hypothermia. They had no choice but to try to head north, back toward the equator.

With the breeze out of the east, they were forced to tack, turning with the steering oar until the wind came from the starboard side of the boat. Prior to reaching Henderson, it had been a maneuver they had accomplished with ease. Now, even though the wind was quite light, they no longer had the strength to handle the steering oar or trim the sails. '[A]fter much labor, we got our boat about,' Chase remembered, 'and so great was the fatigue attending this small exertion of our bodies, that we all gave up for a moment and abandoned her to her own course.'

With no one steering or adjusting the sails, the boat drifted aimlessly. The men lay helpless and shivering in the bilge as, Chase wrote, 'the horrors of our situation came upon us with a despairing force and effect.' After two hours, they finally marshaled enough strength to adjust the sails so that the boat was once again moving forward. But now they were sailing north, parallel to, but not toward, the coast of South America. Like Job before him, Chase could not help but ask, '[What] narrow hopes [still] bound us to life?'

*   *   *

As Chase's men lay immobilized by hunger in the

207

bottom of their boat, yet another member of Hendricks's crew died. This time it was Isaiah Sheppard, who became the third African American to die and be eaten in only seven days. The next day, January 28—the sixty-eighth day since leaving the wreck—Samuel Reed, the sole black member of Pollard's crew, died and was eaten. That left William Bond in Hendricks's boat as the last surviving black in the *Essex*'s crew. There was little doubt who had become the tropic birds and who had become the hawks.

Sailors commonly accepted that eating human flesh brought a person's moral character down to the level of those 'brutish savages' who voluntarily indulged in cannibalism. On Boon Island in 1710, Captain Dean had noticed a shocking transformation among his crew once they began to eat the carpenter's body. 'I found (in a few days) their natural dispositions changed,' Dean wrote, 'and that affectionate, peaceable temper they had all along hitherto, discovered totally lost; their eyes staring and looking wild, their countenances fierce and barbarous.'

But it wasn't the act of cannibalism that lowered a survivor's sense of civility; rather, it was his implacable hunger. During the first leg of their voyage, Chase had noticed that their sufferings had made it difficult for them to maintain 'so magnanimous and devoted a character to our feelings.'

Even under the controlled circumstances of the 1945 Minnesota starvation experiment, the participants were aware of a distressing change in their behavior. A majority of the volunteers were members of the Church of the Brethren, and many

208

had hoped that the period of deprivation would enhance their spiritual lives. But they found just the opposite to be true. 'Most of them felt that the semi-starvation had coarsened rather than refined them,' it was reported, 'and they marveled at how thin their moral and social veneers seemed to be.'

In another notorious case of survival cannibalism, sailors aboard the badly damaged *Peggy* were reaching the final stages of starvation on the stormy Atlantic in 1765. Although they still had more than enough left of the vessel's cargo of wine and brandy, it had been eighteen days since they'd eaten the last of their food. Emboldened by alcohol, the first mate informed the captain that he and the rest of the crew were going to kill and eat a black slave. The captain refused to take part and, too weak to oppose them, overheard the terrifying sounds of the execution and subsequent feast from the cabin. A few days later, the crew appeared at the captain's door, looking for another man to kill. 'I . . . [told them] that the poor Negro's death had done them no service,' Captain Harrison wrote, 'as they were as greedy and as emaciated as ever . . . The answer which they gave to this, was, that they were now hungry, and must have something to eat.'

Like the crew of the *Peggy*, the *Essex* survivors were no longer operating under the rules of conduct that had governed their lives prior to the ordeal; they were members of what psychologists studying the effects of the Nazi concentration camps have called a 'modern feral community'—a group of people reduced to 'an animal state very closely approaching "raw" motivation.' Just as concentration camp inmates underwent, in the words of one psychologist, 'starvation . . . in a state

209

of extreme stress,' so did the men of the *Essex* live from day to day not knowing which one of them would be the next to die.

Under these circumstances, survivors typically undergo a process of psychic deadening that one Auschwitz survivor described as a tendency to 'kill my feelings.' Another woman expressed it as an amoral, even immoral, will to live: 'Nothing else counted but that I wanted to live. I would have stolen from husband, child, parent or friend, in order to accomplish this. Therefore, every day I disciplined myself with a sort of low, savage cunning, to bend every effort, to devote every fiber of my being, to do those things which would make that possible.'

Within a feral community, it is not uncommon for subgroups to develop as a collective form of defense against the remorseless march of horror, and it was here that the Nantucketers—their ties of kinship and religion stitching them together—had an overwhelming advantage. Since there would be no black survivors to contradict the testimonies of the whites, the possibility exists that the Nantucketers took a far more active role in insuring their own survival than has been otherwise suggested. Certainly the statistics raise suspicion— of the first four sailors to be eaten all were black. Short of murdering the black crew members, the Nantucketers could have refused to share meat with them.

However, except for the fact that the majority of the blacks were assigned to a whaleboat commanded by a sickly mate, there is no evidence of overt favoritism in the boats. Indeed, what appears to have distinguished the men of the *Essex* was the great discipline and human compunction they maintained throughout the whole ordeal. If necessity forced them to act like animals, they did so with the deepest regrets. There was a reason why William Bond in Hendricks's boat was the last African American left alive. Thanks to his position as steward in the officers' quarters, Bond had enjoyed a far more balanced and plentiful diet than his shipmates in the forecastle. But now that he was the only black among six whites, Bond had to wonder what the future held.

Given the cruel mathematics of survival cannibalism, each death not only provided the remaining men with food but reduced by one the number of people they had to share it with. By the time Samuel Reed died on January 28, the seven survivors each received close to three thousand calories' worth of meat (up by almost a third since the death of Lawson Thomas). Unfortunately, even though this portion may have been roughly equivalent to each man's share of a Galapagos tortoise, it lacked the fat that the human body requires to digest meat. No matter how much meat they now had available to them, it was of limited nutritional value without a source of fat.

The following night, January 29, was darker than most. The two boat-crews were finding it difficult to keep track of each other; they also lacked the strength to manage the steering oars and sails. That night, Pollard and his men looked up to find that the whaleboat containing Obed Hendricks, William Bond, and Joseph West had disappeared. Pollard's men were too weak to attempt to find the missing boat-either by raising a lantern or firing a pistol. That left George Pollard, Owen Coffin,

211

Charles Ramsdell, and Barzillai Ray—all Nantucketers—alone for the first time since the sinking of the *Essex*. They were at latitude 35° south, longitude 100° west, 1, 500 miles from the coast of South America, with only the half-eaten corpse of Samuel Reed to keep them alive.

But no matter how grim their prospects might seem, they were better than those of Hendricks's boat-crew. Without a compass or a quadrant, Hendricks and his men were now lost in an empty and limitless sea.

*   *   *

On February 6, the four men on Pollard's boat, having consumed 'the last morsel' of Samuel Reed, began to '[look] at each other with horrid thoughts in our minds,' according to one survivor, 'but we held our tongues.' Then the youngest of them, sixteen-year-old Charles Ramsdell, uttered the unspeakable. They should cast lots, he said, to see who would be killed so that the rest could live.

The drawing of lots in a survival situation had long been an accepted custom of the sea. The earliest recorded instance dates back to the first half of the seventeenth century, when seven Englishmen sailing from the Caribbean island of St. Kitts were driven out to sea in a storm. After seventeen days, one of the crew suggested that they cast lots. As it turned out, the lot fell to the man who had originally made the proposal, and after lots were cast again to see who should execute him, he was killed and eaten.

In 1765, several days after the crew of the disabled *Peggy* had eaten the remains of the black slave, lots were drawn to see who would be the next to serve as food. The lot fell to David Flatt, a foremastman and one of the most popular sailors in the crew. 'The shock of the decision was great,' wrote Captain Harrison, 'and the preparations for execution dreadful.' Flatt requested that he be given some time to prepare himself for death, and the crew agreed to postpone the execution until eleven the next morning. The dread of his death sentence proved too much for Flatt. By midnight he had become deaf; by morning he was delirious. Incredibly, a rescue ship was sighted at eight o'clock. But for David Flatt it was too late. Even after the *Peggy*'s crew had been delivered to England, Harrison reported that 'the unhappy Flatt still continued out of his senses.'

Drawing lots was not a practice to which a Quaker whaleman could, in good conscience, agree. Friends not only have a testimony against killing people but also do not allow games of chance. Charles Ramsdell, the son of a cabinetmaker, was a Congregationalist. However, both Owen Coffin and Barzillai Ray were members of Nantucket's Friends Meeting. Although Pollard was not a Quaker, his grandparents had been, and his great-grandmother, Mehitable Pollard, had been a minister.

Faced with similarly dire circumstances, other sailors made different decisions. In 1811, the 139-ton brig *Polly*, on her way from Boston to the Caribbean, was dismasted in a storm, and the crew drifted on the waterlogged hull for 191 days. Although some of the men died from hunger and exposure, their bodies were never used for food; instead, they were used as bait. Attaching pieces of

213

their dead shipmate's bodies to a trolling line, the survivors managed to catch enough sharks to sustain themselves until their rescue. If the *Essex* crew had adopted this strategy with the death of Matthew Joy, they might never have reached the extreme lunge that confronted them now.

When first presented with young Ramsdell's proposal, Captain Pollard 'would not listen to it,' according to an account related by Nickerson, 'saying to the others, "No, but if I die first you are welcome to subsist on my remains."' Then Owen Coffin, Pollard's first cousin, the eighteen-year-old son of his aunt, joined Ramsdell in requesting that they cast lots.

Pollard studied his three young companions. Starvation had ringed their sunken eyes with a dark, smudgelike pigmentation. There was little doubt that they were all close to death. It was also clear that all of them, including Barzillai Ray, the orphaned son of a noted island cooper, were in favor of Ramsdell's proposal. As he had two times before—after the knockdown in the Gulf Stream and the sinking of the *Essex*—Pollard acquiesced to the majority. He agreed to cast lots. If suffering had turned Chase into a compassionate yet forceful leader, Pollard's confidence had been eroded even further by events that reduced him to the most desperate extreme a man can ever know.

They cut up a scrap of paper and placed the pieces in a hat. The lot fell to Owen Coffin. 'My lad, my lad! ' Pollard cried out. '[I]f you don't like your lot, I'll shoot the first man that touches you.' Then the captain offered to take the lot himself. 'Who can doubt but that Pollard would rather have met the death a thousand times,' Nickerson wrote.

'None that knew him, will ever doubt.'

But Coffin had already resigned himself to his fate. 'I like it as well as any other,' he said softly.

Lots were drawn again to see who would shoot the boy. It fell to Coffin's friend, Charles Ramsdell.

Even though the lottery had originally been his idea, Ramsdell now refused to follow it through. 'For a long time,' Nickerson wrote, 'he declared that he could never do it, but finally had to submit.' Before he died, Coffin spoke a parting message to his mother, which Pollard promised to deliver if he should make it back to Nantucket. Then Coffin asked for a few moments of silence. After reassuring the others that 'the lots had been fairly drawn,' he lay his head down on the boat's gunwale. 'He was soon dispatched,' Pollard would later recall, 'and nothing of him left.'

CHAPTER TWELVE

IN THE EAGLE'S SHADOW

Chase and his men lay in the bottom of their boat in a cold drizzle. All they had to shield them from the rain was a piece of tattered, water-soaked canvas. 'Even had it been dry,' Nickerson wrote, '[it] would have been but a poor apology for covering.'

On January 28, 1821, the breeze finally shifted into the west. But it brought them little comfort. 'It had nearly become indifferent to us,' Chase wrote, 'from what quarter it blew.' They now had too far to go and too few provisions to have any hope of reaching land. Their only chance was to be sighted by a ship. '[I]t was this narrow hope alone,' Chase remembered, 'that prevented me from lying down at once to die.'

They had fourteen days of hardtack left, but that assumed they could live two more weeks on only an ounce and a half a day. 'We were so feeble,' Nickerson wrote, 'that we could scarcely crawl about the boat upon our hands and knees.' Chase realized that if he didn't increase their daily portion of bread, they all might be dead in as few as five days. It was time to abandon the strict rationing regime that had brought them this far and let the men eat 'as pinching necessity demanded.'

Success in a long-term survival situation requires that a person display an 'active-passive' approach to the gradual and agonizing unfolding of events. 'The key factor . . . [is] the realization that passivity is itself a deliberate and "active" act,' the survival psychologist John Leach writes. 'There is strength in passivity.' After more than two months of regimenting every aspect of his men's lives, Chase intuitively understood this—that it was now time to give 'ourselves wholly up to the guidance and disposal of our Creator.' They would eat as much bread as they needed to stave off death and see where the westerly wind took them.

By February 6 they were still alive, but just barely. 'Our sufferings were now drawing to a close,' the first mate wrote. '[A] terrible death appeared shortly to await us.' The slight increase in food intake had brought a return to their hunger pangs, which were now 'violent and outrageous.' They found it difficult to talk and think clearly. Dreams of food and drink continued to torment them. '[O]ften did our fevered minds wander to the side of some richly supplied table,' Nickerson remembered. His fantasies always ended the same way—with him 'crying at the disappointment.'

That night, rain squalls forced them to shorten sail. The off-islander Isaac Cole was on watch, and rather than awaken his companions, he attempted to lower the jib himself. But it proved too much for him. Chase and Nickerson awoke the next morning to find Cole despondent in the bilge of the boat. He declared that 'all was dark in his mind, not a single ray of hope was left for him to dwell upon.' Like Richard Peterson before him, he had given up, asserting that 'it was folly and madness to be struggling against what appeared so palpably to be our fixed and settled destiny.'

Even though he barely had the strength to articulate the words, Chase did his best to change Cole's mind. 'I remonstrated with him as effectually as the weakness both of my body and understanding would allow of.' Suddenly Cole sat up and crawled to the bow and hoisted the jib he had lowered, at such cost, the night before. He cried out that he would not give up and that he would live as long as any of them. '[T]his effort was,' Chase wrote, 'but the hectic fever of the moment.' Cole soon returned to the bottom of the boat, where he lay despairing for the rest of the day and through the night. But Cole would not be permitted the dignity of a quiet and peaceful death.

On the morning of February 8, the seventy-ninth day since leaving the *Essex*, Cole began to rant incoherently, presenting to his frightened crew members 'a most miserable spectacle of madness.' Twitching spasmodically, he sat up and called for a napkin and water, then fell down to the bottom of the boat as if struck dead, only to pop up again like a possessed jack-in-the-box. By ten o'clock he could no longer speak. Chase and the others placed him on aboard they had laid across the seats and covered him with a few pieces of clothing.

For the next six hours, Cole whimpered and moaned in pain, finally falling into 'the most horrid and frightful convulsions' Chase had ever seen. In addition to dehydration and hypernatremia (an excess amount of salt), he may have been suffering from a lack of magnesium, a mineral deficiency that, when extreme, can cause bizarre and violent behavior. By four o'clock in the afternoon, Isaac Cole was dead.

It had been forty-three days since they'd left Henderson Island, seventy-eight days since they'd last seen the *Essex*, but no one suggested—at least that afternoon—that they use Cole's body for food. All night the corpse lay beside them, each man keeping his thoughts to himself.

When the crew of the *Peggy* shot and killed a black slave in 1765, one of the men refused to wait for the meat to be cooked. '[B]eing ravenously impatient for food,' the sailor plunged his hand into the slave's eviscerated body and plucked out the liver and ate it raw. 'The unhappy man paid dear for such an extravagant impatience,' Captain Harrison wrote, 'for in three days after he died raving mad.' Instead of eating that sailor's body, the crew, 'being fearful of sharing his fate,' threw it overboard. No one dared to consume the flesh of a man who had died insane.

The next morning, February 9, Lawrence and Nickerson began making preparations for burying

218

Cole's remains. Chase stopped them. All night he had wrestled with the question of what they should do. With only three days of hardtack left, he knew, it was quite possible that they might be reduced to casting lots. Better to eat a dead shipmate—even a tainted shipmate—than be forced to kill a man.

'I addressed them,' Chase wrote, 'on the painful subject of keeping the body for food.' Lawrence and Nickerson raised no objections and, fearful that the meat had already begun to spoil, '[we] set to work as fast as we were able.'

After separating the limbs from the body and removing the heart, they sewed up what remained of Cole's body 'as decently' as they could, before they committed it to the sea. Then they began to eat. Even before lighting a fire, the men 'eagerly devoured' the heart, then ate 'sparingly of a few pieces of the flesh.' They cut the rest of the meat into thin strips—some of which they roasted on the fire, while the others were laid out to dry in the sun.

Chase insisted that he had 'no language to paint the anguish of our souls in this dreadful dilemma.' Making it all the worse was the thought that any one of the remaining three men might be next. 'We knew not then,' the first mate wrote, 'to whose lot it would fall next, either to die or be shot, and eaten like the poor wretch we had just dispatched.'

The next morning they discovered that the strips of flesh had turned a rancid green. They immediately cooked the strips, which provided them with enough meat to last another six or seven days, allowing them to save what little bread they had left for what Chase called 'the last moment of our trial.'

In Captain Pollard's boat, on February 11, only five days after the execution of Owen Coffin, Barzillai Ray died. Ray, whose biblical first name means 'made of iron, most firm and true,' was nineteen years old. It was the seventh death George Pollard and Charles Ramsdell had witnessed in the month and a half since departing Henderson Island.

Psychologists studying the phenomenon of battle fatigue during World War II discovered that no soldiers—regardless of how strong their emotional makeup might be—were able to function if their unit experienced losses of 75 percent or more. Pollard and Ramsdell were suffering from a double burden; not only had they seen seven of nine men die (and even killed one of them), but they had been forced to eat their bodies. Like Pip, the black sailor in *Moby-Dick* who loses his mind after several hours of treading water on a boundless sea, Pollard and Ramsdell had been 'carried down alive to the wondrous depths, where strange shapes of the unwarped primal world glided to and fro.' Now they were alone, with only the corpse of Barzillai Ray and the bones of Coffin and Reed to sustain them.

Three days later, on February 14, the eighty-fifth day since leaving the wreck, Owen Chase, Benjamin Lawrence, and Thomas Nickerson ate the last of Isaac Cole. A week of living off human flesh, combined with their earlier decision to increase their daily ration of hardtack, had strengthened them to the point where they could once again manage the steering oar. But if they were stronger, they were also in a great deal of pain. As if the boils that covered their skin weren't enough, their arms and legs started to swell shockingly. Known as edema, this disfiguring accumulation of fluid is a common symptom of starvation.

Several days of westerly winds had brought them to within three hundred miles of the islands of Masafuera and Juan Fernandez. If they averaged sixty miles a day, they might reach safety in another five days. Unfortunately, they had only three days of hardtack left.

'Matters were now with us at their height,' Chase wrote. '[A]ll hope was cast upon the breeze; and we tremblingly and fearfully awaited its progress, and the dreadful development of our destiny.' Surrendering all prospects, the men were convinced that after two and a half months of suffering they were about to die nearly within sight of salvation.

That night Owen Chase lay down to sleep, 'almost indifferent whether I should ever see the light again.' He dreamed he saw a ship, just a few miles away, and even though he 'strained every nerve to get to her,' she sailed off into the distance, never to return. Chase awoke 'almost overpowered with the frenzy I had caught in my slumbers, and stung with the cruelties of a diseased and disappointed imagination.'

The next afternoon, Chase saw a thick cloud to the northeast—a sure sign of land. It must be the island of Masafuera—at least that was what Chase told Lawrence and Nickerson. In two days, he assured them, they would be on dry land. At first, his companions were reluctant to believe him.

221

Gradually, however, after 'repeated assurances of the favorable appearances of things' on the part of Chase, 'their spirits acquired even a degree of elasticity that was truly astonishing.' The wind remained favorable all night, and with their sails trimmed perfectly and a man tending the steering oar, their little boat made the best time of the voyage.

The next morning the cloud still loomed ahead. The end of their ordeal was apparently only days away. But for fifteen-year-old Thomas Nickerson, the strain of anticipation had become too much. After bailing out the boat, he lay down, drew the mildewed piece of canvas over him like a shroud, and told his fellow crew members that 'he wished to die immediately.'

'I saw that he had given up,' Chase wrote, 'and I attempted to speak a few words of comfort and encouragement to him.' But all the arguments that had served the first mate so well failed to penetrate Nickerson's inner gloom. 'A fixed look of settled and forsaken despondency came over his face,' Chase wrote. '[H]e lay for some time silent, sullen, and sorrowful—and I felt at once . . . that the coldness of death was fast gathering upon him.'

It was obvious to Chase that some form of dementia had seized the boy. Having watched Isaac Cole slip into a similar madness, Chase could not help but wonder if all of them were about to succumb to the temptations of despair. '[T]here was a sudden and unaccountable earnestness in his manner,' he wrote, 'that alarmed me, and made me fear that I myself might unexpectedly be overtaken by a like weakness, or dizziness of nature, that would bereave me at once of both reason and life.'

Whether or not it had been communicated to him through Cole's diseased flesh, Chase also felt the stirrings of a death wish as dark and palpable as the pillarlike cloud ahead.

At seven o'clock the next morning, February 18, Chase was sleeping in the bottom of the boat. Benjamin Lawrence was standing at the steering oar. Throughout the ordeal, the twenty-one-year-old boatsteerer had demonstrated remarkable fortitude. He was the one who, two months earlier, had volunteered to swim underneath the boat to repair a sprung plank. As Lawrence had watched Peterson, Cole, and now Nickerson lose their grip on life, he had clung, as best he could, to hope.

It was something his careworn family had become good at. His grandfather, George Lawrence, had married Judith Coffin, the daughter of a well-to-do merchant. For many years the Lawrences had been part of the island's Quaker elite, but by the time Benjamin came into the world, his grandfather had suffered several financial reversals. The proud old man decided to move to Alexandria, Virginia, where, he told an acquaintance, he could 'descend into a humble sphere among strangers, rather than . . . remain in a place where every object reminded him of his lost prosperity.' When Benjamin was ten years old, his father died during a voyage to Alexandria, leaving his wife with seven children to support.

Safe in Lawrence's pocket was the piece of twine he had been working on ever since they'd left the wreck. It was now close to twelve inches long. He leaned into the steering oar and scanned the horizon.

'There's a sail!' he cried.

Chase immediately scrambled to his feet. Just visible over the horizon was the speck of pale brown that Lawrence had taken for a sail. Chase stared for several suspenseful moments, gradually realizing that, yes, it was a sail—the topgallant of a ship, about seven miles away.

'I do not believe it is possible,' Chase wrote, 'to form a just conception of the pure, strong feelings, and the unmingled emotions of joy and gratitude, that took possession of my mind on this occasion.'

Soon even Nickerson was up on his feet and gazing excitedly ahead.

Now the question was whether they could catch up to the much larger vessel. The ship was several miles to leeward, which was an advantage for the smaller vessel, and heading slightly north of their position, which meant that it might intercept their line of sail. Could their whaleboat reach that crossing point at approximately the same time the ship did? Chase could only pray that his nightmare of the missed rescue ship would not prove true. 'I felt at the moment,' Chase wrote, 'a violent and unaccountable impulse to fly directly towards her.'

For the next three hours they were in a desperate race. Their battered old whaleboat skimmed lightly over the waves at between four and six knots in the northwesterly breeze. Up ahead, the ship's sail plan continued to emerge from the distant horizon, revealing, with excruciating slowness, not only the topgallant sails but the topsails beneath and, finally, the mainsail and foresail. Yes, they assured themselves, they were catching up to the ship.

There was no lookout at the vessel's masthead, but eventually someone on deck saw them approaching to windward and behind. Chase and his men watched in tense fascination as the antlike figures bustled about the ship, shortening sail. Gradually the whaleboat closed the distance, and the hull of the merchantman rose up out of the sea, looming larger and larger ahead of them until Chase could read her quarterboard. She was the *Indian* from London.

Chase heard a shout and through glazed, reddened eyes saw a figure at the quarterdeck rail with a trumpet, a hailing device resembling a megaphone. It was an officer of the *Indian*, asking who they were. Chase summoned all his strength to make himself heard, but his desiccated tongue stumbled over the words: '*Essex* . . . whaleship . . . Nantucket.'

*   *   *

The narratives of shipwreck survivors are filled with accounts of captains refusing to take castaways aboard. In some instances the officers were reluctant to share their already low supply of provisions; in others they were fearful the survivors might be suffering from communicable diseases. But as soon as Chase explained that they were from a wreck, the *Indian*'s captain immediately insisted that they come alongside.

When Chase, Lawrence, and Nickerson attempted to climb aboard, they discovered that they didn't have the strength. The three men stared up at the crew, their eyes wide and huge within the dark hollows of their skulls. Their raw, ulcerated skin hung from their skeletons like noxious rags. As he looked down from the quarterdeck, Captain

William Crozier was moved to tears at what Chase called 'the most deplorable and affecting picture of suffering and misery.'

The English sailors lifted the men from their boat and carried them to the captain's cabin. Crozier ordered the cook to serve them their first taste of civilized food—tapioca pudding. Made from the root of the cassava plant, tapioca is a high-calorie, easy-to-digest food rich in the proteins and carbohydrates that their bodies craved.

Rescue came at latitude 33°45' south, longitude 81°03' west. It was the eighty-ninth day since Chase and his men had left the *Essex*, and at noon they came within sight of Masafuera. Chase had succeeded in navigating them across a 2,500-mile stretch of ocean with astonishing accuracy. Even though they had sometimes been so weak that they could not steer their boat, they had somehow managed to sail almost to within sight of their intended destination. In just a few days the *Indian* would be in the Chilean port of Valparaiso.

Trailing behind on a towline was the whaleboat that had served the Nantucketers so well. Captain Crozier hoped to sell the old boat in Valparaiso and establish a fund for the men's relief. But the next night the weather blew up to a gale, and the boat, empty of men for the first time in three months, was lost.

*   *   *

Three hundred miles to the south, Pollard and Ramsdell sailed on. For the next five days they pushed east, until by February 23, the ninety-fourth

226

day since leaving the wreck, they were approaching the island of St. Mary's just off the Chilean coast. Over a year before, this had been the *Essex*'s first landfall after rounding Cape Horn. Pollard and Ramsdell were on the verge of completing an irregular circle with a diameter of more than three thousand miles.

It had been twelve days since the death of Barzillai Ray. They had long since eaten the last scrap of his flesh. The two famished men now cracked open the bones of their shipmates—beating them against the stone on the bottom of the boat and smashing them with the boat's hatchet—and ate the marrow, which contained the fat their bodies so desperately needed.

Pollard would later remember these as 'days of horror and despair.' Both of them were so weak that they could barely lift their hands. They were drifting in and out of consciousness. It is not uncommon for castaways who have been many days at sea and suffered both physically and emotionally to lapse into what has been called 'a sort of collective confabulation,' in which the survivors exist in a shared fantasy world. Delusions may include comforting scenes from home—perhaps, in the case of Pollard and Ramsdell, a sunny June day on the Nantucket Commons during the sheepshearing festival. Survivors may find themselves in conversation with deceased shipmates and family members as they lose all sense of time.

For Pollard and Ramsdell, it was the bones—gifts from the men they had known and loved—that became their obsession. They stuffed their pockets with finger bones; they sucked the sweet marrow from the splintered ribs and thighs. And they sailed on, the compass card wavering toward east.

Suddenly they heard a sound: men shouting and then silence as shadows fell across them and then the rustle of wind in sails and the creaking of spars and rigging. They looked up, and there were faces.

*   *   *

Of the *Dauphin's* twenty-one-man crew, at least three—Dimon Peters, Asnonkeets, and Joseph Squibb—were Wampanoags from Cape Cod and Martha's Vineyard. As children they had been taught a legend about the discovery of Nantucket that told of how, long before the arrival of the Europeans, a huge eagle appeared over a village on Cape Cod. The eagle would swoop down out of the sky and carry off children in its talons, then disappear over the waters to the south. Finally the villagers asked a benevolent giant named Maushop to find out where the eagle was taking their children. Maushop set off to the south, wading through the water until he came to an island he had never seen before. After searching all over the island, he found the bones of the children piled high beneath a large tree.

On the morning of February 23, the crew of the *Dauphin* made a similar discovery. Looking down from a restless forest of spars and sails, they saw two men in a whaleboat filled with bones.

The men were not much more than skeletons themselves, and the story that would be passed from ship to ship in the months ahead was that they were 'found sucking the bones of their dead mess mates, which they were loath to part with.' The

228

Dauphin's captain, Zimri Coffin, ordered his men to lower a boat and bring the two survivors aboard. Like Chase, Lawrence, and Nickerson before them, Pollard and Ramsdell were too weak to stand and had to be lifted up to the whaleship's deck. Both men were, in the words of a witness, 'very low' when first brought aboard. But after being given some food, Pollard made an astonishing recovery.

At around five o'clock that evening, the *Dauphin* spoke the whaleship *Diana* from New York. The *Diana's* captain, Aaron Paddack, toward the end of a successful voyage, joined Captain Coffin for dinner. Also joining them was Captain George Pollard, Jr., formerly of the *Essex*.

Like many survivors, Pollard was animated by a fierce and desperate compulsion to tell his story. Just as the gaunt, wild-eyed Ancient Mariner of Coleridge's poem poured forth each harrowing detail to the Wedding Guest, so did Pollard tell them everything: how his ship had been attacked 'in a most deliberate manner' by a large sperm whale; how they had headed south in the whaleboats; how his boat had been attacked once again, this time by 'an unknown fish'; and how they had found an island where a 'few fowl and fish was the only sustenance.' He told them that three men still remained on the island. He told of how the rest of them had set out for Easter Island and how Matthew Joy had been the first to die. He told of how Chase's boat had become separated from them in the night and how, in rapid succession, four black men 'became food for the remainder.' Then he told how, after separating from the second mate's boat, he and his crew 'were reduced to the deplorable necessity of casting lots.' He told of how

229

the lot fell to Owen Coffin, 'who with composure and resignation submitted to his fate.' Lastly he told of the death of Barzillai Ray, and how Ray's corpse had kept both him and Ramsdell alive.

Later that night, once he had returned to the *Diana*, Captain Paddack wrote it all down, calling Pollard's account 'the most distressing narrative that ever came to my knowledge.' The question now became one of how the survivors would fare in the dark shadow of their story.

CHAPTER THIRTEEN

HOMECOMING

On February 25, 1821, Chase, Lawrence, and Nickerson arrived in Valparaiso, Chile's largest port, set on a steep hill facing north across a wide bay. At any other time the story of the *Essex* would have captivated the city. But in February and March of that year, the citizens of Valparaiso were tensely awaiting news from the north. Revolutionary forces, having already secured Chile's independence from Spain, were bearing down on Royalists in Lima. It was Peru, not a few American castaways, that demanded Valparaiso's attention, allowing the *Essex* survivors to recuperate in relative privacy.

From the beginning Chase and his men spoke openly about having resorted to cannibalism. On the day of the Nantucketers' arrival, the keeper of the port's official log of incoming and outgoing vessels matter-of-factly reported that the captain of the *Indian* had picked up three men who 'survived with a little water and crackers . . . and with a shipmate that died and that they ate in the term of eight days.'

The U.S. frigate *Constellation* was anchored at Valparaiso, and the acting American consul, Henry Hill, arranged to have Chase, Lawrence, and Nickerson taken to it. Even though it had been a week since their rescue, the survivors still presented an affecting sight. '[T]heir appearance . . . was truly distressing,' wrote Commodore Charles Goodwin Ridgely, commander of the *Constellation*, 'bones working through their skins, their legs and feet much smaller and the whole surface of their bodies one entire ulcer.' Ridgely placed the three men under the care of his surgeon, Dr. Leonard Osborn, who supervised their recovery in the frigate's sickbay deep in the forward part of the third deck. It may have been hot and airless, but for three men who had spent eighty-nine consecutive days beneath the open sky, it was a wonderful comfort.

The crew of the *Constellation* was so profoundly moved by the sufferings of Chase and his men that each sailor donated a dollar toward their assistance. When this was combined with money collected from the American and British residents of Valparaiso, the *Essex* survivors had more than $500 to help defray the costs of their convalescence.

But the men's sufferings were not yet over. As the participants in the Minnesota starvation experiment discovered in 1945, the recovery period was a torturous part of the ordeal. After three months, the Minnesota volunteers still had not

231

returned to their normal weights, even though some were consuming more than five thousand calories a day. They would eat until their stomachs could not take any more, yet they still felt hungry. Many would continue to eat between meals. It wasn't until after six months of 'supernormal eating' that they had regained the bodies they had once possessed.

The *Essex* survivors were in much worse shape than the volunteers in the Minnesota experiment. After three months of abuse, their digestive systems had a difficult time handling the intake of increased quantities of food—a problem shared by Captain David Harrison of the *Peggy* in 1765. Upon his rescue, Harrison was given some chicken broth. It had been thirty-seven days since he'd last had a bowel movement, and soon after drinking some of the broth, he was wracked by excruciating abdominal pain. 'I was . . . at last relieved,' Harrison wrote, 'by the discharge of a callous lump about the size of a hen's egg, and enjoyed a tranquillity of body, notwithstanding all my disorders, with which I was utterly unacquainted for some preceding weeks.'

The day after their arrival in Valparaiso, Chase and his men received a visit from the governor, who had heard rumors that, instead of being the survivors of a wreck, the first mate and his men had killed the *Essex*'s captain in a bloody mutiny. 'For there was a whispering abroad,' Nickerson wrote, 'that foul play had been used by us.' The governor was reassured enough by Chase's story that he allowed the Nantucketers to go freely about the city as soon as they were able.

232

*   *   *

A week and a half later, on March 9, the Nantucket whaleship *Hero* arrived in Valparaiso. While cutting in a whale off St. Mary's Island, she'd been attacked by Spanish pirates. The Spaniards imprisoned the captain and the cabin boy on shore, then locked the rest of the crew belowdecks and began to ransack the ship. When an unknown vessel appeared in the harbor, the pirates returned briefly to shore, allowing first mate Obed Starbuck to burst open the cabin door and retake the ship. Starbuck ordered his men to set sail, and although the pirates came to within yards of catching up to the fleeing whaleship, the Nantucketers were able to reach safety.

As dramatic as that report was, the *Hero* bore even more sensational news. With mate Starbuck acting as skipper, the *Hero* had encountered three whaleships sailing together as an informal group—the *Dauphin*, the *Diana*, and the *Two Brothers*. Captain Zimri Coffin of the *Dauphin* told Starbuck that he had the captain of the *Essex* and another crew member aboard. Shortly afterward, Pollard and Ramsdell were transferred to the *Two Brothers*, which was headed for Valparaiso.

It arrived on March 17. The five survivors had last seen one another on the night of January 12, when their boats had become separated in a howling gale more than two thousand miles out to sea. Since then, two of Chase's crew had died, four of Pollard's, and three of Joy's (then under Hendricks's leadership) before the second mate's boat and the three remaining men disappeared. Only Nantucketers had emerged from Pollard's

233

and Chase's whaleboats alive.

They had all suffered terribly, but it was Pollard and Ramsdell—found clutching the bones of their dead companions—who had come the closest to complete psychic disintegration. Of the anguish each of these two experienced, Pollard's was perhaps the greater. A year and a half earlier, his aunt had entrusted him with the care and protection of her oldest son, Owen. Pollard had not only presided over his cousin's execution but had eaten his flesh, thus participating in what one historian of cannibalism at sea has called the taboo of 'gastronomic incest.'

Pollard had demonstrated remarkable stamina immediately after his rescue, but his urgent need to tell his tale had almost killed him. Soon after that first night, he suffered a relapse. When Captain William Coffin of the Nantucket whaleship *Eagle* offered the *Essex* survivors passage home, Pollard was judged to be too weak for a voyage around Cape Horn. On March 23, Chase, Lawrence, Nickerson, and Ramsdell bid farewell to their captain and left for Nantucket. In May, after two months of recuperation and solitary reflection, Pollard followed them in the whaleship *Two Brothers*.

*   *   *

In the meantime, Commodore Ridgely, commander of the *Constellation*, had made arrangements for the rescue of Chappel, Weeks, and Wright from (as he was told) Ducie Island. Recently arrived in Valparaiso was the *Surry*, a trading vessel from Australia being loaded with fifteen thousand bushels of wheat. Her captain, Thomas Raine, agreed to stop at Ducie on his way back to Sydney and pick up the three *Essex* crew members, assuming, of course, they were still alive.

The *Surry* left South America on March 10. Captain Raine and his crew arrived at Ducie Island less than a month later, only to find the tiny coral atoll uninhabited. The shore was so thick with nesting birds it was impossible to walk without stepping on eggs. Raine decided that no one had visited this necklace of coral in a very long time.

He studied his navigational guide and wondered if the *Essex* officers might have mistaken an island seventy miles to the west for Ducie. A few days later, on April 9, Henderson Island came within view. They approached it from the east, then began to follow the coastline to the north. Upon rounding a rocky headland they found a 'spacious bay' to the west. Raine ordered one of his men to fire a gun.

*   *   *

At that moment, Chappel, Weeks, and Wright had just sat down to eat a tropic bird. Except for some berries and shellfish, birds and eggs were the only food left on Henderson. The landcrabs had disappeared. A few months before, the men had succeeded in catching five green turtles, but by the time they had eaten just one of the turtles, the meat on the other four had spoiled. Over the last four months, the tropic birds had proved exceptionally difficult to find, so the bird they had now was, for them, a bountiful feast. But food was not their gravest concern. What they still needed most was water.

From the day after their seventeen shipmates left for Easter Island, the spring of freshwater never again emerged above the tide line. At low tide they could see freshwater bubbling up to the ocean's surface from the rock, but for the rest of their time on Henderson the spring always remained covered by saltwater.

In desperation, Chappel, Weeks, and Wright dug a series of wells but were unable to reach groundwater. When it rained they would greedily collect the water that accumulated in the hollows of nearby rocks. Dehydration caused their tongues to swell and their lips to crack. After a five-day stretch without water, they reluctantly sucked the blood of a tropic bird but found themselves 'much disordered' by it. While searching the crevices and caves for water, they discovered the remains of the eight unidentified castaways, whose fate they feared would soon be their own. The skeletons lay side by side as if the people had decided to lie down and quietly die together. For Chappel, who had once been the wildest and least responsible of the *Essex*'s crew, it was a sight that helped change his life. From that day forward, he would look to God. 'I found religion not only useful,' he later wrote, 'but absolutely necessary to enable me to bear up under these severe trials.'

When Chappel, Weeks, and Wright, crouched around their tropicbird feast, heard a distant booming, they assumed it was thunder, but one of the men decided to walk down to the beach and have a look. Later he would tell what had happened as soon as he saw the ship: 'The poor fellow,' one of the *Surry*'s crew members reported, 'was so overpowered with the emotions such a sight excited in his breast, he could not go to tell his companions the joyful news.' Finally, however, they, too, grew curious and joined him at the beach.

A high surf was breaking on the ledge of coral surrounding the island. Several times the crew of the *Surry* attempted to land a boat, but the conditions proved too dangerous. The three desperate men stood on the beach, increasingly fearful that their rescuers would decide to abandon them. Finally Chappel, the strongest of the three and the only one who knew how to swim, dove into the sea. His arms were skin and bone but with the adrenaline coursing through him, he reached the launch and was pulled aboard.

The *Surry*'s crew discussed what to do next. They might have to return the following day for the other two men. But Chappel refused to abandon his two shipmates even temporarily. With a rope tied around his waist, he dove into the water and swam back over the coral to the beach. One at a time, the three of them were pulled out to the boat. They suffered many cuts and bruises from the reef, but all made it to the *Surry* alive.

Captain Raine judged that the three of them would have been dead after another month on the island. Their clothes were mere rags; between them they had only a single pair of pants. Somehow one of them had been able to save his seaman's certificate, on which he had kept a record of their days spent on Henderson. They told Raine that Captain Pollard had left several letters in a box nailed to a tree, and the next day Raine was able to land on the island and retrieve the letters.

The only *Essex* crew members not accounted for were the three men—Obed Hendricks, Joseph Vilest, and William Bond—in the second mate's boat, which separated from Pollard's on the night of January 29. Months later, long after Captain Raine had searched Ducie Island, the atoll to the east of Henderson, another ship touched down there. The crew discovered a whaleboat washed up on the brittle shore, with four skeletons inside. In 1825 the British navy captain Frederick William Beechey, who visited both Ducie and Henderson Islands, made the connection between this ghostly vessel of bones and the lost *Essex* boat. If this was indeed the second mate's whaleboat and the skeletons belonged to Hendricks, West, Bond, and perhaps Isaiah Sheppard, the last of the crew to die before the separation from Pollard, then it had drifted for more than a thousand miles, finally coming to rest within a day's sail of where it had started on December 27, 1820.

*   *   *

In 1820–21, as the *Essex* boat-crews struggled east under a blistering sun, their kin on Nantucket were suffering through one of the coldest winters in the island's history. On the day that the three whaleboats left Henderson Island, Obed Macy, Nantucket's historian, recorded in his journal that the harbor was covered with 'porridge ice.' By January 7, the harbor was frozen solid. Ice extended north toward the mainland as far as the eye could see. Supplies of food and especially firewood were already dangerously low. Six feet of snow smothered the outlying areas of the island, making it impossible for the sheep to feed on grass. Macy estimated that as many as half of Nantucket's total herd of about nine thousand sheep would be dead by spring.

On January 13, six men from Martha's Vineyard, who were trapped on Nantucket and desperate to return to their families, launched a whaleboat from the south shore, where the ocean surf had maintained a corridor of open water. The wind remained moderate that day, and people were optimistic that the Vineyarders had reached home safely. There is no record of whether or not they did. On January 25 the temperature dropped to 12 degrees below zero, the lowest ever recorded on the island. 'Many people, especially the old,' Macy wrote, 'could hardly be kept comfortable in bed.'

Four men were added to the town's night watch. With almost all of the island's population crowded into a congestion of old wooden buildings, their fireplaces roaring night and day, there was a high risk of what Macy called a 'disastrous fire.' Adding to the danger was the unusually large amount of sperm oil stored in the town's warehouses that winter. Macy noted that the merchants had taken 'every necessary care to preserve [the oil] from fire.'

Finally, in the beginning of February, the temperature rose above freezing, and it began to rain. 'The ice and snow melts away rapidly,' Macy wrote, 'which seems to animate and give life to business of most kinds. The vessels and men who have been confined here for some weeks begin to move, with some prospects of being released from prison. The people who are so anxious to get off are cutting out the mail packet [from the ice].' On the morning of February 4, the packet sailed from Nantucket with 'the largest mail packages that ever went from here at one time.' On February 17, the day before Chase's rescue, several trading vessels arrived with cargoes of corn, cranberries, hay, fresh pork, beef, turkey, cider, dry fish, and apples. The crisis was over.

The families of the *Essex* crew members had no reason for concern throughout the winter and spring. Letters mailed from the Galapagos post office on Charles Island in late October would not have reached Nantucket until February or March at the earliest. They would have told of a typical whaling voyage reaching its midpoint, with hopes high that a productive season in the Offshore Ground would allow them to return home in the summer of 1822.

What the people of Nantucket did not know was that since late February, a kind of tidal wave of horror had been building in the whale fishery as the story of the *Essex* was passed from ship to ship, gradually making its way around the Horn and up the Atlantic toward Nantucket. Riding the crest of this wave was the *Eagle*, with Chase, Lawrence, Nickerson, and Ramsdell aboard. Before the *Eagle's* arrival, however, a letter reached Nantucket that told of the disaster.

The town's post office was on Main Street, and as soon as the letter arrived, it was read there before an overflowing crowd. The islander Frederick Sanford was a contemporary of the Nantucket teenagers aboard the *Essex*, and he would never forget what he saw and heard that day.

240

The letter, Sanford recalled, told of 'their sufferings in the boats, eating each other, and some of them my old playmates at school!' Despite Nantucket's reputation for Quaker stoicism, the people assembled outside the post office could not conceal their emotions. '[E]veryone was overcome by [the letter's] recital,' Sanford wrote, 'and [wept] in the streets.'

As it turned out, the letter contained an incomplete account of the disaster. Pollard and Ramsdell had been rescued almost a week after Chase's boat-crew, but their account—passed from whaleship to whaleship—was the first to make it home. The letter mentioned the three men left on the island but gave little hope for any other survivors. Pollard and Ramsdell were assumed to be the only Nantucketers left alive.

On June 11, the *Eagle* arrived at the Nantucket Bar. 'My family had received the most distressing account of our shipwreck,' Chase wrote, 'and had given me up for lost.' But standing alongside Ramsdell was not George Pollard; instead, there were three ghosts—Owen Chase, Benjamin Lawrence, and Thomas Nickerson. Tears of sorrow were soon succeeded by amazement and then tears of joy. 'My unexpected appearance,' Chase remembered, 'was welcomed with the most grateful obligations and acknowledgments to a beneficent Creator, who had guided me through darkness, trouble, and death, once more to the bosom of my country and friends.'

Chase discovered that he was the father of a fourteen-month-old daughter, Phebe Ann. For Chase's wife, Peggy, it was an overwhelming sight: the husband whom she had once thought dead holding their chubby-cheeked daughter in his still bony, scab-covered arms.

The community of Nantucket was overwhelmed as well. Obed Macy, the meticulous keeper of Nantucket's historical record, chose not to mention the disaster in his journal. Although articles quickly appeared about the *Essex* in the *New Bedford Mercury*, Nantucket's own fledgling newspaper, the *Inquirer*, did not write about the disaster that summer. It was as if Nantucketers were refusing to commit to an opinion about the matter until they had first had a chance to hear from the *Essex*'s captain, George Pollard, Jr.

* * *

They would have to wait almost two months, until August 5, when Pollard returned to the island aboard the *Two Brothers*. The whaleship was first sighted by the lookout posted at the tower of the Congregational church. As word spread down the lanes and into the grog shops and warehouses and ropewalks and out into the wharves, a crowd formed and began to make its way to the cliff along the north shore. From there they could see the black, sea-worn ship, heavy with oil, her sails furled, anchored at the Nantucket Bar. At 222 tons, the *Two Brothers* was even smaller than the *Essex* had been, and once she'd been relieved of some of her oil, she crossed the Bar at high tide and made her way toward the harbor entrance. The crowd surged back to the waterfront. Soon more than 1,500 people were waiting expectantly at the wharves.

The arrival of a whaleship—any whaleship—was

242

what one Nantucketer called 'an era in most of our lives.' It was the way people learned about the ones they loved—the sons, husbands, fathers, uncles, and friends whose workplace was on the other side of the world. Since no one knew what news the whaleship might bring, islanders greeting a ship tended to hide their eagerness and anxiety behind a veneer of solemnity. 'We feel a singular blending of joy and grief on such occasions,' this same Nantucketer confessed. 'We know not whether to smile or weep. Our emotion at all events is much subdued. We dare not express it *aloud* lest it grate upon the ear of some to whom this ship has been a harbinger of evil. We are disposed to be quiet. And yet at this time we have an irresistible impulse to *utter* our feelings.'

And so, when Pollard first stepped upon the wharf, surrounded by more than a thousand familiar faces, there was an absolute, nerve-shattering quiet. Frederick Sanford, Nickerson's and Ramsdell's old school chum, would later describe the assembly as 'an awe-struck, silent crowd.' As Pollard began to make his way toward home, people moved aside to let him pass. No one said sword.

*   *   *

It was generally acknowledged that a whaling captain bore a much heavier weight of responsibility than a captain in the merchant service. In addition to navigating his vessel around the Horn and back, he was required to train a crew of inexperienced men in the dangerous art of killing and processing whales. And when it was all done, he had to answer to his ship's owners, who expected nothing less than a full hold of oil. It was little wonder, then, that a whaling captain was paid, on average, three times what the commander of a merchant vessel received.

As a mate aboard the *Essex*, George Pollard had known only success; as captain, he had known only disaster. Since a whaleman was paid a portion of the proceeds at the end of the voyage, Pollard, like all the other survivors, had nothing to show for two years of misery and hardship.

Captain Amass Delano knew what it was like to return home after an unsuccessful voyage. '[I]t must be acknowledged, that I never saw my native country with so little pleasure as on my return to it after a disastrous termination of my enterprises and my hopes,' Delano wrote in an 1817 account of his many voyages to the Pacific. 'The shore, on which I would have leaped with delight, was covered with gloom and sadness to my downcast eye and wounded mind . . . [M]y observation was alive to every symptom of neglect or affected pity which might appear in the conduct or salutations of my acquaintance onshore.'

Pollard was inevitably subjected to a lengthy interview by the *Essex*'s owners, Gideon Folger and Paul Macy, a harrowing process during which it would have been difficult for a first-time captain not to sound defensive. 'It is unquestionably true, that the poor and disappointed man is often too jealous on this subject,' Delano wrote, 'and puts an erroneous and unjust construction upon conduct which is neither mercenary nor heartless.' But it wasn't just the *Essex*'s owners to whom Pollard had to answer. There was a member of his own

244

family—Owen Coffin's mother.

*   *   *

Nancy Bunker Coffin, forty-three, was Pollard's aunt, the sister of his mother, Tamar, fifty-seven. Nancy had married into one of Nantucket's oldest and proudest families, one that traced its roots to Tristram Coffin, the patriarch of the island's first English settlement in the seventeenth century. Nancy's father-in-law, Hezekiah Coffin, Sr., had been the captain of one of the ships involved in the Boston Tea Party in 1773. Hezekiah had distinguished himself, according to family legend, as 'the first to throw tea into Boston Harbor.' The family possessed a miniature portrait of Hezekiah. He had wide-set eyes, a sharp nose, and a gentle, slightly embarrassed smile.

Although his son, Hezekiah Jr., had been a birthright Friend, he'd been disowned when he married Nancy Bunker, a non-Quaker, in 1799. Then, in 1812, when Owen Coffin was ten, Hezekiah Jr. officially 'apologized,' and both he and Nancy became members of the North Meeting on Broad Street.

On that August day in 1821, when George Pollard arrived on her doorstep, Nancy's commitment to her adopted faith met the severest possible test. 'He bore the awful message to the mother as her son desired,' Nickerson wrote. Nancy Coffin did not take it well. The idea that the man to whom she had entrusted the care of her seventeen-year-old son was living as a consequence of her boy's death was too much for her to bear. '[S]he became almost frantic with the thought,'

245

Nickerson wrote, 'and I have heard that she never could become reconciled to the captain's presence.'

The verdict of the community was less harsh. The drawing of lots was accepted by the unwritten law of the sea as permissible in a survival situation. 'Captain Pollard was not thought to have dealt unfairly with this trying matter,' Nickerson wrote. Although it did not involve the drawing of lots, a comparable case of survival cannibalism rocked the community of Montevideo, Uruguay, in 1972. The ordeal began when a plane transporting a local soccer team to Santiago, Chile, crashed in the snowy Andes Mountains. Until their rescue ten weeks later, the sixteen survivors sustained themselves on the frozen corpses of the passengers who had died in the crash. Just as had occurred in Nantucket more than 150 years earlier, the residents of Montevideo did not fault the young men's behavior. Soon after their return, Montevideo's Catholic Archbishop declared that since it had been a question of survival, the men were blameless, adding, 'It is always necessary to eat whatever is at hand, in spite of the repugnance it may evoke.'

There is no evidence that Nantucket's religious leaders felt compelled to speak in defense of the *Essex* survivors. The fact remains, however, that no matter how justified it may have been, cannibalism was, and continues to be, what one scholar has termed a 'cultural embarrassment'—an act so unsettling that it is inevitably more difficult for the general public to accept than for the survivors who resorted to it.

For his own part, Pollard did not allow the horror he had experienced in the whaleboat to defeat him, displaying an honesty and directness concerning the disaster that would sustain him all his life. Captain George Worth of the *Two Brothers* was so impressed with the integrity of the former captain of the *Essex* during the two-and-a-half-month voyage back from Valparaiso that he recommended Pollard as his replacement. Soon after his return, Pollard was formally offered command of the *Two Brothers.*

By the time Pollard returned to Nantucket, Owen Chase had begun working on a book about the disaster. Chase had kept a daily log of his ordeal in the boats. He also appears to have obtained a copy of the letter written by the *Diana*'s captain, Aaron Paddack, the night after hearing Pollard's story, which provided him with an account of what had happened on the other two boats after the separation on January 12. But Owen Chase was a whaleman, not a writer. 'There seems no reason to suppose that Owen himself wrote the Narrative,' Herman Melville would write in his own copy of Chase's book. 'It bears obvious tokens of having been written for him; but at the same time, its whole air plainly evinces that it was carefully and conscientiously written to Owen's dictation of the facts.'

Chase had grown up with a boy who, instead of shipping out for the Pacific, had attended Harvard College. William Coffin, Jr., was the twenty-three-year-old son of a successful whale-oil merchant who had also served as Nantucket's first postmaster. After graduating from Harvard, William Jr. had briefly studied medicine, and then, in the words of a friend, followed 'other pursuits more congenial with his enthusiastic love of literature.' Years later, he would ghostwrite Obed Macy's much-praised history of Nantucket; there is also evidence that he helped write an account of the notorious *Globe* mutiny. His published literary career appears to have begun, however, with the narrative of the *Essex* disaster.

Coffin was the ideal person to work with Chase. Well educated and an accomplished writer, Coffin also had a thorough knowledge of both Nantucket and whaling. Being Chase's own age, he could empathize with the young first mate in a way that makes the narrative read, Melville noted, 'as tho' Owen wrote it himself.' The two men worked quickly and well together. By early fall the manuscript was finished. By November 22, almost precisely a year after the sinking, the published book had reached shops on Nantucket.

In a note to the reader, Chase claims that, having lost everything in the wreck, he was desperate to make some money to support his young family. 'The hope of obtaining something of remuneration,' Chase wrote, 'by giving a short history of my sufferings to the world, must therefore constitute my claim to public attention.' But he had other motives as well. Writing the narrative offered him an opportunity to represent himself—a young officer in need of another ship— as positively as possible.

Chase's account is necessarily focused on what happened on his own boat. However, the majority of the deaths—nine out of eleven—occurred on the other two boats, and Chase's description of these deaths is limited to a brief summation at the end of his narrative. It would be difficult for any reader of Chase's book alone to appreciate the true scope of the disaster. In particular, the fact that five out of the first six men to die were black is never commented on by Chase. By keeping many of the most disturbing and problematic aspects of the disaster offstage, Chase transforms the story of the *Essex* into a personal tale of trial and triumph.

It is in his account of the decisions made prior to the ordeal in the whaleboats that the first mate is the most self-serving. He chooses not to mention that he was the one, along with Matthew Joy, who urged Captain Pollard to continue on after the knockdown in the Gulf Stream even though several whaleboats had been lost. He also makes the officers' decision to sail for South America sound as if it were mutually agreed upon from the start when, according to Nickerson, Pollard had initially proposed to sail for the Society Islands. More important, Chase is careful to conceal that he had the opportunity to lance the whale after the first attack—a fact that would not be revealed until the publication of Nickerson's account 163 years later.

Chase's fellow Nantucket survivors, particularly Captain Pollard, undoubtedly felt that their side of the story had not been adequately told in the first mate's account of the disaster. (Herman Melville would later report that Pollard had been moved to write, 'or caused to be [written] under his own name, his own version of the story'—a narrative that has not come to light.) But it wasn't just Chase's fellow crew members who felt slighted by the publication of the *Essex* narrative. As Ralph Waldo Emerson would observe during a visit to the island in 1847, Nantucketers are '[v]ery sensitive to everything that dishonors the island because it hurts the value of stock till the company are

249

poorer.' The last thing they wanted placed before the nation and the world was a detailed account of how some of their own men and boys had been reduced to cannibalism. Chase's account pulled no punches on this issue, employing two exclamation marks when it came to the initial proposal to eat Isaac Cole. No matter how straitened a man's circumstances, many believed, he did not attempt to enrich himself by sensationalizing the sufferings of his own people. Significantly, Chase's next voyage would not be on a Nantucket whaleship. That December he traveled to New Bedford, where he sailed as first mate on the *Florida*, a whaleship without a single Nantucketer in the crew. Even though his family remained on the island, Chase would not sail on a ship from his home port for another eleven years.

George Pollard, however, was given the ultimate vote of confidence. On November 26, 1821, a little more than three months after returning to Nantucket and just a few days after the appearance of Chase's narrative, he set sail for the Pacific as captain of the *Two Brothers*. But perhaps the most extraordinary endorsement Pollard received came from two of his crew members. For Pollard wasn't the only *Essex* man aboard the *Two Brothers;* two others had chosen to serve under him again. One was Thomas Nickerson. The other was Charles Ramsdell, the boy who had spent ninety-four days in a whaleboat with him. If there was someone who had come to know Captain Pollard, it was Charles Ramsdell.

CHAPTER FOURTEEN

CONSEQUENCES

George Pollard took to his second command with optimism that was remarkable, considering what had happened to his first. In the winter of 1822 he successfully brought the *Two Brothers* around the Horn, headed her up the west coast of South America, and provisioned her at the Peruvian port of Payta. In mid-August the *Two Brothers* spoke the U.S. Navy schooner *Waterwitch*. Aboard the *Waterwitch* was a twenty-four-year-old midshipman named Charles Wilkes. As it so happened, Wilkes had finished reading Chase's narrative of the *Essex* disaster only the day before. He asked the captain of the *Two Brothers* if he was any relation to the famous George Pollard of Nantucket. Pollard said that, yes, he was the same man. '[T]his made a great impression on me,' Wilkes said many years later.

Even though Wilkes had already read the published account, Pollard insisted on telling the young midshipman his own version of the story. 'It was to be expected that some effect of his former cruise would have been visible in his manner or conversation,' Wilkes wrote, 'but not so, he was cheerful and very modest in his account.' The midshipman judged Pollard to be 'a hero, who did not even consider that he had overcome obstacles which would have crushed 99 out of a hundred.'

But there was at least one indication that Pollard had not emerged from the ordeal entirely

251

unscathed. Wilkes noted an unusual feature in the captain's cabin. Attached to the ceiling was a large amount of netting, and it was filled with provisions—primarily potatoes and other fresh vegetables. Captain Pollard, the man who had almost starved to death only the year before, could now simply reach over his head and pull down something to eat. Wilkes asked Pollard how, after all that he had suffered, he could dare go to sea again. 'He simply remarked,' Wilkes wrote, 'that it was an old adage that the lightning never struck in the same place twice.' But in the case of Captain Pollard, it did.

In February of 1823 the *Two Brothers* and another Nantucket whaleship, the *Martha*, were sailing west together toward a new whaling ground. In the few years since the start of Pollard's previous voyage, much had changed in the Pacific whale fishery. Soon after the opening up of the Offshore Ground in 1819, Nantucket whaleships had stopped at the Hawaiian island of Oahu for the first time. That same year, Frederick Coffin, captain of the Syren, laid claim to discovering the rich Japan Ground. All of the Pacific, not just its eastern and western edges, had become the domain of the Nantucket whalemen.

The *Two Brothers* and the *Martha* were several hundred miles west of the Hawaiian Islands, headed toward the Japan Ground, when it began to blow. Pollard ordered his men to shorten sail. It was raining hard, and in the high seas, the *Two Brothers* was proving difficult to steer. The *Martha* was the faster of the two whaleships, and as night came on the lookout of the *Two Brothers* could barely see her from the masthead.

They were sailing at about the same latitude as French Frigate Shoals—a deadly maze of rocks and coral reefs to the northwest of the Hawaiian Islands—but both Pollard and Captain John Pease of the *Martha* judged themselves to be well to the west of danger. Since his previous voyage, Pollard had learned how to determine his ship's longitude by lunar observation. However, owing to overcast skies, it had been more than ten days since he had been able to take a lunar, so he had to rely on dead reckoning to determine his ship's position.

It was blowing so hard that the whaleboats had been taken off the davits and lashed to the deck. That night one of the officers remarked that 'the water alongside looked whiter than usual.' Thomas Nickerson was about to retrieve a jacket from down below when he noticed Pollard standing on the ship's railing, staring down worriedly into the sea.

While Nickerson was belowdecks, the ship struck something 'with a fearful crash,' and he was thrown to the floor. Nickerson assumed they had collided with another ship. 'Judge of my astonishment,' he wrote, 'to find ourselves surrounded with breakers apparently mountains high, and our ship careening over upon her broadside and thumping so heavily that one could scarcely stand upon his feet.' The ship was being pounded to pieces on a coral reef. 'Captain Pollard seemed to stand amazed at the scene before him,' Nickerson remembered.

First mate Eben Gardner leaped into the breach. He ordered the men to begin cutting down the masts in hopes of saving the ship. Realizing that the spars would likely fall across and crush the whaleboats tied to the deck, Pollard finally came to life. He commanded the crew to put away their

253

axes and begin readying the boats. 'Had the masts of the ship been cut away at that time,' Nickerson wrote, '[I] would probably have adorned this tale instead of [told] it.'

But by the time the men begun crowding into the two boats, Pollard had lapsed into his former state of mesmerized despair. '[H]is reasoning powers had flown,' Nickerson remembered, and the captain appeared unwilling to leave the ship. The waves threatened to bash the boats against the hull as the men pleaded with their commander to save himself. 'Captain Pollard reluctantly got into the boat,' Nickerson wrote, 'just as they were about to shove off from the ship.'

Nickerson, who at seventeen years old had been promoted to boatsteerer, was standing at the steering oar when a huge wave slammed into the boat and threw him into the sea. One of the mates reached out to him with the blade of the after oar. Nickerson grabbed it and was pulled back into the boat.

The two whaleboats were quickly separated in the darkness. 'Our boat seemed to be surrounded with breakers,' Nickerson remembered, 'and we were compelled to row between them all night for we could see no outlet.' The next morning they saw a ship anchored in the lee of a fifty-foot-high rock. It proved to be the *Martha*, which had narrowly escaped crashing into the rock the night before. Soon both boatcrews had been rescued, and the *Martha* was on her way to Oahu.

*   *   *

Two months later, in the harbor of Raiatea, one of

254

the Society Islands, a missionary named George Bennet boarded the U.S. brig *Pearl* bound for Boston. Among the passengers was George Pollard. The thirty-one-year-old captain had greatly changed since he'd talked to Charles Wilkes less than a year before. His former cheerfulness had disappeared. Yet, anchored in the harbor of an island that he and his men had once spurned in the mistaken fear of cannibals, he insisted on telling Bennet the story of the *Essex* in painful detail. This time, when it came to describing the execution of Owen Coffin, he broke off. 'But I can tell you no more,' he cried out to Bennet, 'my head is on fire at the recollection, I hardly know what I say.'

Pollard finished the conversation by relating how he had recently lost his second whaleship on a shoal off the Hawaiian Islands. Then, in what Bennet called 'a tone of despondency never to be forgotten by him who heard it,' Pollard confessed, '[N]ow I am utterly ruined. No owner will ever trust me with a whaler again, for all will say I am an unlucky man.'

As Pollard predicted, his whaling career was over. The island that had rallied so quickly behind him after the sinking of the *Essex* now turned its back. He had become a Jonah—a twice-doomed captain whom no one dared give a third chance. After returning to his wife, Mary, Pollard made a single voyage in a merchant vessel out of New York. '[B]ut not liking that business,' Nickerson wrote, 'he returned to his home on Nantucket.' He became a night watchman— a position on the lowest rung of the island's social ladder.

A disturbing rumor began to be whispered about the streets of town, a rumor that was still being told

255

on Nantucket almost a hundred years later. It had not been Owen Coffin who had drawn the short piece of paper, the gossipmongers claimed, it had been George Pollard. It was only then that his young cousin, already near death and convinced he would not last the night, offered and even insisted on taking the captain's place. If the rumor had it right, Pollard was not only unlucky, he was a coward, and fate had found him out.

*　　*　　*

The word 'pollard' has two meanings. A pollard is an animal, such as an ox, goat, or sheep, that has lost its horns. But pollard is also a gardening term. To pollard a tree is to prune back its branches severely so that it may produce a dense growth of new shoots. Misfortune had pollarded George Pollard, cutting back his possibilities, but, as if strengthened by the surgery, he created a happy, meaningful life for himself in his native town.

George and Mary Pollard would never have any children of their own, but it might be said that they presided over the largest family on Nantucket. As the town's night watchman, Pollard was responsible for enforcing the nine o'clock curfew, a duty that brought him into contact with nearly every young person on the island. Instead of becoming the dour, embittered man one might expect, he was known for his buoyant, even cheerful, manner. Joseph Warren Phinney was part of the Pollards' extended family. When Phinney's mother and father died, he came to Nantucket to live with his grandparents. His father's first wife had been Mary Pollard's sister, and late in life Phinney left an account of

George Pollard.

'He was a short fat man,' Phinney recalled, 'jolly, loving the good things in life.' Phinney fondly remembered how Mary Pollard would lay her husband down on the kitchen table and measure him for a new pair of pants. Instead of a harpoon, this former whaleman wandered the streets 'with a long hickory pole with an iron hook at the end, under his arm.' The pole not only enabled him to adjust the town's whale-oil street lamps but proved useful in persuading the children to be in their homes by the curfew. Pollard took his duties so seriously that he was known, according to Phinney, as the town 'gumshoe'—a streetwise detective familiar with the intimate details of an island whose population would grow from seven thousand to ten thousand over the next two decades.

Phinney, like every other Nantucketer, knew the story of the *Essex* and had even heard the rumor about how 'the man who drew the lot had his place taken by a young boy.' To Phinney and everyone else who actually knew Pollard, it was impossible that 'this man' could have been George Pollard. (According to the version of the rumor Phinney heard, the man whose place was taken by Owen Coffin 'had a wife and babies,' and as everyone knew, the Pollards were childless.)

There was another rumor about Captain Pollard. It claimed that a newly arrived off-islander innocently asked him if he had ever known a man named Owen Coffin. 'Know him?' Pollard was reputed to have replied. 'Why, I *et* him!'

Pollard's friends didn't credit that story either. They knew that he was incapable of mocking the memory of the men who had died in the *Essex* whaleboats. Even though he had been able to put the tragedy behind him, he never ceased to honor those who had been lost. 'Once a year,' Phinney remembered, 'on the anniversary of the loss of the *Essex*, he locked himself in his room and fasted.'

*   *   *

As a whaleman, Owen Chase would enjoy the success that had eluded George Pollard. His personal life, however, proved less fortunate.

Chase's first voyage after the sinking of the *Essex*, as first mate aboard the New Bedford whaleship *Florida*, lasted less than two years and reaped two thousand barrels of oil. When he returned to Nantucket in 1823, he found a second child, Lydia, toddling in the wake of her older sister, Phebe Ann, now approaching four. Chase chose to remain on-island for the birth of his next child, a son, who was named William Henry. Owen's wife, Peggy did not recover from the delivery. She died less than two weeks later. Owen was now a twenty-seven-year-old widower with three children to care for.

In the fall and winter of 1824–25 he came to know a woman with whom he already shared a special bond. Nancy Slade Joy was the widow of Matthew Joy, second mate of the *Essex*. She and Matthew had been married for two years before her husband had shipped out for the last time. In June of 1825, nine months after the death of Peggy Chase, the widow and widower were married, and Nancy became the stepmother of Owen's three children. Two weeks later, Chase purchased a house from his father on the outskirts of Orange

Street's 'Captain's Row.' In early August, Chase sailed for New Bedford, where he took command of his first vessel, the *Winslow*. He was twenty-eight years old, the same age Pollard had been when he had become captain of the *Essex*.

The *Winslow* was a small whaleship and carried only fifteen men. On July 20, 1827, after a voyage of almost two years, she returned to New Bedford with 1,440 barrels of oil. Chase returned to Nantucket, paid off the $500 mortgage on his house, and was back in New Bedford by the second week in August. The emotions of Nancy Chase, who had lived with her husband for less than two months back in the summer of 1825, can only be imagined when she learned that Owen was departing almost immediately on another voyage aboard the *Winslow*.

Soon after her departure, the *Winslow* was damaged in a tremendous gale and limped back to New Bedford in October for repairs. The owners decided to take the opportunity to enlarge the ship to 263 tons, allowing Chase to spend nine months with his wife and three children back on Nantucket. Leaving again in July 1828, he filled his newly modified ship in two years and was back on Nantucket in the summer of 1830.

It is naturally tempting to read into Chase's post-Essex career an Ahab-like quest for revenge. There is, in fact, a tiny shred of evidence to indicate that even if Chase was not motivated by a desire to find and kill the whale that had sunk the *Essex*, other whalemen said he was.

In 1834, seventeen years before the publication of *Moby-Dick*, the poet and essayist Ralph Waldo Emerson shared a coach with a sailor who told of a whale (and a white whale at that) known for bashing up whaleboats with its jaw. The seaman claimed that a whaleship had been fitted out of New Bedford called the *Window* or the *Essex*, he wasn't sure which, to kill this whale and that the creature had been finally dispatched off the cost of South America. One can only wonder if Emerson recorded a garbled account of how Owen Chase, the new captain of the *Winslow* and the former first mate of the *Essex*, succeeded in avenging himself on the whale that had caused him so much hardship and pain.

Whatever the case may be, Chase's almost decade-long professional banishment from Nantucket ended soon after his return from his second full voyage as captain of the *Winslow*. At the age of thirty-three he was offered command of what was to be one of the largest ships in the Nantucket whale fishery. Until then, almost all the island's ships were built on the mainland in places such as Rochester and Hanover, Massachusetts. But whaling had brought a tremendous surge of wealth to the island. The profit margins were now high enough that it was deemed economically feasible to build a whaleship at the island's Brant Point Shipyard, even though all the materials had to be transported across Nantucket Sound. Over the next two years, the 376-ton, copper-fastened whaleship *Charles Carroll* took shape under Chase's experienced eye, and with an investment of $625 he was given a 1/32 owners' share in the vessel.

*   *   *

Chase's first voyage as captain of the *Charles Carroll* was a financial success. After three and a half years, he returned in March 1836 with 2,610 barrels of oil, almost twice the return of his first voyage as captain aboard the *Winslow*. But the voyage came at a great personal cost. Nine months after her husband left the island, Nancy Chase gave birth to a daughter, Adeline. A few weeks later, Nancy was dead. Greeting their father at the wharf in the spring of 1836 were Phebe Ann, almost sixteen; Lydia, thirteen; William Henry, eleven; and Adeline, two and a half—a girl who had no memory of her mother and had never known her father.

Chase wasn't home a month before he had remarried. Eunice Chadwick was just twenty-seven years old, and she now had four stepchildren to care for. By the end of August, after less than five months of marriage, she was waving good-bye to her new husband. This was to be Chase's last voyage as a whaling captain. He was forty years old and, if all went well, would be able to retire to his house on Orange Street.

Also in the Pacific during this period was a young man whose whaling career was just beginning. Herman Melville first signed on in 1840 as a hand aboard the New Bedford whaleship *Acushnet*. During a gam in the Pacific, he met a Nantucketer by the name of William Henry Chase—Owen Chase's teenage son. Melville had already heard stories about the *Essex* from the sailors aboard the *Acushnet* and closely questioned the boy about his father's experiences. The next morning William pulled out a copy of Owen's *Essex* narrative from his sea chest and loaned it to

Melville. 'The reading of this wondrous story upon the landless sea,' Melville remembered, 'and so close to the very latitude of the shipwreck had a surprising effect upon me.'

Later in the voyage, during a gam with another whaleship, Melville caught a glimpse of a Nantucket whaling captain whom he was told was none other than Owen Chase. 'He was a large, powerful well-made man,' Melville would later write in the back pages of his own copy of Chase's narrative, 'rather tall; to all appearances something past forty-five or so; with a handsome face for a Yankee, and expressive of great uprightness and calm unostentatious courage. His whole appearance impressed me pleasantly. He was the most prepossessing-looking whalehunter I think I ever saw.' Although Melville appears to have mistaken another whaling captain for Chase, his description is remarkably similar to a surviving portrait of Owen Chase. It depicts a confident, almost arrogant face—a man completely at ease with the responsibility of command. But Chase's professional assurance would not prepare him for the news he heard midway through his final voyage.

*　　　*　　　*

Sixteen months after her husband sailed aboard the *Charles Carroll*, Eunice Chase, Owen Chase's third wife, gave birth to a son, Charles Fredrick. Herman Melville would be told of how Chase received the news, and inevitably the future author of *Moby-Dick* would compare the plight of the former first mate of the *Essex* to that of George Pollard. 'The miserable pertinaciousness of misfortune which

262

pursued Pollard the captain, in his second disastrous and entire shipwreck did likewise hunt poor Owen,' Melville wrote, 'tho' somewhat more dilatory in overtaking him the second time.' Melville was told that Chase had received letters 'informing him of the certain infidelity of his wife . . . We also heard that his receipt of this news had told most heavily upon Chase, and that he was a prey to the deepest gloom.'

A matter of days after his return to Nantucket in the winter of 1840, Chase filed for divorce. On July 7, the divorce was granted, with Chase taking over legal guardianship of Charles Frederick. Two months later, Chase was married for the fourth time, to Susan Coffin Gwinn. In the previous twenty-one years, he had spent only five at home. He would now remain on Nantucket for the rest of his life.

*   *   *

The other *Essex* survivors also returned to the sea. Once they'd been delivered to Oahu after the wreck of the *Two Brothers*, Thomas Nickerson and Charles Ramsdell soon found berths on other whaleships. In the 1840s Ramsdell served as captain of the *General Jackson* out of Bristol, Rhode Island; he would marry twice and have a total of six children. Nickerson eventually tired of the whaling life and became a captain in the merchant service, relocating to Brooklyn, New York, where he and his wife, Margaret, lived for a number of years. They had no children.

Benjamin Lawrence served as captain of the whaleships *Dromo* and *Huron*, the latter out of

Hudson, New York, home of the *Essex*'s second mate, Matthew Joy. Lawrence had seven children, one of whom would die at sea. In the early 1840s, Lawrence, like Chase, retired from the whaling business and purchased a small farm at Siasconset, on the east end of the island of Nantucket.

Less is known about the three off-islanders rescued from Henderson Island. The two Cape Codders, Seth Weeks and William Wright, continued as crew members on the *Surry*, voyaging throughout the Pacific until they made their way to England and back to the United States. Wright was lost at sea in a hurricane off the West Indies. Weeks eventually retired to Cape Cod, where he would outlive all the other *Essex* survivors.

The Englishman Thomas Chappel returned to London in June 1823. There he contributed to a religious tract that wrung every possible spiritual lesson from the story of the *Essex* disaster. Nickerson later heard of the Englishman's death on the fever-plagued island of Timor.

*   *   *

Although townspeople continued to whisper about the *Essex* well into the twentieth century, it was not a topic a Nantucketer openly discussed. When the daughter of Benjamin Lawrence was asked about the disaster, she replied, 'We do not mention this in Nantucket.'

It wasn't just the fact that the men had resorted to cannibalism. It was also difficult for Nantucketers to explain why the first four men to be eaten had been African American. What made this a particularly sensitive topic on Nantucket was the island's reputation as an abolitionist stronghold—what the poet John Greenleaf Whither called 'a refuge of the free.' Instead of the *Essex*, Nantucket's Quakers preferred to talk about how the island's growing black community to the south of town, known as New Guinea, participated in the booming whaling economy.

In 1830 Captain Obed Starbuck and his almost all-black crew returned after a voyage of only fourteen and a half months with 2,280 barrels of oil. A headline in the *Nantucket Inquirer* announced, 'GREATEST VOYAGE EVER MADE.' Spirits ran so high that the black sailors in the crew paraded up Main Street proudly shouldering their harpoons and lances. Less than ten years later, an escaped slave living in New Bedford was invited to speak at an abolitionist meeting at the island's Atheneum library. The African American's name was Frederick Douglass, and his appearance on Nantucket marked the first time he had ever spoken before a white audience. This was the legacy Nantucket's Quaker hierarchy wanted the world to remember, not the disturbing events associated with the *Essex*.

For a time, at least, off-islanders seemed to have forgotten about the tragedy. In 1824 Samuel Comstock led the crew of the Nantucket whaleship *Globe* in a bloody mutiny and public attention was directed away from the *Essex*. Ten years later, however, with the publication of an article about the wreck in the *North American Review*, interest returned. Over the next two decades, numerous accounts of the *Essex* disaster appeared. One of the most influential versions of the story was included in a popular children's schoolbook, William H.

McGuffey's *The Eclectic Fourth Reader*. It would become difficult to grow up in America without learning some form of the *Essex* story.

In 1834 Ralph Waldo Emerson wrote in his journal of his conversation with the seaman about the white whale and the *Essex*. When Emerson visited Nantucket in 1847, he met Captain Pollard and, in a letter to his young daughter back home in Concord, Massachusetts, described the sinking of the *Essex*: '[A] great sperm whale was seen coming with full speed toward the vessel: in a moment he struck the ship with terrible force, staving in some planks and causing a leak: then he went off a little way, and came back swiftly, the water all white with his violent motion, and struck the ship a second frightful blow.'

In 1837 Edgar Allan Poe made use of the more ghoulish aspects of Chase's account in his *Narrative of Arthur Gordon Pym*. Lots are drawn, men are eaten, and one sailor dies in horrible convulsions. Decades before the Dormer Party became snowbound in the foothills of the Sierras, the *Essex* brought a scandalous tale of cannibalism to the American public.

But it would be left to Herman Melville to make the most enduring use of the whaleship's story. *Moby-Dick* contains several detailed references to the attack of the whale on the *Essex*, but it is the climax of the novel that draws most heavily on Chase's narrative. 'Retribution, swift vengeance, eternal malice were in his whole aspect,' Melville writes of the white whale's assault on the *Pequod*. Upon impact, the whale, just as Chase describes in his account, dives beneath the ship and runs 'quivering along its keel.' But instead of attacking

266

the already sinking ship for a second time, Moby Dick turns his attention to the whaleboat of Captain Ahab.

Moby-Dick proved to be both a critical and financial disappointment, and in 1852, a year after its publication, Melville finally visited Nantucket. He traveled to the island in July with his father-in-law, Justice Lemuel Shaw, the same judge who had granted Owen Chase's divorce twelve years earlier. Like Emerson before him, it wasn't Chase, now a retired whaling captain living off the income from his investments, whom Melville sought out, but rather George Pollard, the lowly night watchman.

Melville appears to have stayed at the Ocean House, on the corner of Centre and Broad Streets, diagonally across from the home in which George and Mary Pollard had been living for decades. Late in life Melville wrote of the *Essex*'s captain: 'To the islanders he was a nobody—to me, the most impressive man, tho' wholly unassuming even humble—that I ever encountered.'

In the years to come, Melville's professional life as a novelist would go the way of Pollard's whaling career. Without a readership for his books, the author of *Moby-Dick* was forced to take a job as a customs inspector on the wharves of New York City. Although he ceased writing novels, he continued to write poetry, in particular a long, dark poem called *Clarel*, in which there is a character based on Pollard. After two disastrous voyages, the former captain becomes 'A night patrolman on the quay / Watching the bales till morning hour / Through fair and foul.' Melville felt a powerful kinship with the captain of the *Essex*, and his description of the old seaman is based as much upon himself as it is on the man he met on the streets of Nantucket:

> Never he smiled;
> Call him, and he would come; not sour
> In spirit, but meek and reconciled:
> Patient he was, he none withstood;
> Oft on some secret thing would brood.

By 1835, when Obed Macy published, with the assistance of William Coffin, Jr., his *History of Nantucket*, New Bedford had eclipsed the island as America's leading whaling port. The Nantucket Bar—a mere nuisance in the early days of the Pacific whale fishery—had developed into a major obstacle to prosperity. The whaleships had become so large that they could no longer cross the Bar without being almost completely unloaded by lighters—a time-consuming and expensive process. In 1842, Peter Folger Ewer designed and built two 135-foot 'camels'—giant wooden water wings that formed a floating dry dock capable of carrying a fully loaded whaleship across the Bar. The fact remained, however, that New Bedford's deep-water harbor gave the port an unassailable advantage, as did its nearness to the newly emerging railroad system, on which increasing numbers of merchants shipped their oil to market.

But Nantucketers also had themselves to blame for the dramatic downturn the whaling business would take on the island in the 1840s. As whalemen from New Bedford, New London, and Sag Harbor opened up new whaling grounds in the North Pacific, Nantucketers stuck stubbornly to the long-since depleted grounds that had served them so well in past decades.

There were also problems at home. Quakerism, once the driving cultural and spiritual force of the community, fractured into several squabbling sects. Throughout the 1830s and 1840s, there were more meetinghouses than ever on the island, yet the total number of Quakers on Nantucket dwindled with each passing year. As the strictures of Quakerism relaxed, Nantucketers were free to display the wealth they had once felt obliged to conceal. Main Street became lined with elegant brick estates and giant clapboard Greek Revival mansions— monuments to the riches islanders had, in the words of Herman Melville, 'harpooned and dragged up hither from the bottom of the sea.' Even though the annual return of oil had been steadily diminishing for a number of years, there was little visible reason for concern on the streets of Nantucket in the early summer of 1846. Then, at eleven o'clock on a hot July night, someone shouted the dreaded word 'Fire!'

It had been one of the driest summers on record. The wooden buildings were as parched as tinder. In a few short minutes, the flames had spread from a hat factory on Main Street to an adjoining structure. At this time Nantucket was without a municipal fire department, relying instead on privately organized fire companies. As the fire made its way up Main Street with alarming rapidity, individual homeowners started bidding for the fire companies' services so as to protect their own houses. Instead of working together as a coordinated unit, the companies split off in different directions, allowing the blaze to build into an uncontrollable conflagration.

269

The immense upward flow of heat created wind currents that rushed through the narrow streets, spreading the fire in all directions. Chunks of burning debris flew into the air and landed on houses that had been assumed safe. In an attempt to contain the blaze, the town's fire wardens dynamited houses, the explosions adding to the terrifying confusion of the night. Owen Chase's Orange Street home was far enough south to escape the fire, but Pollard's house on Centre Street was directly in its path. Miraculously, the tornado-like convection currents turned the fire east, toward the harbor, before it reached the night watchman's house. Pollard's residence survived, even though all the houses on the east side of the street were destroyed.

Soon the fire reached the waterfront. Oil warehouses billowed with black smoke, then erupted into flame. As the casks burst, a river of liquid fire poured across the wharves and into the harbor. One fire company had run its engine into the shallows of the anchorage and was pumping seawater onto the wharves. The men belatedly realized that a creeping slick of oil had surrounded them in fire. Their only option was to dive underwater and swim for their lives. Their wooden fire engine was destroyed, but all the men made it to safety.

By the next morning, more than a third of the town—and almost all the commercial district—was a charred wasteland. But it was the waterfront that had suffered the most. The sperm oil had burned so fiercely that not even cinders remained. The leviathan, it was said, had finally achieved his revenge.

The town was quickly rebuilt, this time largely in brick. Nantucketers attempted to reassure themselves that the disturbing dip in the whaling business was only temporary. Then, just two years later, in 1848, came the discovery of gold in California. Hundreds of Nantucketers surrendered to the lure of easy wealth in the West. Abandoning careers as whalemen, they shipped out as passengers bound for San Francisco, packed into the same ships in which they had once pursued the mighty sperm whale. The Golden Gate became the burial ground of countless Nantucket whaleships, abandoned by their crews and left to rot on the mudflats.

Long before Edwin Drake struck oil in Titusville, Pennsylvania, in 1859, Nantucket's economic fate had been determined. Over the next twenty years, the island's population would shrink from ten thousand to three thousand. 'Nantucket now has a "body-o'-death" appearance such as few New England towns possess,' one visitor wrote. 'The houses stand around in faded gentility style- the inhabitants have a dreamy look, as though they live in the memories of the past.' Even though whaling would continue out of New Bedford into the 1920s, the island whose name had once been synonymous with the fishery had ceased to be an active whaling port only forty years after the departure of the *Essex*. On November 16, 1869, Nantucket's last whaling vessel, the *Oak*, left the harbor, never to return.

*   *   *

The world's sperm-whale population proved

271

remarkably resilient in the face of what Melville called 'so remorseless a havoc.' It is estimated that the Nantucketers and their Yankee whale-killing brethren harvested more than 225,000 sperm whales between 1804 and 1876. In 1837, the best year in the century for killing whales, 6,767 sperm whales were taken by American whalemen. (As a disturbing point of comparison, in 1964, the peak year of modern whaling, 29,255 sperm whales were killed.) Some researchers believe that by the 1860s whalemen may have reduced the world's sperm-whale population by as much as 75 percent; others claim that it was diminished by only 8 to 18 percent. Whatever figure is closer to the truth, sperm whales have done better than other large cetaceans hunted by man. Today there are between one and a half to two million sperm whales, making them the most abundant of the world's great whales.

As late as 1845, whalemen were confident that the sperm whale stocks were in no danger of diminishing. They did comment, however, on how the behavior of the whales had changed. 'They have indeed become wilder,' one observer wrote, 'or as some of the whalers express it, "more scary," and, in consequence, not so easy to capture.' Like the whale that had attacked the *Essex*, an increasing number of sperm whales were fighting back.

In 1835 the crew of the English whaleship *Pusie Hall* were forced into full retreat by what they termed a 'fighting whale.' After driving away four whaleboats, the whale pursued them back to the ship. The men hurled several lances at the whale 'before it could be induced to retire.' In 1836, the

Lydia, a Nantucket whaleship, was struck and sunk by a sperm whale, as was the *Two Generals* a few years later. In 1850, the *Pocahontas*, out of Martha's Vineyard, was rammed by a whale but was able to reach port for repairs. Then, in 1851, the year that *Moby-Dick* was published, a whaleship was attacked by a sperm whale in the same waters where the *Essex* had been sunk thirty-one years before.

*   *   *

The *Ann Alexander*, a whaleship out of New Bedford, was under the command of one of the fishiest captains in the Pacific, John DeBlois. In a letter to the ship's owner, DeBlois boasted that he had succeeded in killing every whale he had ever fastened to. But in August of 1851, just to the south of the equator and about five hundred miles east of the Galapagos, Captain DeBlois met his match.

It was a large solitary bull, what DeBlois called 'a noble fellow!' Two boats were lowered, and the fight was on. Almost immediately the whale rushed after the mate's boat. '[I]n an instant [the boat] was crushed like so much paper in his mighty jaws,' DeBlois wrote. After rescuing the first mate's crew, DeBlois was joined by the second mate in another whaleboat. They divided the men among them and resumed the chase. Almost immediately, however, the whale attacked the mate's boat and immediately destroyed it. DeBlois was forced to stop the pursuit, pick up the scattered crew, and return to the *Ann Alexander*.

By this point, DeBlois recounted, 'my blood was up, and I was fully determined to have that whale,

273

cost what it might.' As he stood at the ship's bow with a lance in his hand, the captain told the helmsman where to steer. The whale was, DeBlois wrote, an 'artful beast,' allowing them to gain, only to hurry ahead before the captain could throw his weapon.

Suddenly the whale sank, then turned and surfaced only yards in front of the ship. DeBlois hurled the lance, but it was too late. The whale's massive head struck the bow of the ship, knocking DeBlois off his feet. Convinced that the *Ann Alexander* had been stove, he ran below to check for damage, but all proved tight.

DeBlois ordered his men to lower another boat. The mate objected, insisting that to do so would be suicide. Since it was already close to dusk, DeBlois reluctantly decided to wait until morning. 'Just as I gave these orders,' the captain remembered, 'I caught a glimpse of a shadow as it seemed to me.' It was the whale hurtling through the water toward the *Ann Alexander.* It struck the ship 'a terrible blow,' DeBlois wrote, 'that shook her from stem to stern.'

Even before he went below to inspect the damage, he could hear water pouring into the hold. The captain rushed to his cabin to get the navigational instruments they would need in the whaleboats. As the mates readied the two remaining boats, DeBlois went below one more time, but the cabin was so full of water that he was forced to swim to safety. By the time he returned to the deck, both whaleboats had rowed clear of the ship. He leaped from the railing and swam to the mate's boat.

Almost immediately his men began, in DeBlois's

274

words, '[to] upbraid me, saying, "O Captain, you ran too much risk of our lives!"'

'"Men," I replied, "for God's sake, don't find fault with me! You were as anxious as I to catch that whale, and I hadn't the least idea that anything like this would happen."'

The next morning they returned to the wreck. As soon as DeBlois scrambled up the side, he saw 'the prints of the [whale's] teeth on the copper . . . The hole was just the size of the whale's head.' As DeBlois cut away the masts to right the ship, the ship's bell continued to clang with the rhythmic heave of the sea. '[A] more mournful sound never fell on my ears,' he remembered. 'It was as though it was tolling for our deaths.'

The ship was almost completely submerged, and the waves broke over the captain's head. Eventually he was joined by the mate, and the two of them attempted to cut through the deck and locate some provisions and fresh water. By noon, about half the crew of twenty-four had found the courage to climb aboard the wreck and search for food. Several of the men had begun to grumble that they should immediately set sail for the Marquesas, two thousand miles to the west. DeBlois told the crew to assemble at the rail of the ship, where he asked 'if they wanted me to advise them.' A majority of the men nodded their heads. Although he knew it wasn't what they wanted to hear, he told them that there weren't enough provisions to reach the Marquesas. Instead, they should sail their boats (which possessed centerboards) north toward the equator, where they might be spotted by a ship bound for California. Begrudgingly, the men agreed. Before they left, DeBlois took up a nail and scratched a message into the ship's taffrail: 'Save us—we poor souls have gone in two boats to the north on the wind.'

The mate had twelve men in his boat, the captain thirteen. The crew wanted to stay together, but once again DeBlois overruled them. ' "No" says I, "my object is to have one boat go ahead, if it sails faster, and the other follow in the same course, so that if the first boat is picked up, say, a hundred miles ahead, their rescuers can bear down to the other boat." '

'Our parting was a solemn sight,' he wrote, 'if ever there was one in this world. We never expected to meet again on earth, and the strong men who had braved all sorts of dangers, broke down and wept like children.' The mate's boat soon surged ahead. It wasn't long before DeBlois's men 'became clamorous for food.' They had had nothing to eat or drink for twenty-four hours. But their captain felt it was too early to begin eating what little food they had. 'My mind was filled with all the stories I had ever heard of shipwrecks,' he remembered, 'where the famishing men had been often driven to eating their shipmates' bodies.' He thought, of course, of the *Essex* and how some of the men had drawn lots. 'Pictures of this sort were enough to drive one wild,' he wrote, 'when he felt that the same ordeal was before him.'

At dusk, DeBlois stood up on the stern of his whaleboat for one final look before darkness came on. In the distance, ahead of the mate's boat, he saw the sail of a ship. 'I tried to sing out, "Sail ho," ' he recalled, 'but I couldn't speak a word.' By nightfall all of the crew were safely aboard the whaleship *Nantucket.*

Five months later, the crew of the *Rebecca Simms* succeeded in killing the whale that sank the *Ann Alexander.* By then the bull appeared 'old, tired, and diseased.' Its sides were shaggy with twisted harpoons and lances; huge splinters were found embedded in its head. The whale yielded between seventy and eighty barrels of oil.

When Herman Melville received word of the sinking of the *Ann Alexander*, he could not help but wonder if the writing of his *Essex*-based novel had mystically conjured up the reappearance of a ship-ramming whale. 'Ye Gods!' he wrote a friend. 'What a Commentator is this *Ann Alexander* whale . . . I wonder if my evil art has raised this monster.'

*   *   *

Nantucket, once the whaling capital of the world, was all but a ghost town by the time the last survivors of the *Essex* disaster began to pass away. Charles Ramsdell was the first of the Nantucketers to die, in 1866. Throughout his life he was known for his reticence concerning the *Essex*, in part, one islander surmised, because of his role as Owen Coffin's executioner.

Old age was not kind to Owen Chase. His memory of his sufferings in an open boat never left him, and late in life he began hiding food in the attic of his house on Orange Street. By 1868 Chase was judged 'insane.' The headaches that had plagued him ever since the ordeal had become unbearable. Clutching an attendant's hand, he would sob, 'Oh my head, my head.' Death brought an end to Chase's suffering in 1869.

277

George Pollard followed his former first mate the next year. The obituary was careful to note that Pollard had been known on the island as something more than the captain of the *Essex:* 'For more than forty years he has resided permanently among us; and leaves a record of a good and worthy man as his legacy.'

In the 1870s, Thomas Nickerson returned to Nantucket and moved into a house on North Water Street, not far from where his parents were buried in the Old North Burial Ground. Instead of whales, Nantucketers were now after summer visitors, and Nickerson developed a reputation as one of the island's foremost boardinghouse keepers. One of his guests was the writer Leon Lewis, who, after hearing Nickerson tell about the *Essex*, proposed that they collaborate on a book about the disaster.

Nickerson had talked with Charles Ramsdell about his experiences in the whaleboat with Pollard; he had also spoken with Seth Weeks on Cape Cod about his time on Henderson Island. As a consequence, Nickerson's narrative provides information that was unavailable to Chase. He also includes important details about the voyage prior to the whale attack. But Nickerson, like Chase before him, was not above adjusting his account to suit his own purposes. Not wanting to be remembered as a cannibal, he claims that the men in Chase's boat did not eat the body of Isaac Cole. Instead, he insists, it was the extra bread made available to them by the deaths of Cole and Peterson that 'enabled us to exist until relieved.' He also chose not to recount how, toward the end of the ordeal, he suddenly decided it was his turn to die.

In April 1879, Nickerson's last surviving crew member in the first mate's boat, Benjamin Lawrence, died. All his life, Lawrence had kept the piece of twine he'd made while in the whaleboat. At some point it was passed on to Alexander Starbuck, the Nantucketer who had taken over Obed Macy's role as the island's historian. In 1914, Starbuck would donate the piece of twine, wound four times into a tiny coil and mounted in a frame, to the Nantucket Historical Association. Written within the circle of twine was the inscription 'They were in the Boat 93 Days.'

Eighteen years earlier, in 1896, the Nantucket Historical Association had received another donation associated with the *Essex*. Sometime after the ship sank in November 1820, a small chest, ten by twenty inches, was found floating in the vicinity of the wreck. Leather-bound and studded with brass nails, it may have been used by Captain Pollard to store the ship's papers. It was picked up by the crew of a passing ship and sold to John Taber, a whaleman then on his way home to Providence, Rhode Island. In 1896, Taber's daughter, who had since moved to Garrettsville, Ohio, decided that the chest rightfully belonged on Nantucket and donated the artifact to the historical association.

It was all that remained of the whaleship *Essex*— a battered box and a ragged piece of string.

EPILOGUE

BONES

Early on the morning of December 30, 1997, Edie Ray, coordinator of the Nantucket Marine Mammal Stranding Team, received a telephone call. A whale had washed upon the eastern extreme of the island at Siasconset, just off a low plain of sand known as Codfish Park. A spout was puffing from the top of the whale's head: it was still alive. Soon Ray was in her car and headed down Milestone Road, a straight, seven-mile spine of asphalt that connects Nantucket town to the eastern brim of the island. It was bitterly cold and blowing a gale, and the car was slammed by the icy blasts of wind.

Ray knew the surf would be ugly at Codfish Park. In the last decade, winter storms had eroded nearly fifty yards from this end of the island. Waves with a fetch that reached all the way to Portugal, three thousand miles to the east, regularly thundered onto the beach, and in just six years, sixteen houses had either been moved, torn down, or washed away by the sea. This time, however, the waves had brought something with them.

Ray soon saw the whale, a huge black hulk, off the northern edge of Codfish Park. It was a sperm whale, a cetacean almost never seen in these waters, stranded on a shoal about 150 yards off the beach. Its block shaped head was pointed toward shore, and it was being pummeled by the waves, its tail flopping forward with each hit. The high surf

281

was making it difficult for the whale to breathe.

It would be later determined that, long before the whale washed up on Nantucket, it had broken several ribs in a collision, either with a ship or another whale. Sick, weak, and disoriented, this forty-six-foot adult male—half the length of the whale that sank the *Essex*—did not have the strength to fight free of the breakers. For Ray it was a distressing sight. She had been trained to assist stranded mammals, including pilot whales and seals, and she and her fellow team members were now powerless to help this giant creature.

Word began to spread throughout the island that a live sperm whale had washed up on Codfish Park. By the afternoon, a crowd had assembled, despite the frigid winter weather. Many onlookers were upset that nothing was being done to assist the whale. Lacerations were now visible around its mouth and eyes, and blood clouded the water. Ray and others explained that the severe surf and the whale's size made it impossible to do anything but watch.

By the afternoon, staff members from the New England Aquarium, which monitors whale strandings along the region's 2,500 miles of coast, had flown in from Boston. As the tide rose, the whale was able to free itself from the shoal, only to be washed back by the waves. Each time it swam free, the rip swept the whale south, and the crowd, often cheering it on, followed it along the beach. Just before sunset, the whale finally escaped the breakers and swam out into open water. Ray and several New England Aquarium people rushed to her car and drove out to Tom Never's Head, a bluff to the south, toward which the whale was last seen swimming. They glimpsed it several times but finally lost sight of it in the fading light.

The next morning, December 31, the whale was found washed up on Low Beach, between Codfish Park and Tom Never's Head. The wind had eased to the point that Stranding Team members and aquarium staffers could now approach the whale, which was still alive, but just barely. By noon it was dead.

The Nantucket Whaling Museum, housed in a former sperm candle factory, already had one of the world's greatest collections of whaling equipment, scrimshaw, and artifacts from the South Seas. It even had the skeleton of a finback whale that had washed up in the 1960s. To add the skeleton of a sperm whale—the species upon which the island's fame had been founded—would provide the museum with the ultimate draw. More important, a sperm-whale skeleton would allow Nantucketers to appreciate firsthand the might and grace of the whale, to pay homage to the creature their forefathers had once dedicated their lives to killing.

On January 2, a team of scientists, many from the New England Aquarium, began a necropsy—measuring and photographing the carcass and collecting blood and tissue samples that would later help them determine what the whale had been suffering from. It soon became clear that the whale was decomposing much more quickly than expected, an indication of just how sick it had been before it died. Using scalpels, forceps, and large knives, the team took samples from the lungs, the three stomachs, the bowling-ball-sized heart, the liver, the spleen, and the ears, about the size of a man's fist and situated far back in the head.

As one group worked at the whale's midsection, a New England Aquarium staff member climbed up on top of the whale. With a long-handled Japanese flensing tool, he made an experimental six-foot slice into the intestinal cavity, unleashing a gaseous explosion of gore that blew him off the whale and drenched the others in blood. For the next few minutes, ropelike intestines continued to bubble out of the incision. Even though the whale had been dead for several days and the outdoor temperature was well below freezing, the blubber-encased body steamed in the cold January air.

The necropsy was finished by three o'clock in the afternoon. Now there was the job of removing more than forty tons of putrefying blubber, meat, and guts from the skeleton. By this point, Jeremy Slavitz and Rich Morcom, two staff members from the Nantucket Historical Association, which owns and maintains the island's whaling museum, had become deeply involved in the whale stranding. Morcom asked his boss if he could borrow some tools from the Whaling Museum's collection. After some quick research, he decided that a boarding knife, a cutting spade, and a bone spade were what he needed. Soon the artifacts, their blades long tarnished with age, were once again sharp and glittering.

Even though the Nantucketers were now ideally equipped, it was backbreaking work, giving all of them an appreciation for the amount of sheer labor whaling in the nineteenth century had required. The blubber was not only difficult to cut, even with the sharpest tools, but also remarkably heavy. A single four-foot-square slab of eight-inch-thick blubber weighed as much as four hundred pounds. The smell was, both Morcom and Slavitz agreed, beyond description. Their eyes watered constantly. They gagged as they worked. Each night both of them left their clothes outside their front doors and ultimately, when the cutting was finished, threw them away. Even after long showers, they could still smell the rotting flesh. One evening, Morcom's wife, knowing that he had spent a vacation day working from dawn till dusk, cooked him up a big steak, but the smell of frying meat nauseated him. A whale wasn't a fish, he now knew all too well, but a mammal.

On January 3 they punctured the whale's bulbous head, and the spermaceti flowed out. At first it was 'as clear as vodka,' Morcom remembered; then, upon exposure to the air, the fluid magically congealed into a cloudy, almost waxlike substance. In a few short hours every available bucket and barrel had been filled with spermaceti, and there were still hundreds of gallons remaining. An island fisherman happened to have his dinghy in the back of his pickup truck and offered it as a spermaceti receptacle. Soon it was filled to the gunwale with oil. They ultimately collected about a hundred gallons of spermaceti and were forced to leave an estimated three hundred more on the beach.

By the end of the day they had cut away most of the flesh and blubber from the skeleton, dumping the offal in a hole dug in the beach and temporarily storing the bones under a tarp. A job that had taken as many as three weeks at other whale strandings had been accomplished in only three days.

The bones were eventually buried in a pit, the location of which was kept undisclosed. The jaw and its valuable teeth were buried in Morcom's backyard, but only after his wife and children were sworn to secrecy. With advice from a variety of experts in the field, the Nantucketers decided to build cages for the bones and place them in the harbor the following spring, in expectation that marine scavengers would strip the bones of remaining flesh. The day after Mother's Day, Morcom, Slavitz, and others disinterred the bones, which smelled as bad as, if not worse than, they had when they'd been buried in January. The team loaded them into cages, and the cages were lowered into the harbor, near Brant Point-comparatively still waters, where all manner of devourers, from crabs to fish, could dine undisturbed. Except for a few barnacles, the bones were clean when they emerged from the harbor six months later.

Today the bones reside in a shed designed for the storage of Nantucket Historical Association artifacts. In the center of a room lined with curios such as an antique sleigh and the first sewing machine to come to Nantucket are the grayish-white pieces of the sperm-whale skeleton: the wishbone of the jaw, the disks of the backbone, the bulky ribs and the fingerlike bones from the fins. The bone that is by far the largest, the cranium—over a ton in weight—sits outside on its own boat trailer.

The bones are sopping with oil. A sperm whale

skeleton installed at Harvard University a century ago still oozes grease. Morcom, whose job description as properties manager has grown to include whales, is bathing the Nantucket bones in ammonium hydroxide and hydrogen peroxide, a mixture that extracts oil. The Nantucket Historical Association has already completed plans to build a new museum with the sperm-whale skeleton as its centerpiece.

*   *   *

The island has changed greatly in recent decades. What was a generation or so ago a decrepit fishing village with a famous past and a few tourists in July and August has become a thriving summer resort. After a century of neglect, downtown Nantucket has been restored. Instead of sail lofts, grocers, and barbershops, however, the buildings now house art galleries, designer clothing boutiques, and T-shirt shops, all of which would have appalled the good gray Quakers of the whaling era. Spurning the cobblestoned elegance of Main Street, Nantucket's latest crop of millionaires build their 'trophy houses' by the beach. People still gaze from the tower of the Congregational church, but instead of scanning the horizon for oil-laden whaleships, the tourists—who have paid two dollars to sweat their way up the ninety-four steps to the belfry—watch high-speed ferries bringing cargoes of day-trippers from Cape Cod.

At the height of its influence more than 150 years ago, Nantucket had led the new nation toward its destiny as a world power. 'Let America add Mexico to Texas, and pile Cuba upon Canada,'

Melville wrote in *Moby-Dick*, 'let the English overswarm all India, and lay out their blazing banner from the sun; two thirds of this terraqueous globe are the Nantucketer's.' But if the island's inhabitants once ventured to the far corners of the world, today it seems as if the world has made its way to Nantucket. It is not whaling, of course, that brings the tourists to the island, but the romantic glorification of whaling—the same kind of myths that historically important places all across America have learned to shine and polish to their economic advantage. Yet, despite the circus (some have called it a theme park) that is modern Nantucket, the story of the *Essex* is too troubling, too complex to fit comfortably into a chamber of commerce brochure.

Unlike, say, Sir Ernest Shackleton and his men, who put themselves in harm's way then had the luck to live out an Edwardian fantasy of male camaraderie and heroism, Captain Pollard and his crew were simply attempting to make a living when disaster struck in the form of an eighty-five-foot whale. After that, they did the best they could. Mistakes were inevitably made. While Captain Pollard's instincts were sound, he did not have the strength of character to impose his will on his two younger officers. Instead of sailing to Tahiti and safety, they set out on an impossible voyage, wandering the watery desert of the Pacific until most of them were dead. Like the Dormer Party, the men of the *Essex* could have avoided disaster, but this does not diminish the extent of the men's sufferings, or their bravery and extraordinary discipline.

Some have praised the officers of the *Essex* for

288

their navigational skills, but it was their seamanship, their ability to keep their little boats upright and sailing for three months in the open ocean, that is even more astonishing. Captain Bligh and his men sailed almost as far, but they had the coast of Australia and a string of islands to follow, along with favorable winds. Bligh's voyage lasted forty-eight days; the *Essex* boats were out for almost twice as long.

From the beginning the Nantucketers in the crew took measures to provide one another with the greatest possible support without blatantly compromising the safety of the others. Although rations appear to have been distributed equally, it was almost as if the Nantucketers existed in a protective bubble as off-island crew members, first black then white, fell by the wayside until the Nantucketers had, in the case of Pollard's crew, no choice but to eat their own. The *Essex* disaster is not a tale of adventure. It is a tragedy that happens to be one of the greatest true stories ever told.

*   *   *

Evidence of the disaster and of the men who survived it can still be found on the streets of Nantucket. Captain Pollard's red-shingled house on Centre Street has long since become a gift shop. On the corner of the building a small plaque reads, 'Built by Captain William Brock in 1760. Later owned by Captain George Pollard Junior of the whaling ship *Essex*. Herman Melville spoke to Captain Pollard, whose story was the basis for *Moby-Dick*.' In an age when most of the island's historic houses have been renovated several times over, Owen Chase's home remains one of the last unchanged houses on Orange Street, its dark green trim and water-stained clapboards evoking the somber disquiet of the captain's final years. The boarding house where Thomas Nickerson once entertained his guests with tales of the *Essex* still stands on North Water Street—one of many buildings now associated with a large hotel.

The Whaling Museum devotes a small exhibit to the story of the ship that was sunk by a whale. There is a crew list from the *Essex*'s next-to-last voyage that includes the signatures of George Pollard, Owen Chase, Obed Hendricks, Benjamin Lawrence, and Thomas Chappel. There is Obed Macy's wharf book, in which the merchant and historian recorded the financial details involved in selling the *Essex*'s oil in 1819. For some reason, the ship's trunk found bobbing in the Pacific after the sinking is not on view. The one personal memento of the tragedy, probably used because it takes up so little display space in the crowded museum, is Benjamin Lawrence's tiny piece of twine.

But it is the newly acquired skeleton of the sperm whale, oozing oil in the Nantucket Historical Association shed, that speaks most powerfully to the tragedy of the whaleship *Essex*. The nourishing, lifesaving bones of their dead comrades were what Pollard and Ramsdell clung to so fiercely even after their ordeal had ended. And it is bones that Nantucketers cling to now, tangible reminders of a time when the island was devoted to the business of transforming whales into money.

In *Moby-Dick* Ishmael tells of seeing the skeleton of a sperm whale assembled in a grove of palm trees on a South Pacific island. 'How vain and

290

foolish,' he says, 'for timid untraveled man to try to comprehend aright this wondrous whale, by merely poring over his dead attenuated skeleton . . . Only in the heart of quickest perils; only when within the eddyings of his angry flukes; only on the profound unbounded sea, can the fully invested whale be truly and livingly found out.' But, as the survivors of the *Essex* came to know, once the end has been reached and all hope, passion, and force of will have been expended, the bones may be all that are left.

NOTES

For anyone wanting to know more about the *Essex* disaster, there is no better resource than Thomas Farel Heffernan's *Stove by a Whale: Owen Chase and the* Essex. In addition to the complete text of Chase's narrative, Heffernan's book includes (with the notable exception of the Nickerson narrative) all the relevant accounts left by other survivors. Heffernan's chapters of analysis—including discussions of what happened to the survivors and how the story of the *Essex* was disseminated—are models of scholarly rigor and readability. Edouard Stackpole's pamphlet *The Loss of the* Essex, *Sunk by a Whale in Mid-Ocean* provides a useful summary of the ordeal, as does his chapter about the disaster in *The Sea-Hunters*, an important book for anyone wanting to know more about Nantucket and whaling. Stackpole's introduction to Thomas Nickerson's *The Loss of the Ship 'Essex' Sunk by a Whale* published by the Nantucket Historical Association (NHA) is also essential. A new edition of Nickerson's narrative is now available from Penguin. Henry Carlisle's novel *The Jonah Man* contains a fascinating treatment of the *Essex* disaster. If Carlisle takes a novelist's license with some of the facts (Pollard, for example, is depicted as the son of a farmer, when it was Chase whose father was a 'yeoman'), his account provides a convincing portrayal of both the ordeal and the community of Nantucket.

The NHA's collections contain a myriad of documents relating to the *Essex*. In addition to

Obed Macy's 'wharf book,' in which he recorded how much the oil was sold for after the ship's return in April 1819 and how the money was divided among the owners and crew, there are documents detailing the leftover provisions that were sold at auction that month, along with costs associated with repairs performed in South America. From documents in the NHA's Edouard Stackpole collection, it is possible to recreate, in part, the makeup of the crews aboard the *Essex* prior to her last voyage.

I would also like to direct the reader's attention to the works of two underappreciated whalemen-turned-authors. Because he was often critical of the Quaker whalemen of Nantucket, William Comstock has been virtually ignored by island historians. Yet his *A Voyage to the Pacific, Descriptive of the Customs, Usages, and Sufferings on Board of Nantucket Whale-Ships* and *Life of Samuel Comstock* (William's brother and infamous leader of the bloody *Globe* mutiny) contain some of the best existing accounts of whaling in the early nineteenth century. William Hussey Macy was one of the most insightful and articulate whalemen Nantucket ever produced. Unfortunately, Macy's book, *There She Blows!* has been forgotten, even though several subsequent and widely read authors relied upon it for information. Originally promoted as a book for children, Macy's work is much more than that, providing a detailed and vivid account of a boy's introduction to both the town of Nantucket and life aboard a whaler.

PREFACE: FEBRUARY 23, 1821

My account of the rescue of the second *Essex* whaleboat is based largely on the description provided in Charles Murphey's 220-stanza poem published in 1877, a copy of which is at the NHA. Murphey was the third mate of the *Dauphin* and tells how the boat was sighted to leeward before the *Dauphin* bore down to determine its identity. Commodore Charles Goodwin Ridgely's journal records that the two *Essex* survivors were 'in a most wretched state, they were unable to move when found sucking the bones of their dead Mess mates, which they were loath to part with' (cited in Heffernan, p. 99). For an account of the discovery of Thomas Nickerson's manuscript, see Edouard Stackpole's foreword in the edition of the narrative published by the NHA in 1984 (p. 7) and Bruce Chadwick's 'The Sinking of the *Essex*' in *Sail*. A brief biography of Leon Lewis is in volume 2 of Albert Johannsen's *The House of Beadle and Adams* (pp. 183–86). Charles Philbrick's poem about the *Essex*, 'A Travail Past,' is in *Nobody Laughs, Nobody Cries* (pp. 111–27).

CHAPTER ONE: Nantucket

Thomas Nickerson's remarks are from his original holograph manuscript entitled *The Loss of the Ship 'Essex' Sunk by a Whale* (NHA Collection 106, Folder 1). In some instances, the spelling and punctuation have been adjusted to make

Nickerson's prose more accessible to a modern-day audience.

According to Walter Folger, Jr., a part-owner of the *Essex*, there were a total of seventy-seven 'ships and vessels employed in the whale fishery in 1819 from Nantucket' in both the Atlantic and Pacific Oceans, with seventy-five ships in the Pacific Ocean alone in 1820 (NHA Collection 118, Folder 71). In 'A Journal of the most remarkable events commenced and kept by Obed Macy' (NHA Collection 96, Journal 3, Nov. 13, 1814–April 27, 1822), Macy (who acted as the town's census taker in August 1820) records that 7,266 people lived on the island.

Josiah Quinsy compares Nantucket to Salem in 1801 (Crosby, p. 114). Joseph Sansom details the appearance of the Nantucket waterfront in 1811 (Crosby, p. 140); another good description of the wharves is found in William H. Macy's *There She Blows!* (pp. 12–15, 19–21). William Comstock's *Voyage to the Pack* (pp. 6–7) describes a voyage during the same time frame as the *Essex*. The account of the young Nantucket boys on the waterfront is from Macy (p. 20).

The *Essex*'s specifications are spelled out in her original 1799 register, describing her as having 'two decks and three masts and that her length is eighty seven feet, seven inches her breadth twenty five feet her depth twelve feet six inches and that she measures two hundred thirty eight tons; and seventy two ninety fifths that she is a square sterned ship has no Gallery and no figure head' (in Heffernan, p. 10). In a roster of Nantucket vessels that sailed in 1815, the *Essex* is listed as having left the island on July 13, with Daniel Russell as

Master, George Pollard, Jr., as second mate, and Owen Chase as part of the crew; she returned on November 27, 1816, and sailed again on June 8, 1817 (NHA Collection 335, Folder 976). Her complete crew list for the 1817 voyage is in NHA Collection 15, Folder 57.

In his invaluable *Nantucket Scrap-Basket* (which is greatly indebted to William H. Macy's earlier *There She Blows!*), William F. Macy provides this definition of a walk: 'A raised platform on the roof of many old Nantucket houses, from which to look off to the sea. *Never* called "Widow's Walk," "Captain's Walk," or "Whale Walk," as often written nowadays [in 1916], but *always* just "the walk." Writers and others please note.' Obed Macy mentions the comet in his journal on July 7 and 14, 1819. The *New Bedford Mercury* speaks of the comet in its July 9 and July 23 editions. A part-owner of the *Essex* is mentioned in connection with the comet in a letter (dated July 16) from a contributor in Plymouth. 'Mr. Walter Folger, of Nantucket, has been here this week, in attendance on the Court, as a witness, and has here continued his observations on the comet, which had been commenced at home. He brought with him a sextant and a small telescope.' The sea serpent is mentioned in the June 18 and August 6 editions of the *Mercury*. I talk about the development of Indian debt servitude on Nantucket in *Abram's Eyes* (pp. 157–60). See also Daniel Vickers 'The First Whalemen of Nantucket,' *William and Mary Quarterly*.

For an account of Burke's speech about the American whale fishery, see my 'Every Wave Is a Fortune': Nantucket Island and the Making of an

American Icon' in *New England Quarterly*. William Comstock begins his description of a whaling voyage on a Nantucket whaler with a pointed discussion of the way in which islands foster a unique cultural attitude: 'Islands are said to be nurseries of Genius, an assertion which would be wonderfully supported, if we could prove Greece and Rome to have once been two snug little detached parcels of land, situated in the midst of the Mediterranean Sea; and Germany a resurrection of the quiescent Atlanta. I am rather inclined to attribute this opinion to the overweening patriotism of our neighbor, John Bull, whose sea washed isle produced better things than all the rest of the world can afford; although, perhaps America can match him in thunder and lightning' *(Voyage to the Pack* p. 3). Ralph Waldo Emerson was on Nantucket in 1847; he also records in his journal 'A strong national feeling' (vol. X, p. 63) on the island.

In his *History*, Obed Macy tells of the whaling prophecy and the appearance of Ichabod Paddock (p. 45), Hussey's killing of the first sperm whale (p. 48), and the exhibition of a dead whale on the Nantucket waterfront in 1810 (p. 151). J. Hector St. John de Crèvecoeur described Nantucket as an oil-fertilized sandbank in *Letters from an American Farmer (p.* 142). For an account of the coming of Quakerism to Nantucket, see my *Away Offshore (pp.* 78–87) and also *Quaker Nantucket* by Robert Leach and Peter Gow (pp. 13–30). Peleg Folger's poem is quoted in Obed Macy's *History* (pp. 279–81).

Welcome Greene was the Quaker visitor to Nantucket in 1821 who made the disparaging remark about the state of the streets and observed the use of quarterboards as fences. Joseph Sansom wrote about the naming of the town's streets (Crosby, p. 142). Walter Folger's comparison of the community to a family is in Crosby (p. 97); Obed Macy's remarks concerning the Nantucketers' 'consanguinity' is in his *History* (p. 66). For a more detailed description of downtown Nantucket, see my *Away Offshore* (pp. 7–10); see also Edouard Stackpole's *Rambling Through the Streets and Lanes of Nantucket.* According to an article in the *Nantucket Inquirer and Mirror* (February 14, 1931), a grand total of 134 sea captains have lived on Orange Street.

In 1807 James Freeman remarked that 'not more than one half of the males and two thirds of the females, who attend the Friends' meetings, are members of the society' (Crosby, p. 132). Charles Murphey (the same man who was on the *Dauphin* when the *Essex* boat was discovered) wrote the poem about gazing upon the women during a Quaker meeting; it is in his journal of a voyage on the ship *Maria*, 1832–1836, on microfilm at the NHA. In the same poem Murphey tells of being 'With girls o'er mill hills promenading.' The Nantucketer William Coffin, father of the man who probably ghostwrote Owen Chase's narrative of the *Essex*, spoke of how rarely he strayed from town in 1793 (NHA Collection 150, Folder 78).

Walter Folger tells of Nantucket children learning Wampanoag whaling phrases 'as soon as they can talk' (Crosby, p. 97); the anecdote about the boy harpooning the family cat is in William F. Macy's *ScrapBasket* (p. 23); on Nantucket's secret women's society, see Joseph Hart's *Miriam Coffin*,

299

where he states, 'The daughter of a whale-fisherman loses *caste*, and degrades herself in the eyes of her acquaintance, if she unites her destiny to a landsman' (p. 251). Although the poem that begins 'Death to the living' had been in common use long before, it appears in a sequence of toasts delivered at a banquet in celebration of the voyage of the *Loper* in 1830 *(Nantucket Inquirer*, September 25). The statistics concerning widows and fatherless children appear in Edward Byers's *Nation of Nantucket* (p. 257). The gravestone inscriptions for Nickerson's parents are recorded in NHA Collection 115, Box II. All genealogical information concerning the Nantucket crew members of the *Essex* comes from the NHA's newly computerized Eliza Barney Genealogy; information about the Nickersons is from *The Nickerson Family* (Nickerson Family Association, 1974).

In his *Letters from an American Farmer*, Crèvecoeur speaks of Nantucket's 'superior wives' and their 'incessant visiting' (p. 157), as well as their use of opium (p. 160) and the effects of marriage (p. 158). Lucretia Mott's comments concerning the socializing of husbands and wives on Nantucket is in Margaret Hope Bacon's *Valiant Friend* (p. 17). Eliza Brock's journal containing the 'Nantucket Girl's Song' is at the NHA; she kept the journal while on a whaling voyage with her husband from May 1853 to 1856. I discuss the validity of Crèvecoeur's remarks about opium use in 'The Nantucket Sequence in Crèvecoeur's *Letters from an American Farmer*' in the *New England Quarterly*. For a discussion of he's-at-homes, see my *Away Offshore* (p. 257); for an account of the discovery of a he's-at-home on Nantucket, see Thomas Congdon's 'Mrs. Coffin's Consolation' in *Forbes M.*

Crèvecoeur records, 'I was much surprised at the disagreeable smell which struck me in many parts of the town; it is caused by the whale oil and is unavoidable; the neatness peculiar to these people can neither remove or prevent it' (p. 111). The smell apparently emanated from right-whale oil as opposed to sperm oil; see Clifford Ashley's *The Yankee Whaler* (p. 56). Owen Chase in his narrative of the *Essex* disaster claims that the upperworks of the *Essex* were entirely overhauled prior to her leaving in the summer of 1819. William H. Macy describes ships being coppered in Nantucket Harbor (p. 14). On the life span of a whaleship, see *In Pursuit of Leviathan* by Davis et al. (p. 240). Roger Hambidge, shipwright at Mystic Seaport, spoke to me about the phenomenon of iron sickness in whaleships and stated that twenty years was about the average life of a ship, a statement corroborated by the statistical analysis in Davis et al. (p. 231). Obed Macy's concerns about the condition of whaleships is in a January 1822 entry in his journal. A listing of Nantucket vessels and their owners in 1820 has Gideon Folger and Sons as owning both the *Essex* and the *Aurora* (NHA Collection 335, Folder 976).

William Comstock makes the derogatory remark concerning Nantucket Quakers in *The Life of Samuel Comstock* (pp. 39–40), where he also speaks of the owners' tendency to underprovision their ships (p. 73). Davis et al. have calculated the return on investment shipping agents typically received in New Bedford (*In Pursuit of Leviathan*,

p. 411); Nantucket owners in the boom year of 1819 were undoubtedly reaping a similar, if not higher, profit. The description of poor economic times on the mainland is in the *New Bedford Mercury* (June 4, 1819), which quotes from an article in the *Baltimore Federal Republican*. The comings and goings of the Nantucket whaling fleet can be traced in Alexander Starbuck's *History of Nantucket* (pp. 428–33).

William H. Macy speaks of the 'grand plaza of Nantucket' (p. 15) and how the island's boys would taunt the green hands (p. 21). William F. Macy defines 'watching the pass' (p. 140); he also defines 'foopaw' (p. 126), 'rantum scoot' (p. 134), 'manavelins' (p. 131), and the idiom used to describe someone who is cross-eyed (p. 121). William Comstock tells of the whittling code on Nantucket (*Voyage to the Pacific*, p. 68). More than fifty years earlier, Crèvecoeur remarked on the Nantucketers' almost compulsive need to whittle: '[T]hey are never idle. Even if they go to the market-place, which is (if I may be allowed the expression) the coffee-house of the town, either to transact business or to converse with their friends, they always have a piece of cedar in their hands, and while they are talking, they will, as it were, instinctively employ themselves in converting it into something useful, either in making bungs or spoils for their oil casks, or other useful articles' (p. 156). Joseph Sansom tells of how everyone on the island used sea phrases (Crosby, p. 143). A sampling of the unique pronunciations of Nantucketers is recorded in 'Vocabulary of English Words, with the corresponding terms as used by the Whalemen' in *The Life of Samuel Comstock* (p. 57).

The green hand Addison Pratt tells of how he was examined by the shipowner and the captain (p. 12); William H. Macy speaks of how the owners and captains judged the men by their eyes and build (p. 19). William Comstock tells of green hands whose ignorance led them to insist on the longest lay possible (*Voyage to the Pack*, pp. 11–12). William H. Macy explains how first-time captains were the lowest in the pecking order in finding a crew (p. 19).

I have used the time frame described by Nickerson to calculate when the *Essex* was floated over the Nantucket Bar. Pratt provides a detailed description of the loading of a Nantucket whaleship during this period (p. 13). According to Richard Henry Dana, 'The average allowance, in merchant vessels, is six pounds of bread a week, and three quarts of water, and one pound and a half of beef, or one and a quarter of pork, a day, to each man' (*The Seaman's Friend*, p. 135). William H. Macy tells of how a whaleship was always full, whether it was with provisions or oil (pp. 33–34).

It is difficult to determine exactly how many whaleboats the *Essex* was originally equipped with since Nickerson and Chase seem to disagree on the subject. She had a minimum of two spare boats; that it wasn't uncommon for a ship of this period to have three spares is indicated by Comstock. 'Two spare boats, placed on a frame over head, shaded the quarter deck, while another, placed on spars which projected over the stern, was ready to be cleared at a moment's warning' (*Voyage to the Pacific*, p. 14).

Pratt describes taking a packet from Boston to Nantucket (p. 11). According to James and Lois

Horton, there were three African American communities in Boston at this time: the 'black' section of Beacon Hill in West Boston (where the Museum of Afro-American History is now located); to the north in the area now occupied by the Massachusetts General Hospital; and near the wharves of the North End. The Hortons say that the North End neighborhood 'had once been the largest black neighborhood in the city,' but was losing ground to the other areas as of 1830 (pp. 4–5). In Dana's *Two Years Before the Mast*, there is a black cook whose wife lives on Robinson's Alley (between Hanover and Unity streets) in the North End (pp. 179–80). For a summary discussion of the relative equality enjoyed by blacks on shipboard, see W. Jeffrey Bolster's *Black Jacks* (pp. 1–6). James Freeman provides the 1807 description of how blacks had replaced Indians as a workforce in the Nantucket whale fishery (Crosby, p. 135). Comstock tells of the harsh treatment of African Americans in *The Life of Samuel Comstock* (pp. 37–38). William H. Macy claims that the packet delivering green hands from New York to Nantucket was commonly referred to as 'the Slaver' (pp. 9, 17).

William F. Macy defines gam as a 'social visit and talk. Originally this term was applied to a school of whales, and its use by the whalemen is doubtless derived from that source. Whaleships meeting at sea often hove to, and the captains would visit back and forth during the time the ships were in company. Under certain conditions the crews were allowed the privilege also' (p. 126). At the onset of his voyage, the green hand narrator of William H. Macy's *There She Blows!* feels 'that pride in my floating home springing up within me, which every seaman feels for his vessel' (p. 36). According to Ashley, a sailor's mattress, filled with either corn husks or straw, was called a 'Donkey's Breakfast' (p. 54). On August 16, 1819 (four days after the *Essex* left Nantucket), Obed Macy recorded: 'The grasshoppers have destroyed the greater part of the turnips'; he also mentions them in September. Information concerning the *Chili* comes from Starbuck (p. 432).

CHAPTER TWO: **Knockdown**

The letter written by the *Essex* owners to Captain Daniel Russell is at the NHA. The marriage of George Pollard and Mary Ridden (June 17, 1819) is recorded in the Church Records of the South Congregational (now Unitarian) Church on Nantucket, as are the marriages of Owen Chase (the first mate of the *Essex*) and Peggy Gardner (on April 28, 1819) and Matthew Joy (second mate) and Nancy Slade (August 7, 1817). Curiously, the minister was paid $2.00 for Joy's marriage, $1.50 for Chase's, and $1.25 for Pollard's.

For a description of the division of duties among a ship's officers while weighing anchor, see Richard Henry Dana's *Seaman's Friend* (pp. 139–40). Information on Captain Pollard's appearance comes from Joseph Warren Phinney's 'Nantucket, Far Away and Long Ago,' in *Historic Nantucket* (p. 29), with notes by his granddaughter Diana Taylor Brown, to whom I am grateful for providing me with a copy of Phinney's original manuscript. Owen Chase's appearance is based on information in the crew list of the *Florida* (his first ship after the *Essex):* 'five feet, ten inches tall, dark complexioned and brown haired' (Heffernan, p. 120). In the Nantucket Registry of Deeds Grantee Book 22 (p. 262), Owen Chase's father, Judah, is listed as a 'husbandman.' Owen Chase's remarks concerning the number of voyages required to become a commander are from his narrative, as are all subsequent quotations attributed to him. While Chase claimed it took just two voyages to qualify to be a captain, the evidence suggests that four was the usual minimum number of voyages (Stuart Frank, personal communication, Oct. 25, 1999). Clifford Ashley, in *The Yankee Whaler*, describes the use of a whaler's windlass (pp. 49–50), as does Falconer in his *Marine Dictionary.*

Reuben Delano, in *The Wanderings and Adventures of Reuben Delano*, speaks of the dramatic sea change that occurred among the officers once a Nantucket whaleship left the island (p. 14). William Comstock defines 'spit-fire' in *The Life of Samuel Comstock* (p. 71); he also tells of how Nantucketers stuck together aboard a whaleship (p. 37). William H. Macy describes the competition among the officers when it came to picking whaleboat crews (p. 39); he also speculates that Noah may have been the first captain to address his crew (p. 40). Pratt's comments about blacks being relegated to the forecastle of a Nantucket whaleship is in his *Journals (pp.* 14–15). Richard Henry Dana tells of his preference for the forecastle in *Two Years Before the Mast* (p. 95).

W. Jeffrey Bolster speaks of 'yarning' and other activities in the forecastle in *Black Jacks* (pp. 88–89).

William H. Macy describes the seasickness cure

306

common among Nantucketers (p. 19). My thanks to Don Russell, a descendant of *Essex* captain Daniel Russell, who mentioned to me a family tradition concerning this same cure. According to Ashley, the lookouts positioned themselves inside hoops installed on the fore and main royal-masts chest-high above the crosstrees (p. 49). However, at this relatively early period in the fishery, there is no evidence of hoops having been installed on the masts of Nantucket whaleships. In *Voyage to the Pack*, Comstock writes: 'Two jack cross trees were made by the captain, and placed over the top gallant heads, one at the fore, the other at the main. One man was stationed on each, to look out for whales, and relieved every two hours. One of the boatsteerers was kept continually aloft with the man on the main top gallant cross trees, so that while one watched, the other covertly slept' (p. 20).

My discussion of studding sails and the knockdown is based largely on John Harland's invaluable *Seamanship in the Age of Sail.* According to Harland, the danger of dipping a studding-sail boom into the water even applied to a topgallant studding sail. Darcy Lever's 1819 seamanship guide provides a detailed and illustrated description of taking in studding sails (pp. 82–83); he also has a section entitled 'A Ship on Her Beam Ends' (pp. 96–97). Benjamin Franklin's chart of the Gulf Stream is in Everett Crosby's *Nantucket in Print* (pp. 88–89). According to Harland, when shortening sail, '[t]he most lofty, and the most cumbersome sail was got off first, ideally before the squall hit. Studdingsails (particularly topgallant and lower) . . . were particularly at risk if the ship were caught unprepared' (p. 222). The naval saying

307

concerning squalls is in Harland (p. 221), as are the other quoted sources.

Harland discusses what happens as a heeling ship approaches the point of no return. '[W]ith greater angles, the righting arm increases rapidly with the angle up to about 45 degrees, after which it decreases and at a certain critical angle, disappears' (p. 43). In his nautical dictionary Falconer provides this definition of 'beam-ends': 'A ship is said to be on her beam-ends when she inclines very much on one side, so that her beams approach to a vertical position; hence also a person lying down is said to be on his beam-ends.' Addison Pratt tells of a knockdown off Cape Horn: '[W]e were knocked down upon our beam-ends by a heavy squall of wind. All hands were called to reduce sail, as the decks . . . were nearly perpendicular, the leescuppers being knee deep under water. All the way we could get fore and aft was by holding onto the weather rail, the vessel was pitching heavily and the night being very dark' (p. 17). My thanks to Chuck Gieg, who shared with me his personal experience of a knockdown on the training ship *Albatross* in the 1960s (the basis for the movie *White Squall*) . Harland discusses the perils of a ship sailing backward (pp. 70, 222).

CHAPTER THREE: **First Blood**

The American Consul at Maio in the Cape Verde Islands may have known the *Essex*'s second mate. Both Ferdinand Gardner and Matthew Joy were from Nantucket families that had moved to Hudson, New York, the improbable location of a

Nantucket-spawned whaling port started in the aftermath of the Revolution.

My description of a whale hunt is based on many accounts, but primarily those provided by William H. Macy, Clifford Ashley, Willits Ansel in *The Whaleboat*, and the remarkable amount of information assembled in the 'Whaleboat Handbook' used by the Mystic Seaport Whaleboat demonstration staff. My thanks to Mary K. Bercaw for making the handbook available to me. The description of how the sighting of a whale 'enlivened' the crew is from Charles Nordhoff's *Whaling and Fishing* (p. 100). Ansel speaks of the roles of the different oarsmen (p. 26) and the relative speeds of a whaleboat and a sperm whale (pp. 1617). Ashley tells of whaleboat crews bent on 'whaling for glory': 'They raced and jockeyed for position, and in a close finish, with boats jammed together at the flank of a whale, have been known deliberately to foul one another; to dart harpoons across each other's boats, imperiling both the boats and the lives of all concerned, and then to ride blithely off, fast to the whale, waving their hands or thumbing noses to their unfortunate comrades struggling in the water' (p. 110). Comstock recounts the mate's exhortation to his whaleboat crew in *Voyage to the Pacific* (pp. 23–24). In 'Behavior of the Sperm Whale,' Caldwell, Caldwell, and Rice record a whaleman's observation that the spout of a whale smelled 'fetid' and stung a man's skin
(p. 699). Ansel relates Charles Beetle's account of a novice boatsteerer fainting at the prospect of harpooning a whale (p. 21).

According to Clifford Ashley, who shipped out

on a whaling voyage in the early twentieth century, sperm whales were capable of dragging whaleboats along at bursts of up to twenty-five miles per hour. He adds, 'I have been in motor speed boats at better than forty-five miles per hour, and found it a tame performance after a "Nantucket Sleighride"' (p. 80).

Francis Olmsted describes the use of a spade to cripple a fleeing sperm whale (p. 22). The lance had a line attached to the end of it, enabling the mate to retrieve it after every throw (Ashley, p. 87). Caldwell et al. speak of dying whales vomiting 'pieces of squid the size of whaleboats' (p. 700). Enoch Cloud's horrified response to the death of a whale occurred during a voyage in the 1850s and is in *Enoch's Voyage* (p. 53). Ansel speaks of dead whales being towed back to the ship headfirst (p. 23).

In his *History*, Obed Macy provides a step-by-step description of cutting up (including the removal of the head) and boiling a whale (pp. 220–24). According to Clifford Ashley, early cutting stages were 'short fore-and-aft planks hung overside, one forward and one aft of the gangway' (*The Yankee Whaler*, p. 97). Just how greasy the deck of a whaleship could become is indicated by Charles Nordhoff: 'The oil washes from one side to the other, as the ship lazily rolls in the seaway, and the safest mode of locomotion is sliding from place to place, on the seat of your pantaloons' (p. 129); Nordhoff also describes the stench of the tryworks smoke. Davis et al. speak of ambergris (*In Pursuit of Leviathan*, pp. 29–30). According to Obed Macy, 'The ambergris is generally discovered by probing the intestines with a long pole' (p. 224). Although whalemen would soon be pioneering the folk art of scrimshaw by carving designs on the teeth of sperm whales, it is highly unlikely that the crew of the *Essex* in 1819 were saving their whales' teeth (Stuart Frank, personal communication, July 1999). J. Ross Browne recounts the 'murderous appearance' of a whaleship at night (p. 63). William H. Macy gives the description of appropriate 'trying-out clothes' (p. 80).

Richard Henry Dana tells of how a crew's morale can deteriorate in *Two Years Before the Mast* (p. 94). For a discussion of the differences in shipboard fare served to those in the cabin and the forecastle, see Sandra Oliver's *Saltwater Foodways* (pp. 97–99, 113). Oliver provides the information concerning the average caloric intake of a sailor in the nineteenth century (p. 94). Moses Morrell was the green hand who lamented his gradual starvation aboard a Nantucket whaleship; his journal is at the NHA. If Pollard appears to have overreacted to his men's complaints about food, it was nothing compared to the response of Captain Worth aboard the *Globe:* 'When any man complained to Captain Worth that he was suffering with hunger, he would tell him to eat iron hoops; and several times gagged the complainants' mouths with pump-bolts' (*Life of Samuel Comstock*, p. 73).

CHAPTER FOUR: **The Lees of Fire**

Captain Bligh abandoned his attempt to round Cape Horn after thirty days (the time it took the whaleship *Essex* to double the Horn); that the decision was made under extreme duress is made clear by Sir John Barrow: '[T]he ship began to complain, and required pumping every hour; the decks became so leaky that the commander was obliged to allot the great cabin to those who had wet berths' (p. 41). David Porter tells of rounding the Horn in his *Journal* (p. 84). Although the *Beaver* was the first Nantucket whaleship to enter the Pacific, the *Emilia*, a British ship captained by James Shield, was the first whaler to round the Horn in 1788 (Slevin, p. 52).

Captain Swain's words about the scarcity of whales are cited in Edouard Stackpole's *The Sea Hunters* (p. 266). Obed Macy's mention of the need for a new whaling ground was recorded on September 28, 1819; his journal also reveals that he followed the political situation in South America closely.

Robert McNally characterizes the whalemen's attitude toward whales as a 'tub of lard' in *So Remorseless a Havoc* (p. 172). Charles Nordhoff refers to the old whalemen's delight in trying out (p. 131), while William H. Macy speaks of how 'boiling' inspired thoughts of home (p. 87). The events that occurred on Nantucket in December 1819 are from Obed Macy's journal. William H. Macy testified to how long it took for mail to reach the Pacific: '[N]ews from home even a year old was heartily welcomed; while the advent of a whaler five or six months out was a perfect windfall' (p. 154). For an account of the discovery of the Offshore Ground, see Stackpole (pp. 266–67).

Francis Olmsted's description of the delights of Atacames (pp. 161–63) includes an interesting account of a chapel: 'Down the sides of the altar, the drippings of sperm candles used in the service, had run like the stalactites of some subterranean cavern' (p. 171).

As far as I know, this is the first time that the name of the deserter, Henry Dewitt, has appeared in print. The name is recorded in a crew list that seems to have been written down soon after Pollard left on his subsequent voyage in the fall of 1821 (Pollard is listed as 'Capt. Two Brothers'). The list includes all twenty of the previously known *Essex* crew members plus 'Henry De Wit—runaway' (NHA Collection 64, Scrapbook 20). In his discussion of the number of shipkeepers aboard the *Beaver* in 1791, Clifford Ashley makes the claim that 'two men would have been insufficient to handle' a ship of 240 tons (p. 60).

William H. Macy records the unique pronunciation of Galapagos (p. 167). Colnett's account of his explorations in the Pacific include a diagram of how to cut up a sperm whale that Obed Macy would use in his *History*; Colnett describes the Galapagos as a sperm-whale nursery (*A Voyage to . . . the South Paces Ocean*, p. 147). My summary of Hal Whitehead's observations of sperm-whale society are taken from his articles 'Social Females and Roving Males' and 'The Behavior of Mature Male Sperm Whales on the Galapagos Islands Breeding Grounds.' Whitehead did not see whales copulating in the Galapagos grounds. 'That we never saw copulation is not surprising,' he writes. 'Although there are reports in the literature of sperm whales being observed copulating, these reports are few, somewhat contradictory, and not always convincing' (p. 696). Whitehead cites a description made by A. A. Berzin of a male approaching a female from underneath (p. 694).

The account of repairing a leak on the *Aurora* is in Stackpole's *The Sea-Hunters* (pp. 305–6). According to Reginald Hegarty, 'Sea-boring worms could not penetrate metal but if a small piece of copper was accidentally torn off, quite a section of sheathing would soon be so honeycombed that it would wash off, taking more copper with it. The planking would then be exposed and in a short time a section of planking would have its strength eaten away' (p. 60). For an exhaustive description of how leaks were repaired on wooden vessels, see Harland (pp. 303–4).

Herman Melvilles description of the Galapagos appears in 'The Encantadas' (p. 126). On the tortoise's cool body temperature, see Charles Townsend's 'The Galapagos Tortoises' (p. 93); Townsend also speaks of 'Port Royal Tom' (p. 86). For a summary of the history of the post office on Charles Island, see Slevin's 'The Galapagos Islands' (pp. 108–11). Charles Townsend records that 'the terrapin on Charles Island were exterminated very early' (p.89).

CHAPTER FIVE: **The Attack**

My description of the scale of the Pacific Ocean is based largely on Ernest Dodge's *Islands and Empires* (p. 7); see also Charles Olson's *Call Me Ishmael*, especially his concluding chapter 'Pacific Man' (pp. 113–19). For an account of the whalers' activities in the western Pacific in the early nineteenth century, see Stackpole's *Sea-Hunters* (pp. 254–56). Hezekiah Coffin's death in the vicinity of Timor is referred to in Mary Hayden

Russell's journal of a whaling voyage; after mentioning the island of 'Aboyna,' she writes: '[Here] your dear Father in a former voyage had the misfortune to bury his Mate, Hezekiah Coffin, and where he only escap'd the jaws of death himself' (NHA Collection 83). For the islands listed in Pollard's copy of Bowditch's Navigator, see Heffernan's *Stove by a Whale* (pp. 243–46). Stackpole tells of the first whalers at Hawaii and the Society Islands in The *Sea-Hunters* (pp. 275–89).

William Comstock's description of a mate taking over the harpoon from his boatsteerer is in *Voyage to the Pacific* (pp. 24–25). Niekerson's narrative claims that Chase was at the steering oar—not, as Chase claims, at the bow with the harpoon in his hand—during their last two attempts to fasten to whales. In this instance I have decided to trust Chase's account, although the possibility exists that he was, in fact, at the steering oar and that the ghostwriter introduced an error. Adding to the uncertainty is an earlier statement Chase makes in his narrative: 'There are common sailors, boat-steerers, and harpooners: the last of these is the most honorable and important. It is in this station, that all the capacity of the young sailor is elicited; on the dexterous management of the harpoon, the line, and the lance, and in the adventurous positions which he takes alongside of his enemy, depends almost entirely the successful issue of his attack' (p. 17). Contrary to what Chase states in this passage, it was the boatsteerer who threw the harpoon and the mate or boatheader (never called a harpooner, a term used instead to describe the boatsteerer) who was considered the 'most honorable and important.' This may be, once again, a case of the ghostwriter's confusing the assigned roles in a whaleboat, but for the purposes of this narrative I have taken it to be Chase's description of the role he created for himself on his whaleboat: a mate who threw both the harpoon and the lance and directed the boatsteerer from the bow.

D.W. Rice in 'Sperm Whale' (pp. 203–4) describes a sperm whale's diving habits and mentions the whaler's rule of thumb for judging how long a sperm whale would be underwater. Obed Macy tells of the sinking of the *Union* in his History (pp. 230–35). Chase and Nickerson have very different versions of what happened after the first whale attack. Chase claims that the ship began to sink almost immediately. Nickerson makes no mention of the *Essex* taking on water after the first collision and is careful to point out that Chase had the opportunity to lance the whale after the first attack, something Chase chose not to mention. I have decided to side with Nickerson, who clearly felt compelled to correct the first mate's account in his own narrative. Both Chase (p. 31) and Herman Melville in 'The Battering Ram' chapter of *Moby-Dick* discuss how a sperm whale is well adapted for attacking a ship head-on. An article in the *Sydney Gazette*, apparently based on information provided by the three *Essex* survivors who elected to stay on Henderson Island and were later taken to Australia, states: 'The vessel was going at the rate of 5 knots, but such was the force when [the whale] struck the ship, which was under the cat-head, that the vessel had stern-way, at the rate of 3 or 4 knots; the consequence was, that the sea rushed into the cabin windows, every man on deck was knocked down, and worse than all, the bows were stove completely in' (Heffernan, p. 240). A pamphlet written after the disaster by the boatsteerer Thomas Chappel also refers to the ship being driven backward; Chappel claims the whale 'knocked off a great part of the false keel' when it bumped the ship with its back (Heffernan, p. 218). Although neither account mentions the whale's tail still moving after the second impact—in effect pushing the ship backward after the collision had stopped the ship—this appears to be the only way to reconcile Chase's relatively low estimate of the whale's speed at impact (six knots) with the other accounts of the ship being driven backward.

Hal Whitehead discusses how whalers would seek out bulls in 'The Behavior of Mature Sperm Whales on the Galapagos Islands Breeding Grounds' (p. 696). Concerning the size reached by large bull sperm whales, Alexander Starbuck writes in his *History of the American Whale Fishery*, 'Sperm whales which yield 100 barrels are considered very large, but this yield is occasionally exceeded' (p. 155). He then quotes Davis's *Nimrod of the Sea*, in which a whale of ninety feet that yielded 137 barrels is mentioned; Davis also claimed that a New Bedford whaler took a sperm whale on the Offshore Ground that produced 145 barrels of oil. Starbuck asserts that in 1876 the bark *Wave* out of New Bedford took a sperm whale that yielded 162 barrels and 5 gallons of oil (p. 155). Clearly an eighty-five-foot bull sperm whale is within the realm of possibility.

For a detailed discussion of the brain size and intelligence of sperm whales, see Carl Zimmer's *At*

317

the Water's Edge (pp. 219–26). Richard Ellis, in *Men and Whales*, also speaks eloquently about a sperm whale's brain (p. 29). Hal Whitehead and Linda Weilgart in 'Moby's Click' talk about how whales use clicks both for echolocation and communication; they tell of sperm whales being known as 'carpenter fish' (p. 64). Linda Weilgart, Hal Whitehead, and Katherine Payne write about the remarkable similarities between sperm whales and elephants in 'A Colossal Convergence.' The description of the battle between the two bull sperm whales is in Caldwell et al. (pp. 692–93). In Henry Carlisle's novel *The Jonah Man*, Pollard theorizes that the whale heard Chase's hammering through the air: 'Carried on the easterly wind, the clatter of hammers could be heard more than a mile to westward' (p. 106). But, as Whitehead confirms in a personal e-mail communication, the sperm whale would have most likely heard the hammering through the water, the medium to which its ears were best adapted and which transmits sounds with a much greater efficiency than air. In fact, the whale that attacked the *Essex* would have also heard the chaos being wreaked by Pollard and Joy in the shoal of sperm whales several miles to leeward. While this might seem to corroborate Chase's belief that the whale was 'fired with revenge for their sufferings,' Whitehead points out that 'it is important to understand that we now know that relationships between large male sperm whales and groups of females are brief and impermanent. Thus . . . it is very unlikely that the male had any attachment to the females being killed' (personal communication, August 5, 1998).

Whitehead theorizes that the whale may have

first struck the *Essex* by mistake and that 'this contact greatly disturbed the animal, resulting in the second event, which does read like an "attack"' (personal communication, August 5, 1998). Many whalemen in the nineteenth century apparently agreed with Whitehead. According to a remark concerning the *Essex* (from the *North American Review*) cited by Francis Olmsted in *Incidents of a Whaling Voyage:* 'But no other instance is known, in which the mischief is supposed to have been malignantly designed by the assailant [the whale], and most experienced whalers believe that even in this case, the attack was not intentional' (p. 145).

Other whalemen, however, thought differently. An old Nantucket captain in William H. Macy's *There She Blows.* states: 'We have all heard of the *Essex* affair . . . I remember it well, for I was cruising on *Chili* at that time in the *Plutarch*, and from the statements of the survivors, it is plain enough that the whale went to work deliberately and with malice prepense, as the lawyers would say, to destroy the ship' (p. 133).

My description of how the *Essex* was constructed is based on several sources. John Currier in 'Historical Sketch of Ship Building on the Merrimac River' claims that ships constructed in Amesbury at the time of the *Essex* were 'built almost entirely of oak; their decks alone being of native white pine. The ribs, planking, ceiling, beams and knees were cut from oak timber, floated down the river or drawn by ox teams from within a radius of ten or fifteen miles' (p. 34). My thanks to Roger Hambidge and Ted Kaye of Mystic Seaport for directing me to a specifications list of the whaleship *Hector* in Albert Cook Church's *Whale*

319

Ships and Whaling (pp. 174–79). Thanks also to Mark Starr at the Shipyard Documentation Office of Mystic Seaport for providing me with the specifications of the *Charles W. Morgan*. I also relied on Reginald Hegarty's *Birth of a Whaleship*.

My thanks to Professor Ted Ducal of the Physics Department at Wellesley College for speaking to me about the physics of whales in general and the wreck of the *Essex* in particular. My thanks also to Peter Smith, a naval architect at Hinckley Yachts, who calculated the potential forces involved in a collision between an 80-ton whale and a 238-ton ship, and the strength of a whaleship's construction (personal communications, December 18 and 23, 1998).

CHAPTER SIX: **The Plan**

In *Survival Psychology*, John Leach writes of the apathy that commonly affects survivors in the immediate aftermath of a disaster, known as the 'recoil period' (pp. 24–37, 129–134). In 'Disaster: Effects of Mental and Physical State,' Warren Kinston and Rachel Rosser discuss the reluctance of survivors to leave the scene of a disaster (p. 444). Concerning whaleboats in the early nineteenth century, Erik Ronnberg, Jr., states, 'Depictions of boats from this period—in the form of paintings, lithographs, and logbook sketches—make it clear that rowing was the usual if not exclusive form of propulsion. Those sources that do show whaleboats under sail indicate that the sprit rig was most favored and the boats were guided with a steering oar with no rudder in evidence. This compounded by the lack of a centerboard, would have severely handicapped the boats' abilities to sail to windward; indeed, this rig and steering configuration would be efficient only in the pursuit of whales downwind' (*To Build a Whaleboat*, p . 1). As Ronnberg also points out, these early boats were of clinker or lapstrake construction, not the batten-seam construction that typified boats in later years. Instead of being white (as were almost all whaleboats by the middle of the nineteenth century), the *Essex* boats were probably quite colorful—perhaps dark blue and red, the color of the ship's flag; see Ansel (p. 95).

Caleb Crain's 'Lovers of Human Flesh: Homosexuality and Cannibalism in Melville's Novels' contains an excellent synopsis of early-nineteenth-century accounts of Marquesan cannibalism and homosexuality (p. 30). For a discussion of the kinds of stories about native cannibalism that were told by the seamen of the era, see Gananath Obeyesekere's 'Cannibal Feasts in Nineteenth-Century Figi: Seamen's Yarns and the Ethnographic Imagination,' in *Cannibalism and the Colonial World*, edited by Francis Barker, Peter Hulme, and Margaret Iversen. There was also a disturbing racial aspect to the rumors of cannibalism that sailors swapped in the forecastles of whaleships. A Maori chief from New Zealand who had been brought to London in 1818 insisted that 'black men had a much more agreeable flavor than white' (in Tannahill's *Flesh and Blood*, p. 151). Suggesting that this was accepted as a fact among Nantucket whalemen was the experience of Captain Benjamin Worth off the coast of New Zealand in 1805. Worth told of how when a gale threatened to drive his ship ashore, the blacks in the crew begged him to do everything he could to make for open ocean since 'the natives preferred Negro flesh to that of the white man' (in Stackpole's *The Sea-Hunters*, pp. 399–400). The officers of the *Essex* were between voyages when the stories about the peaceful state of the natives of Nukahivah appeared in the *New Bedford Mercury* (April 28, 1819). Melville's statement about the *Essex* crew's decision 'to gain a civilized harbor' is part of the comments he wrote in the back pages of his own copy of Chase's narrative, a transcript of which is included in the Northwestern-Newberry edition of *Moby-Dick* (pp. 978–95). Ernest Dodge in *Islands and Empires* speaks of the gigantic royal mission chapel in Tahiti, built in 1819, the same year the *Essex* left Nantucket (p. 91).

Obed Macy's remarks about the Nantucketers' intimate knowledge of the sea is in his *History* (p. 213). Such was not, apparently, the case when it came to the landmasses of the world. William Comstock recounts an incident that reveals just how geographically ignorant a Nantucketer could be. At one point the officer of a Nantucket whaleship 'very honestly desired to be informed whether England was on the continent, or "stood alone by itself," and on being answered by another officer that it was in the County of Great Britain, wanted to know how far it was from London' (*The Life of Samuel Comstock*, p. 57). If a whaleman could be this vague about an island with which Nantucket had always had a close commercial connection, it is little wonder that the men of the *Essex* were without any information concerning the islands of the Central Pacific. For a detailed drawing of the launch Captain Bligh and his men sailed to the island of Timor, see A. Richard Mansir's edition of Bligh's *The Journal of* Bounty*'s Launch*.

Leach in *Survival Psychology* discusses the differences between authoritarian and social leaders (p. 140), while Glin Bennet in *Beyond Endurance: Survival at the Extremes* speaks of the different personality types required in what he calls the escape and survival periods following a disaster (pp. 210–11). The analysis of a career first mate versus a 'fishy' man is based on William H. Macy's words about the first mate Grafton, whom Macy describes as a man of rather thoughtful cast of mind, of much intelligence, and possessed of an extensive stock of information upon many subjects, with a habit of generalizing and a clearness of expression which rendered him an agreeable companion to all with whom he came in contact. Though a good whaleman, Grafton [the first mate] was not what is known to the *connoisseur* as a 'fishy man' (pp. 44–45). John Leach in Survival Psychology writes about the importance family connections take on during a disaster (p. 156), as well as the relationship of strong leadership to survival (p. 139).

CHAPTER SEVEN: **At Sea**

See Ronnberg's *To Build a Whaleboat* for an excellent analysis of the difficulties of sailing an early-nineteenth-century whaleboat (pp. 1–4). Concerning the sound made by a clinker-style whaleboat, Clifford Ashley writes in *The Yankee*

Whaler: '[T]he name [of clinker] was formed in imitation of the sound made by the boat while going through water. I have frequently noted this in a clinker-built tender. As the whale grew wary [later in the nineteenth century], the noise was found objectionable, and therefore a smooth-sided boat, to glide more silently upon the unsuspecting animal, was adopted' (p. 61).

Ashley records the location of the Offshore Ground as latitude 5° to 10° south, longitude 105° to 125° west (p. 41). Thomas Heffernan has identified at least seven whaleships that were in the neighborhood of the *Essex* at the sinking: three from Nantucket (the *Governor Strong*, the *Thomas*, and the *Globe);* three from New Bedford (the *Balaena*, the *Persia*, the *Golconda);* and one from England (the *Coquette)* (p. 77).

For information on hardtack, see Sandra Oliver's *Saltwater Foodways* (p. 107). The nutritional content of the hardtack rations and Galapagos tortoises, as well as the estimate of how much weight the men would lose over the course of sixty days, were determined with the help of Beth Tornovish and Dr. Timothy Lepore on Nantucket. Statistics relating to the body's water needs come from *Understanding Normal and Clinical Nutrition*, by Eleanor Whitney et al. (pp. 272–75). As a point of comparison, Captain Bligh set his men's initial daily rations at one ounce of bread (as opposed to six ounces for the men of the *Essex)* and a quarter pint (compared to a half pint) of water (*Bounty*'s *Launch*, p. 36). Francis Olmstead observed that many of the crew aboard the whaleship on which he sailed had 'laid in from fifty to seventy pounds of tobacco as their solace for the voyage, and will probably have to obtain a fresh supply from the captain before they return home' (pp. 83–84).

Warren Kinston and Rachel Rosser speak of the effects of a 'tormenting memory' and cite William James's reference to the San Francisco earthquake in 'Disaster: Effects on Mental and Physical State' (pp. 443–44). Hilde Bluhm in 'How Did They Survive? Mechanisms of Defense in Nazi Concentration Camps' speaks of the importance of self-expression in promoting psychic survival (p. 10). John Leach, in *Survival Psychology*, refers to activities such as Lawrence's creation of a piece of twine as 'tasking,' which he defines as 'the breaking down of the person's aim or purpose into simple tasks so that life can be handled one step at a time' (p. 152); he refers to one subject who dealt with a particularly long-term situation by making himself 'a rudimentary set of golf clubs and wooden balls' (p. 153).

My discussion of navigation is based in large part on J. B. Hewson's *A History of the Practice of Navigation*, especially his chapter on navigation by latitude and dead reckoning (pp. 178–225). Francis Olmsted in *Incidents of a Whaling Voyage* also provides an interesting account of navigation on a whaleship (pp. 43–44). My thanks to Donald Treworgy of Mystic Seaport for sharing his expertise with me; according to Treworgy in a personal communication: 'If Pollard of the *Essex* did not learn to work a lunar until the next voyage, it seems very unlikely that he would have had a chronometer for doing a time sight in 1819. Marine chronometers in 1819 were still handmade, costly and not always reliable.' According to Obed Macy, who speaks of Nantucket's whaling captains' being 'lunarians' in his History, by the 1830s the island's whaleships were 'generally furnished with chronometers' (p. 218). On Captain Bligh's remarkable feat of navigation in an open boat, see Bounty's *Launch* (pp. 24, 60–61).

In his History Obed Macy tells how the crew of the *Union* tied their two whaleboats together (p. 233). In Survive *the Savage Sea*, Dougal Robertson recounts how his wooden sailing yacht was rammed repeatedly and sunk by several killer whales. Robert Pitman and Susan Chivers describe how a pod of killer whales attacked and killed a sperm whale in 'Terror in Black and White,' *Natural History*, December 1998 (pp.26–28). The description of Chase's dissection of a tortoise is based, in part, on Dougal Robertson's detailed account of cutting up a green turtle (p. 109).

Chase calls the conditions they experienced on December 8 as a 'perfect gale.' Dean King's *A Sea of Words* defines gale as a 'wind of an intensity between that of a strong breeze and a storm. In the 19th century, it was more precisely defined as blowing at a speed of between 28 and 55 nautical miles per hour. In a gale, the waves are high with crests that break into spindrift, while in a strong gale the crests topple and roll and dense streaks of foam blow in the wind' (p. 202). Richard Hubbard's *Boater's Bowditch: The Small Craft American Practical Navigator* includes a table that puts the theoretical maximum of waves with unlimited fetch in Force 9 (41–47 knots) at 40 feet (p. 312). William Van Dorn's *Oceanography and Seamanship* also includes a useful table that indicates the rate of sea state growth as a function of wind speed and duration (p. 189).

John Leach speaks of the 'perceptual narrowing' that occurs in the aftermath of a disaster (p. 124), a factor that undoubtedly contributed to the *Essex* survivors' unswerving commitment to their original plan, even though heading for the Society Islands remained a possibility throughout the first month after the sinking.

CHAPTER EIGHT: **Centering Down**

The best accounts of the sufferings of the people aboard the *Medusa* raft are from two of the survivors, J. B. Henry Savigny and Alexander Correard, in *Narrative of a Voyage to Senegal;* see also Alexander McKee's *Death Raft.* W J. McGee's analysis of the sufferings of Pablo Valencia in the southwestern Arizona desert appears in his now famous article, 'Desert Thirst as Disease.'

My description of gooseneck barnacles is based on information provided by James Canton, Director of the Williams-Mystic Program at Mystic Seaport (personal communication, October 1998). For a description of how the crustaceans are commonly eaten, see the *Epicurious Dictionary* (http://www2.condenet.com). My thanks to James McKenna on the faculty of the Williams-Mystic Program for providing me with detailed information on why some portions of the Pacific support less life than others (personal communication, March 23, 1999). M. F. Maury's chart indicating the 'Desolate Region' appears in plate five of his *Wind and Current Charts.*

Willits Ansel, in *The Whaleboat,* tells how to

clench a nail (pp. 88–89). W. Jeffrey Bolster discusses the 'blacks' spiritual leadership' aboard a ship in *Black Jacks* (p. 125); he also recounts the story of the black cook's praying for the deliverance of a whaleship. My description of how Quakers 'centered down' is based on Arthur Worrall's *Quakers in the Colonial Northeast* (pp. 91–95). For an excellent summary of the effects of starvation on disaster victims, see John Leach's *Survival Psychology* (pp. 87–99). Throughout their narratives, Chase and Nickerson occasionally contradict themselves concerning the amount of water and, especially, bread rations. In this and other chapters I have assumed that the downward progression of their daily rations of bread was from six ounces to three ounces and, finally (after leaving Henderson Island), to one and a half ounces, while the daily water ration remained at half a pint.

CHAPTER NINE: **The Island**

For an account of the Nantucketer Mayhew Folger's 'discovery' of Pitcairn Island, see Greg Dening's *Mr. Bligh's Bad Language* (pp. 307–38) and Walter Hayes's *The Captain from Nantucket and the Mutiny on the* Bounty (pp. 41–47). To this day, Pitcairners rely on miro and tau wood harvested at Henderson to produce the wood carvings they sell to tourists; see Dea Birkett's *Serpent in Paradise* for a description of a modern-day wood-collecting voyage from Pitcairn to Henderson (pp. 81–96). From 1991 to 1992, a team of scientists under the aegis of the Sir Peter Scott

Commemorative Expedition to the Pitcairn Islands set up a base camp on the north beach of Henderson Island—almost exactly where the *Essex* survivors landed more than 170 years earlier. The scientists flew to Tahiti, then sailed the two thousand miles to Henderson on a chartered yacht. Supplies of food and water were shipped in every three months from Auckland, New Zealand. I have relied heavily on the book the expedition produced, *The Pitcairn Islands: Biogeography, Ecology and Prehistory*, edited by Tim Benton and Tom Spencer, for information about Henderson Island.

The presence of a 'fresh water lens' beneath a coral island is discussed in William Thomas's 'The Variety of Physical Environments Among Pacific Islands' in *Man's Place in the Island Ecosystem: A Symposium*, edited by F. R. Fosberg (pp. 26–27). Thomas Heffernan cites Robert McLoughlin's account of the medical examination of the skeletons on Henderson Island in *Stove by a Whale* (pp. 84–85). The behavior between the man-of-war hawks and tropic birds can still be observed on Henderson Island. See J. A. Vickery and M. De L. Brooke's 'The Kleptoparastic Interactions Between Great Frigatebirds and Masked Boobies on Henderson Island, South Pacific' in *The Condor*. Although a great frigatebird is another name for a man-of-war hawk, a masked boobie is a different species from a tropic bird, the kind of bird Nickerson claimed to have seen on Henderson.

T. G. Benton and T. Spencer describe how flora and fauna spread throughout the Pacific Islands in 'Biogeographic Processes at the Limits of the Indo-West Pacific Province' in *The Pitcairn Islands* (pp.

243–44). My account of human habitation on Henderson is indebted to T. Spencer and T. G. Benton's 'Man's Impact on the Pitcairn Islands' (pp. 375–76) and Marshall Weisler's 'Henderson Island Prehistory: Colonization and Extinction on a Remote Polynesian Island,' also in *The Pitcairn Islands* (pp. 377–404). In 'Obesity in Samoans and a Perspective on Its Etiology in Polynesians,' in *The American Journal of Clinical Nutrition*, Stephen McGarvey writes:

> Polynesian settlement required long ocean voyages into prevailing trade winds and unknown waters. The sailors on these early voyages of indeterminate length and unclear destinations may have experienced a significant risk of starvation and death when on-board food supplies dwindled and ceased. Overweight individuals and/or those with efficient metabolisms, presumably mediated by hyperinsulinemia, may have better survived such voyages because of their large store of energy reserves in the form of adipose tissue . . . Surviving sailors of these discovery voyages and, thus, the first settlers may have been those able to use and store food energy efficiently, perhaps via thrifty genotype mechanisms. (p. 1592S)

McGarvey theorizes that this is why modern-day Samoans are characterized by 'massive adiposity and high prevalence of obesity.' See also his article 'The Thrifty Gene Concept and Adiposity Studies in Biological Anthropology.' When it comes to the men in the *Essex* whaleboats, McGarvey postulates in a personal communication (May 11, 1999) that the health and nutrition of the men before the whale attack, not any racial or genetic predisposition, were the primary factors influencing their ability to survive. The statistics concerning the relative life spans of black and white infants are from Barbara M. Dixon's *Good Health for African Americans* (p. 27).

Pollard's public letter left on Henderson was quoted from in the *Sydney Gazette* (June 9, 1821). Other accounts claim that Owen Chase also left a letter; one source says it was addressed to his wife, another to his brother. As extra protection, Pollard placed the letters in a small lead case before putting them in a wooden box nailed to the tree.

CHAPTER TEN: **The Whisper of Necessity**

Statistical information on wind directions in trade-wind zones comes from William Thomas's 'The Variety of Physical Environments Among Pacific Islands,' in *Man's Place in the Island Ecosystem*, edited by F. R. Fosberg (p. 31). My thanks to the Nantucket Quaker expert Robert Leach for providing me with information on Matthew Joy's background (personal communication, May 28, 1998). According to Aaron Padlock's letter (based on Pollard's account and at the NHA): 'Matthew P. Joy (second officer) died through debility & costiveness.'

The findings of the Minnesota starvation experiment are contained in the two-volume *Biology of Human Starvation*, by Ancel Keys et al. A readable summary and analysis of the findings are contained in Harold Guetzkow and Paul Bowman's *Men and Hunger: A Psychological Manual for Relief Workers*, a guide still in use today. The term 'stomach masturbation' is referred to by Hilde Bluhm in 'How Did They Survive?' (p. 20). Guetzkow and Bowman speak of starvation and 'so-called American characteristics' in *Men and Hunger* (p. 9).

One example of the claims made for dehydration and starvation as a 'natural and quite tolerable' way to die can be found on the Web site http://www.asap-care.com/fluids.htm: 'Dehydration and starvation have proven to be very tolerable while dying. This is easy to understand because people have been dying comfortably for thousands of years without artificial tube feedings and fluid supports . . . [These] are natural events that should be allowed to occur when death is imminent, not fought relentlessly and avoided at any and all costs.'

CHAPTER ELEVEN: Games of Chance

Chase's narrative and Aaron Padlock's letter disagree slightly concerning the timing of events on Pollard's and Hendricks's boats after their separation from Chase. Since Paddack wrote his letter on the night of Pollard's rescue after listening to the captain's own account, I have taken it to be a more reliable source concerning the sequence of events on these two boats.

The reference to survival cannibalism at sea being so widespread in the nineteenth century is from Brian Simpson's *Cannibalism and the*

Common Law (p. 121). The second canto of Byron's *Don Juan*, published in the summer of 1819, illustrates the attitudes and assumptions of the time:

LXVI

'Tis thus with people in an open boat,
They live upon the love of life, and bear
More than can be believed, or even thought,
And stand like rocks the tempest's wear and
    tear;
And hardship still has been the sailor's lot,
Since Noah's ark went cruising here and
    there . . .

LXVII

But Man is a carnivorous production,
And must have meals, at least one meal a day;
He cannot live, like woodcocks, upon suction,
But, like the shark and tiger, must have prey;
Although his anatomical construction
Bears vegetables, in a grumbling way,
Your laboring people think beyond all question,
Beef, veal, and mutton, better for digestion.

LXVIII

And thus it was with our hapless crew . . .

The most comprehensive treatment of the *Nottingham Galley* is contained in a scholarly edition of Kenneth Roberts's novel *Boon Island.* I have used Captain Dean's earliest edition of his narrative published in 1711, reprinted in Donald Wharton's *In the Trough of the Sea. Selected American Sea-Deliverance Narratives, 1670–1766* (pp. 153–55). Edward Leslie's *Desperate Journeys, Abandoned Souls: True Stories of Castaways and Other Survivors* contains an excellent discussion of the *Nottingham Galley* wreck, along with other famous incidences of maritime cannibalism, including the *Essex* disaster. Also see chapter five, 'The Custom of the Sea,' in Simpson's *Cannibalism and the Common Law* (pp. 95–145).

Christy Turner and Jacqueline Turner's *Man Corn: Cannibalism and Violence in the Prehistoric American Southwest* provides a detailed analysis of how much meat an average human would provide (pp. 34–35), as does Stanley Garn and Walter Block's 'The Limited Nutritional Value of Cannibalism,' in *American Anthropologist* (p. 106). In *The Biology of Human Starvation*, Ancel Keys et al. cite autopsies of starvation victims in which 'adipose tissues contained no cells with fat globules' (p. 170); they also cite information on the percentage weight losses of the organs of starvation victims (p. 190). My thanks to Beth Tornovish and Tim Lepore for their estimates of the amount of meat and calories the *Essex* starvation victims would have provided. For a modern-day survivalist's guide to cannibalism (complete with a diagram of a human body indicating the preferred cuts of meat and even a list of recipes), see Shiguro Takada's *Contingency Cannibalism: Superhardcore Survivalism's Dirty Little Secret.*

According to P. Deurenberg et al., in 'Body Mass Index and Percent Body Fat: A Meta Analysis Among Different Ethnic Groups,' in the *International Journal of Obesity*, 'Blacks have lower body fat for the same Body Mass Index (BMI) compared to Caucasians' (pp. 1168–69). For accounts of the Dormer Party and the increased survival rates of the women relative to the men, see George Stewart's *Ordeal by Hunger* and Joseph King's *Winter of Entrapment*. Another example of women outlasting men in a starvation situation is found in Ann Saunders's account of her ordeal after the ship on which she was a passenger (along with only one other woman) became disabled on its way from New Brunswick to Liverpool in 1826. After twenty-two days in the rigging of the waterlogged ship, the six survivors (all of whom resorted to cannibalism) included the two women passengers. In addition to a physiological advantage, Pollard's age may have given him an attitudinal edge when it came to long-term survival. According to John Leach, 'Those under twenty-five suffer because they have not yet learned to conserve energies. They have difficulty pacing themselves for the long haul . . . [P]assivity does not come naturally to youth' *(Survival Psychology*, p. 172).

Both Glin Bennet in *Beyond Endurance* (pp. 205–9) and John Leach in *Survival Psychology* speak of Shackleton's unique ability to embody different leadership styles. According to Leach, Shackleton was 'a rare man who was capable of both types of leadership. He was clearly a dominant character capable of decisive initial leadership while possessing an incredible degree of perseverance' (p. 141). Frank Worsley makes the comments concerning Shackleton's sensitivity to his men in *Shackleton's Boat Journey (pp.* 169–70).

In *Biology of Starvation*, Keys provides a summary of the physiological effects of starvation that includes a poor tolerance to cold temperatures and a darkening of the skin, particularly about the face (pp. 827–28). Brian Simpson, in *Cannibalism and the Common Law*, tells of the 'belief that cannibalism, once practiced, easily becomes a habit' (p. 149). Guetzkow and Bowman speak of how semistarvation had 'coarsened' the men in the Minnesota experiment (p. 32). David Harrison's account of the sufferings aboard the Peggy appears in Donald Wharton's *In the Trough of the Sea* (pp. 259–77); although the sailors claimed that the black slave was picked to be killed by lottery, Captain Harrison had 'some strong suspicions that the poor Ethiopian was not altogether treated fairly; but on recollection, I almost wondered that they had given him even the appearance of an equal chance with themselves' (p. 269). Herbert Bloch describes 'modern feral communities' in 'The Personality of Inmates of Concentration Camps' (p. 335). Hilde Bluhm in 'How Did They Survive?' refers to the inmate who spoke of 'killing' his feelings (p. 8); Bluhm also quotes from the female prisoner who took on a 'savage cunning' in order to survive in the death camps (p. 22). While living with the Ihalmiut in the Northwest Territory, Farley Mowatt learned the vital importance of fat to a people living on an all-meat diet. In *People of the Deer* he writes, 'an eternal craving for fat is part of the price of living on an all-meat diet' (p. 85).

The first recorded instance of drawing lots in a survival situation at sea was published in 1641; see Simpson's *Cannibalism and the Common Law* (pp. 122–23). The description of David Flatt's reaction to his death sentence aboard the *Peggy* is told by Harrison (Wharton, pp. 271–76). See also H. Bluestone and C. L. McGahee's 'Reaction to

Extreme Stress: Impending Death by Execution.' My thanks to Friends Robert Leach and Michael Royston for their insights regarding Quakerism's stand on gambling and killing (personal communication, June 3, 1998). Leach also provided me with information regarding the Quaker background of George Pollard (personal communication, May 22, 1998). R. B. Forbes, in the pamphlet *Loss of the Essex, Destroyed by a Whale*, refers to how the men aboard the *Polly* fished for sharks with people's body parts (pp. 13–14). My account of the drawing of lots and execution of Owen Coffin is based not only on testimonies from Pollard (as recorded by George Bennet, in Heffernan [p. 215]), Chase, and Nickerson but also on a letter Nickerson wrote to Leon Lewis dated October 27, 1876 (at the NHA). In the letter Nickerson claims that Pollard was Coffin's executioner, which contradicts his own account in the narrative, where he says that it was Ramsdell who shot Coffin. Since other accounts claim it was Ramsdell, I have assumed that Nickerson was mistaken in the letter.

CHAPTER TWELVE: **In the Eagle's Shadow**

John Leach speaks of the active-passive approach to a long-term survival situation in *Survival Psychology* (p. 167). Eleanor Whitney et al., in *Understanding Normal and Clinical Nutrition*, describe the effects of an extreme magnesium deficiency: 'convulsions, bizarre muscle movements (especially of the eye and facial muscles), hallucinations, and difficulty in swallowing'

(p. 302). Captain Harrison's account of the sailor who died insane after eating the raw liver of a black slave is in Donald Wharton's *In the Trough of the Sea* (p. 269). A version of this story apparently made its way into the lore surrounding the *Essex* ordeal. In his pamphlet *Loss of the Essex*, R. B. Forbes, who depended greatly on information provided by the often unreliable Frederick Sanford, claimed that 'when a black man died in one of the boats, another one partook of his liver, became mad, and jumped overboard' (p. 11).

The meaning of 'Barzillai' comes from Alfred Jones's 'A List of Proper Names in the Old and New Testaments' in *Cruden's Complete Concordance* (p. 791). Warren Kinston and Rachel Rosser write of the psychological effects of suffering high losses in battle in 'Disaster: Effects on Mental and Physical State' (pp. *445–46)*. Ancel Keys et al. discuss what they call the 'edema problem' in *The Biology of Human Starvation* (pp. 935–1014).

Robert Leach provided me with the information concerning Benjamin Lawrence's Quaker upbringing (personal communication, May 22, 1998). Josiah Quinsy wrote of his conversation with the financially humbled Captain Lawrence (Benjamin's grandfather) in 1801, recording: 'Lawrence had seen better days, and had been upon a level in point of property, with the principal inhabitants of the island. But misfortunes had beset his old age, and he was just preparing to remove his family to Alexandria' (Crosby, p. 119). As Leach reveals, Benjamin's father died during a voyage to Alexandria in 1809.

Concerning the sailing speed of a whaleboat,

Willits Ansel writes, in *The Whaleboat:* '[F]our to six knots was a good average for a boat beating or running over a period of time on a number of headings' (p. 17). In 1765 the crew of the *Peggy* watched helplessly as the captain of a potential rescue ship ordered his men to sail away from the disabled craft (Wharton, p. 265). As Edward Leslie writes in *Desperate Journeys, Abandoned Souls:* '[R]escuing castaways entailed risks and offered no tangible rewards; indeed, taking survivors on board would deplcte already limited supplies of food and water' (p. 218). According to Beth Tornovish, tapioca pudding is 'a soft food that would be easy for these starving men to digest. It is high in calories and protein . . . [and] high-protein, high-calorie foods are recommended to postoperative surgical patients to promote healing and regain nutrient losses experienced prior to and during surgery' (personal communication, March *28, 1999).*

Christy Turner and Jacqueline Turner discuss techniques for extracting marrow from human bones in *Man Corn* (pp. 33–38). MacDonald Critchley, in *Shipwreck Survivors: A Medical Study,* writes of deliriums among castaways that are 'shared in . . . actual content . . . , leading to a sort of collective confabulation' (p. 81). Charles Murphey, third mate on the *Dauphin,* tells how Pollard's boat was discovered in his 220-stanza poem published in 1877; Murphey also provides a crew list that indicates the Native Americans who were aboard the *Dauphin.* For an account of the Indian legend of how the giant Maushop followed a giant eagle to Nantucket, see my *Abram's Eyes: The Native American Legacy of Nantucket Island*

(p. 35). Melville retells a version of this legend in Chapter 14 of *Moby-Dick*. Commodore Charles Ridgely of the *Constellation* recorded the account of how Pollard and Ramsdell were found sucking the bones of their shipmates (Heffernan, p. 99). As Heffernan points out, Ridgely would have heard this account from the Nantucketer Obed Starbuck, first mate of the *Hero* (p. 101). A story in the *Sydney* Gazette, (June 9, 1821) claimed that 'the fingers, and other fragments of their deceased companions, were in the pockets of the Capt. and boy when taken on board the whaler.' An incomplete photocopy of Aaron Paddack's letter describing Pollard's account of the *Essex* disaster is in NHA Collection 15, Folder 57. In the letter, Paddack writes: 'Captain Pollard, though very low when first taken up has immediately revived I regret to say that young Ramsdell has appeared to fail since taken up.' Claude Rawson, the Maynard Mack Professor of English at Yale University, spoke to me about the tendency of those who have been reduced to survival-cannibalism to speak openly about the experience—often to the horror of their listeners (personal communication, November 13, 1998). The loquacity of the sixteen survivors of an airplane crash in the Andes in 1972 made possible Piers Paul Read's now famous account of survival-cannibalism, *Alive: The Story of the Andes Survivors.*

CHAPTER THIRTEEN: Homecoming

In *Stove by a Whale* Thomas Heffernan provides a detailed account of the political situation in Chile at the time of the *Essex* survivors' arrival in Valparaiso (pp. 89–91). The NHA *Essex* blue file contains a transcript from the National Archives in Chile of the February 25 entry describing the ordeal of Chase, Lawrence, and Nickerson. Nickerson speaks of the acting American consul Henry Hill's efforts on their behalf. Commodore Ridgely's account of the survivors' appearance and their treatment by Dr. Osborn is cited by Heffernan (pp. 100–1). Ridgely claims that the sailors aboard the *Constellation* originally offered to donate an entire month's pay to the treatment of the *Essex* survivors (which would have totaled between two and three thousand dollars), but realizing that American and English residents of Valparaiso had also created a fund, Ridgely limited his men to a dollar each (Heffernan, p. 100).

Ancel Keys et al. tell of the painful process by which the participants in the Minnesota starvation experiment regained the weight they had lost in *The Biology of Human Starvation* (p. 828). Captain Harrison's account of the difficulties he had in regaining use of his digestive tract are described in his narrative of the *Peggy* disaster (Wharton, p. 275). Nickerson provides a detailed account of the troubles the *Hero* ran into off St. Mary's Island; also see my *Away Off Shore* (pp. 161–62). *My* description of how Pollard and Ramsdell made their way to Valparaiso is indebted to Heffernan's *Stove by a Whale* (pp. 95–109), as is my account of the rescue of the three men on Henderson Island (pp. 109–15). Brian Simpson writes of 'gastronomic incest' in *Cannibalism and the Common Law* (p. 141).

Chappel tells of their travails on Henderson in a
341

pamphlet titled 'Loss of the *Essex,*' reprinted in Heffernan (pp. 218–24). Nickerson talked to Seth Weeks about his time on the island, and Weeks confirmed that the freshwater spring never again appeared above the tide line. According to the oceanographer James McKenna, it is more than likely that an exceptionally high (and low) spring tide, combined with other factors such as the phase of the moon and variations in the orbital patterns of the sun and moon, were what gave the *Essex* crew temporary access to the spring in late December of *1820* (personal communication, May 10, *1999*). Captain Beechey writes of the missing *Essex* boat: 'The third [boat] was never heard of; but it is not improbable that the wreck of a boat and four skeletons which were seen on Ducie's Island by a merchant vessel were her remains and that of her crew' (in *Narrative*, vol. 1, pp. 59–61). Heffernan, who cites the Beechey reference, doubts that the whaleboat referred to could have belonged to the *Essex* (*Stove by a Whale*, p. 88).

Obed Macy's account of what happened on Nantucket during the winter and spring of 1821 are in the third volume of his journals in NHA Collection 96. Frederick Sanford's description of the letter regarding the *Essex* survivors being read 'in front of the post-office in a public way' is in a brief article titled 'Whale Stories' that apparently appeared in an off-island newspaper in or around 1872. An undated copy of the article is on file at the NHA; my thanks to Elizabeth Oldham for bringing the story to my attention. Sanford also includes a somewhat overheated account of the whale attack: '[A] large whale (sperm) came upon the ship, and with such violence as to make her heel and shake like an aspen leaf. The whale glanced off to windward and when two miles to windward turned and came down upon the ship and struck her a most deadly blow on the bows which caused her to heel over and to fill and sink!'

The *New Bedford Mercury* (June 15, 1821) includes two stories about the *Essex*. The first comes from a Captain Wood, of the *Triton*, who had heard about the disaster from Captain Paddack of the *Diana* and reports that Pollard and Ramsdcll had been picked up by the *Dauphin;* the second story tells of a letter just received from Nantucket reporting on the arrival of the *Eagle* with Chase, Lawrence, Nickerson, and Ramsdell as passengers. Nantucket's own paper, the *Inquirer*, did not begin publication until June 23, 1821, almost two weeks after the arrival of the first group of *Essex* survivors. The letter describing Chase's inability to speak about the disaster is dated June 17, 1821 and is the possession of Rosemary Heaman, a descendant of Barnabas Sears, to whom the letter was addressed. My thanks to Mrs. Heaman for bringing the letter to my attention. Mention of Pollard's reception is limited to a single sentence: 'Capt. Pollard, late Master of the ship *Essex*, arrived here in the *Two Brothers*, last Sunday' (August 9, 1821). Frederick Sanford's account of Pollard's arrival is in Gustav Kobbé's 'The Perils and Romance of Whaling,' *The Century Magazine*, August 1890 (p. 521); he also writes of Pollard's return to Nantucket in the *Inquirer* (March 28, 1879). Although many writers have mistakenly attributed Sanford's account of a silent reception to the arrival of Chase and company, it was Pollard's return that elicited this response. The description of a Nantucketer's reaction to the arrival of a whaleship is from the *Nantucket Inquirer* (May 14,1842).

Lance Davis et al. speak of the greater responsibilities and pay of a whaling captain compared to a merchant captain (*In Pursuit of Leviathan*, pp. 175–85). Amasa Delano's memories of his return after an unsuccessful voyage are in his *Narrative of Voyages and Travels* (pp. 252–53). Edouard Stackpole writes of Owen Coffin's grandfather Hezekiah and his involvement in the Boston Tea Party in *Whales and Destiny*, (p. 38). Robert Leach provided me with information regarding the Coffin family and the Friends Meeting (personal communication, May 20, 1998). Thomas Nickerson's account of Nancy Coffin's response to George Pollard is in his letter to Leon Lewis.

Piers Paul Read speaks of the Montevideo Archbishop's judgment of the Andes survivors in *Alive!* (p. 308). Another Catholic official did insist, however, that, contrary to the claims of one of the Andes survivors, the eating of human flesh under these circumstances was not equivalent to Holy Communion (p. 309). Documents relating to the rise of Quakerism on Nantucket mention a religious discussion that makes an intriguing reference to cannibalism and communion. In the spring of 1698, several years before Quakerism took hold on the island, an itinerant Friend named Thomas Chalkley visited Nantucket and recorded his conversation with one of the community's first settlers, Stephen Hussey. Hussey had once lived in the Barbados, where he had heard a Quaker claim that 'we must eat the spiritual flesh, and drink the spiritual blood of Christ.' Hussey asked, 'Is it not a contradiction in nature, that flesh and blood should be spiritual?' When Chalkley pointed out that Christ had been speaking figuratively when he told the apostles, 'Except ye eat my flesh and drink my blood ye have no life in you,' Hussey indignantly replied, 'I don't think they were to gnaw it from his arms and shoulders' (Starbuck, *History of Nantucket*, p. 518). One can only wonder how Chalkley and Hussey would have responded to the all-too-literal story of the *Essex*. Claude Rawson refers to cannibalism as a 'cultural embarrassment' in a review of Brian Simpson's *Cannibalism and the Common Law* in the *London Review of Books* (January 24, 1985, p. 21). Concerning survivors who have resorted to cannibalism, John Leach writes, 'If it can be accepted, justified or in cases rationalized, then the act of enforced cannibalism can be accommodated with little or no psychological dysfunction' (*Survival Psychology*, p. 98).

Thomas Heffernan has pointed out the similarities between Chase's account of what happened on Pollard's and Joy's boat and what is described in Aaron Paddack's letter (*Stove By a Whale*, p. 231). Herman Melville wrote about Owen Chase's authorship of his narrative in the back pages of his own copy of the book (see Northwestern-Newberry *Moby-Dick*, p. 984). Yet another aspect of the disaster not mentioned by Chase is whether he ever followed Richard Peterson's dying wishes and contacted the sailor's widow in New York. The family of William Coffin, Jr., had something of a tradition of writing controversial publications. Five years earlier, his father, who twenty years before had been wrongly accused by the island's Quaker hierarchy of robbing the Nantucket Bank, wrote an eloquent defense that proved the crime had been committed by off-islanders; see my *Away Off Shore* (pp. 156–59). I also speak of William Coffin, Jr.'s qualifications as ghostwriter of Chase's narrative in *Away Offshore* (pp. 158, 249). The statement regarding William Coffin's 'enthusiastic love of literature' appeared in an obituary in the *Nantucket Inquirer* (May 2, 1838). An announcement concerning the publication of Chase's narrative appeared in the *Inquirer* (November 22, 1821).

Melville recorded having heard of a narrative by Captain Pollard in the back pages of his copy of Chase's book (Northwestern-Newberry *Moby-Dick*, p. 985). Ralph Waldo Emerson's remarks concerning the Nantucketers' sensitivity to 'everything that dishonors the island' appears in his 1847 journal entries about the island (p. 63). In 1822, an anonymous letter would appear in a Boston paper questioning the religious character of the island's inhabitants. An irate Nantucketer responded in words that might have been applied to Owen Chase: 'We have a spy amongst us, who, like other spies, sends abroad his cowardly reports where he thinks they can never be disproved' *(Nantucket Inquirer* [April 18, 1822]). According to Alexander Starbuck's list of whaling voyages in the *History of Nantucket*, the *Two Brothers* left Nantucket on November 26, 1821. Nickerson speaks of being a part of the *Two Brothers'* crew (along with Charles Ramsdell) in a poem titled 'The Ship *Two Brothers*' (NHA Collection 106, Folder 31/2).

CHAPTER FOURTEEN: Consequences

My account of the *Two Brothers'* last voyage is based primarily on Nickerson's poem 'The Ship *Two Brothers'* and his prose narrative 'Loss of the Ship *Two Brothers* of Nantucket,' both previously unpublished and in NHA Collection 106, Folder *31/2*. The first mate of the *Two Brothers*, Eben Gardner, also left an account of the wreck, which is at the NHA. Charles Wilkes, the midshipman on the *Waterwitch* who recorded his conversation with George Pollard, would become the leader of the United States Exploring Expedition. As Heffernan points out, there is the possibility that Wilkes also met Owen Chase in 1839 when four of the expedition's ships, along with the *Charles Carroll*, were anchored for several weeks at Tahiti (pp. 130–31). Wilkes's account of his meeting with Captain Pollard is included in *Autobiography of Rear Admiral Charles Wilkes, U.S. Navy*, 1798–1877 and is quoted at length in Heffernan (pp. 146–48).

Edouard Stackpole tells of Frederick Coffin's discovery of the Japan Ground in *The Sea-Hunters* (p. 268); not all whaling scholars are convinced that Coffin was the first to find the whaling ground. George Pollard may have been taught how to perform a lunar observation by the *Two Brothers'* former captain, George Worth, during the two-and-a-half-month cruise back to Nantucket from Valparaiso in the spring and summer of 1821. Although both Pollard and Captain Pease of the *Martha* were convinced that they had run into an uncharted shoal, Nickerson reveals in his letter to

Leon Lewis that both he and the *Martha's* first mate, Thomas Derrick, believed it to be French Frigate Shoal, an already well-known hazard to the west of the Hawaiian Islands.

George Bennet's account of his meeting with George Pollard originally appeared in *Journal of Voyages and Travels by the Rev. Daniel Tyerman and George Bennet, Esq. Deputed from the London Missionary Society*. Concerning a character based on Pollard, Melville writes in the poem *Clarel:*

A Jonah is he?—And men bruit
The story. None will give him place
In a third venture.

Nickerson tells of Pollard's single voyage in the merchant service in his 'Loss of the Ship *Two Brothers* of Nantucket.' The rumor about George Pollard's switching lots with Owen Coffin is recorded by Cyrus Townsend Brady in 'The Yarn of the *Essex*, Whaler' in *Cosmopolitan* (November 1904, p. 72). Brady wrote that even though the tradition was 'still current in Nantucket,' he doubted its veracity.

My thanks to Diana Brown, granddaughter of Joseph Warren Phinney, for providing me with a copy of the relevant portions of the original transcript of Phinney's reminiscences, recorded by his daughter, Ruth Pierce. Ms. Brown has published a selection of her grandfather's reminiscences under the title 'Nantucket, Far Away and Long Ago,' in *Historic Nantucket* (pp. 23–30). In a personal communication (August 9, 1998), she explains Phinney's relation to Captain Pollard: 'Captain Warren Phinney, his father, married

348

Valina Worth, the daughter of Joseph T. Worth and Sophronia Riddell (June 6, 1834). Sophronia Ridden was, I believe, the sister of Mary Ridden who married Captain Pollard. After bearing three daughters, she died in 1843. Shortly after that, he was married to Henrietta Smith, who died the end of 1845, the year Joseph Warren was born. His father died about five years after this in a ship disaster on one of the Great Lakes, so he was then brought up by his grandmother and grandfather Smith. He of course was not a blood relative to the Pollards, but they were part of his extended family.' The rumor about George Pollard's making light of having eaten Owen Coffin is recorded in Horace Beck's *Folklore and the Sea* (p. 379). As late as the 1960s, the tradition was still being repeated on Nantucket; my thanks to Thomas McGlinn, who attended school on the island, for sharing with me his memory of the Pollard anecdote.

What is known about Owen Chase's life after the *Essex* disaster is recounted by Heffernan in *Stove by a Whale* (pp. 119–45). Emerson recorded his conversation with the sailor about the white whale and the *Winslow/Essex* on February 19, 1834 (*Journals*, vol. 4, p. 265). Melville's memories of meeting Chase's son and seeing Chase himself are in the back pages of his copy of the *Essex* narrative (Northwestern-Newberry *Moby-Dick*, pp. 981–83). Although Melville did apparently meet Owen Chase's son, he went to sea *after* Owen had retired as a whaling captain and mistook someone else for the former first mate of the *Essex*. Even if Melville didn't actually scc Chase, he thought he did, and it would be Melville's sensibility that would largely determine how future generations viewed the *Essex* disaster: through the lens of *Moby-Dick*. Melville's remarks concerning Chase's learning of his wife's infidelity are also recorded in his copy of the narrative (Northwestern-Newberry *Moby-Dick*, p. 995).

In 'Loss of the Ship *Two Brothers* of Nantucket,' Nickerson tells of what happened after the crew was taken to Oahu on the *Martha*: 'all of the crew of the *Two Brothers* were safely landed and as the whaling fleet were at the time in that port, each took their own course and joined separate ships as chances offered.' Heffernan speaks of Ramsdell's being captain of the *General Jackson* in *Stove by a Whale* (p. 152); the computerized genealogical records at the NHA show that Ramsdell's first wife, Mercy Fisher, bore four children and died in 1846, and that his second wife, Elisa Lamb, had two children. The Brooklyn City Directory lists a Thomas G. Nickerson, shipmaster, living on 293 Hewes as late as 1872. Benjamin Lawrence's obituary appeared in the *Nantucket Inquirer and Mirror* (April 5, 1879). Nickerson writes in his narrative about the fates of William Wright and Thomas Chappel. Seth Weeks's obituary appeared in the *Nantucket Inquirer and Mirror* (September 24, 1887); it concludes: 'He became blind for some years past, and ended his life in sweet peace and quiet among his own people, always highly respected and honored.'

Edouard Stackpole recounts the anecdote about Nantucketers' not talking about the *Essex* in 'Aftermath' in the NHA edition of Nickerson's narrative (p. 78). For an account of the island's reputation as a Quaker abolitionist stronghold, see my ' "Every Wave Is a Fortune": Nantucket Island

and the Making of an American Icon'; Whittier writes about Nantucket in his ballad 'The Exiles,' about Thomas Macy's voyage to the island in 1659. I discuss the success of the almost all-black crew of the *Loper* in *Away Offshore* (pp. 162–63). Frederick Douglass ends the first edition of the narrative of his life with his speech at the Nantucket Atheneum.

Thomas Heffernan traces the literary uses of the *Essex* story in his chapter 'Telling the Story' (pp. 155–82). The author of an article in the *Garrettsville* (Ohio) *Journal* (September 3, 1896) about the return of the *Essex* trunk to Nantucket provides convincing evidence of the impact the *Essex* story had on America's young people: 'In McGuffey's old "Eclectic Fourth Reader" we used to read that account. It told about whalers being in open whale-boats two thousand miles from land . . . Such accounts as that make impressions on the minds of children which last.' Testifying to how far the story of the *Essex* spread is a ballad titled 'The Shipwreck of the *Essex*,' recorded in Cornwall, England. The ballad takes many liberties with the facts of the disaster, claiming, for example, that lots were cast no less than eight times while the men were still on Ducie Island (in Simpson's *Cannibalism and the Common Law*, pp. 316–17). Emerson's letter to his daughter about the *Essex* is in his collected letters, edited by Ralph Rusk, vol. 3 (pp. 398–99). On Melville's one and only visit to Nantucket, see Susan Beegel's 'Herman Melville: Nantucket's First Tourist.' Melville recorded his impressions of George Pollard in the pages of Chase's *Narrative* (Northwestern-Newberry *Moby Dick*, pp. 987–88).

On Nantucket's decline as a whaling port and

the Great Fire of 1846, see my *Away Off Shore* (pp. 195–98, 203–4, 209–10). Christopher Hussey, in *Talks About Old Nantucket*, writes about how the burning slick of oil surrounded the firefighters in the shallows of the harbor (p. 61); see also William C. Macy's excellent account of the fire in Part III of Obed Macy's *History of Nantucket* (pp. 287–89). Concerning the *Oak*, Nantucket's last whaling vessel, Alexander Starbuck writes: 'Sold at Panama, 1872; sent home 60 bbls sperm, 450 bbls. [right] whale. Nantucket's last whaler' (p. 483).

The statistics concerning the number of sperm whales killed in the nineteenth and twentieth centuries are from Dale Rice's 'Sperm Whale' (p. 191); see also Davis et al.'s *In Pursuit of Leviathan* (p. 135) and Hal Whitehead's 'The Behavior of Mature Male Sperm Whales on the Galapagos Islands Breeding Grounds' (p. 696). Charles Wilkes (the same man who, as a midshipman, talked with George Pollard) recorded the observation that sperm whales had 'become wilder' in vol. 5 of *Narrative of the United States Exploring Expedition* p.493). Alexander Starbuck collected accounts of whale attacks on ships in *History of the American Whale Fishery* (pp. 114–25). Captain DeBlois's description of his encounter with the whale that sank the *Ann Alexander* is in Clement Sawtell's *The Ship* Ann Alexander *of New Bedford 1805–1857* (pp. 61–84). Melville speaks of the '*Ann Alexander* whale' in a letter dated November 7,1851, to Evert Duyekinek in his *Correspondence* (pp. 139–40).

In a letter dated November 15, 1868, to Winnifred Battie, Phebe Chase tells of seeing Owen Chase: '[H]e called me cousin Susan (taking me for sister Worth) held my hand and sobbed like a child, saying O *my head, my head[.]* [I]t was pitiful to see the strong man bowed, then his personal appearance so changed, didn't allow himself decent clothing, fears he shall come to want' (NHA Collection 105, Folder 15). For information concerning Nickerson, see Edouard Stackpole's foreword to the NHA edition of Nickerson's narrative (pp. 8–11). My thanks to Aimee Newell, Curator of Collections at the NHA, for providing me with information about Benjamin Lawrence's circle of twine and the *Essex* chest. See 'A Relic of the Whaleship *Essex*' in the *Nantucket Inquirer and Mirror* (August 22, 1986) and 'A Valuable Relic Preserved' in the *Garrettsville Journal* (September 3, 1896).

EPILOGUE: **Bones**

Information on the sperm whale that washed up on Nantucket at the end of 1997 comes from the following sources: articles by Dionis Gauvin and Chris Warner in the *Nantucket Inquirer and Mirror* (January 8, 1998); articles by J. C. Gamble in the *Nantucket Beacon* (January 6, 1998); 'The Story of Nantucket's Sperm Whale' by Cecil Barron Jensen in *Historic Nantucket* (Summer 1998, pp. 5–8); and interviews conducted in May and June of 1999 with Edie Ray, Tracy Plant, Tracy Sundell, Jeremy Slavitz, Rick Morcom, and Dr. Karlene Ketten. Dr. Wesley Tiffney, Director of the University of Massachusetts-Boston Field Station, spoke with me about erosion at Codfish Park (personal communication, June 1999).

The whale necropsy was supervised by Connie Marigo and Howard Krum of the New England Aquarium. The cutting up of the whale was directed by Tom French of the Massachusetts Division of Fisheries and Wildlife. Working with French were David Taylor, a science teacher at Triton Regional High School in Newburyport, Massachusetts, and three of Taylor's students. It was fitting that Taylor and his students were from Newburyport, which was where many of Nantucket's first settlers had come from in the seventeenth century. The Nantucket Historical Association was officially granted the whale skeleton by the National Marine Fisheries Service in the winter of 1998.

According to Clay Lancaster's *Holiday Island*, Thomas Nickerson operated a guest house on North Water Street in the mid-1870s (when he met the writer Leon Lewis), but had relocated to North Street (now Cliff Road) by 1882 (p. 55). An advertisement in the *Inquirer and Mirror* (June 26, 1875) announces Nickerson's having opened 'a family boardinghouse [with] several large airy and commodious rooms, with all the comforts of a home.' My thanks to Elizabeth Oldham for bringing this ad to my attention.